Revisiting Dewey

Best Practices for Educating the Whole Child Today

Daniel W. Stuckart and Jeffrey Glanz

Foreword by Maurice R. Berube

ROWMAN & LITTLEFIELD EDUCATION

A division of
ROWMAN & LITTLEFIELD PUBLISHERS, INC.
Lanham • New York • Toronto • Plymouth, UK

Published by Rowman & Littlefield Education
A division of Rowman & Littlefield Publishers, Inc.
A wholly owned subsidary of The Rowman & Littlefield Publishing Group, Inc.
4501 Forbes Boulevard, Suite 200, Lanham, Maryland 20706
http://www.rowmaneducation.com

Estover Road, Plymouth PL6 7PY, United Kingdom

British Library Cataloguing in Publication Information Available

Library of Congress Cataloging-in-Publication Data

Stuckart, Daniel W., 1965–
    Revisiting Dewey : best practices for educating the whole child today / Daniel W.
Stuckart and Jeffrey Glanz.
        p. cm.
    Includes bibliographical references.
    ISBN 978-1-60709-028-1 (cloth : alk. paper) — ISBN 978-1-60709-029-8 (pbk. : alk.
paper) — ISBN 978-1-60709-030-4 (electronic)
    1. Holistic education—United States. 2. Dewey, John, 1859–1952. I. Glanz, Jeffrey.
II. Title.
LC995.S78 2010
370.11—dc22   2010024255

∞ ™ The paper used in this publication meets the minimum requirements of American
National Standard for Information Sciences—Permanence of Paper for Printed Library
Materials, ANSI/NISO Z39.48-1992.

Printed in the United States of America

Contents

Foreword

At the end of every blind alley we seem to find Dewey.

—Richard Rorty

John Dewey profoundly transformed American education. Philosopher, educator, and social activist, Dewey established the bedrock of a distinctly American public school system. Dewey prescribed an education that had as its focus the development of the whole child: intellectually, morally, aesthetically, and socially. He defined intelligence as the ability to solve real problems and based his curricula on experiential learning. His legacy still stands, albeit, at times, in truncated form.

At the moment Dewey's influence has been challenged. One of his critics, E. D. Hirsch, Jr., would acknowledge that Dewey was "the writer who has most deeply affected American educational history and practice" but Hirsch feels that Dewey was "deeply mistaken" about curriculum. Hirsch advocated a content-specific curriculum that would be accompanied by national standards and high-stakes testing. This national reform movement triggered by the U.S. Department of Education's jeremiad *A Nation at Risk* in 1983 was directly opposite the Dewey model.

Still, Dewey's influence is being felt in academic circles. The American Educational Research Association has a Special Interest Group on Dewey scholarship, and a companion academic journal, *Educational Theory*, carries the Dewey torch. Moreover, prominent educational (critical) theorists such as Henry A. Giroux, Michael Apple, and Peter McClaren have absorbed Deweyan ideas in their work.

The authors of *Revisiting Dewey: Best Practices for Educating the Whole Child Today* have solicited comments from Dewey scholars on Dewey's relevance today. These distinguished writers surveyed are in agreement that Dewey's ideas are still pertinent. But the quintessential observation was made by the eminent educator John I. Goodlad who scolds the Deweyites for "[quoting] Dewey endlessly but neglecting to implement his ideas."

Revisiting Dewey seeks to apply Deweyan ideas to contemporary educational issues. It is an admirable map to meld Dewey into the classroom against a backdrop of the No Child Left Behind Act of 2001 (NCLB) and high-stakes testing. And the book succeeds in giving a virile account of how powerful those Deweyan ideas still are for American education.

The world—and education—has dramatically progressed since Dewey's contribution at the turn of the twentieth century and his death in 1952. We have had a technological revolution that has consumed the ways and means we educate youngsters. And we have broadened our horizons to include children with special needs in our schools. All the more reason to apply Dewey's insights to these new worlds. *Revisiting Dewey* does just that.

Glanz and Stuckart bring to the conversation a solid grounding in contemporary educational research. And that research coupled with Deweyan principles points to the shortcomings of the current reform movement and its centerpiece of legislation, the No Child Left Behind Act. NCLB sets up a narrow curriculum, almost wholly math and English, and equally narrow high-stakes testing that virtually ignores Dewey's emphasis on developing abstract thinking.

Revisiting Dewey is an easy-to-read guide to Deweyan neoprogressive education reform. I recommend the book to academics already converted to Dewey's thought for a fresh perspective on the Dewey canon. But *Revisiting Dewey* has also a special place for practitioners who are suffocating from the content-specific curriculum that fails to address the concerns of the whole child.

The authors could not have written a more timely or more important book.

Maurice R. Berube is Eminent Scholar Emeritus of Education from Old Dominion University and coauthor of *The End of School Reform*.

Preface

Antagonists often interpret Dewey out of context, which is ironic because the bedrock of Deweyan philosophy is context, specifically the social interaction of people in place and time. In his final years, Dewey spent increasing amounts of energy clarifying and defending what he had written over his long lifetime. For example, when influential members of an offshoot progressive movement reinterpreted his writings about the central role of children's interests in guiding learning, Dewey stepped forward to speak against an education that solely followed the dictates of children.

Yet, the idea that Dewey succumbed to child interest, and his educational followers instituted curricular changes to reflect the preeminence of that interest in the United States (and other parts of the world), gained traction in the public consciousness throughout the 1960s and 1970s. Critics lamented the expansion of elective courses at the expense of students mastering the fundamentals of reading, writing, and arithmetic. Unwittingly, Dewey became one of the ideological undercurrents setting the stage for the Assessment and Accountability Movement and the No Child Left Behind Act of 2001. In the 1970s, a resurgence of interest in Deweyan principles emerged.

Over two decades after his death, the editors of the *History of Education Quarterly* devoted the spring 1975 issue to revisiting some of his ideas and offering interpretations of his writings and actions. Three years prior, in the spring 1972 issue, an article in the same journal ignited a firestorm of controversy by questioning Dewey's commitment to democracy, despite a vast compendium of evidence suggesting otherwise. Today, well over a century has passed since Dewey began writing some of his seminal works and nearly 60 years have passed since his death, yet Dewey is still reviled and admired at the same time in different quarters. So, what was it about Dewey that made him larger than life?

Dewey was a voracious scholar of history and philosophy who articulated a cogent view of life and applied that view to his understanding of human nature. According to Dewey, individuals engaged in transactions with the external environment. He described in minute detail, voluminous manuscripts, and frequent articles how human beings interacted with others and the natural environment to grow, which in a formal sense defined education.

His astute observations provided meaning and pathways to greater growth. The fact that he lived so long, wrote so much, and achieved vast notoriety spoke to the prolific nature of the man. However, ultimately, it is the philosophy that has stood the test of time, often perceived as obfuscations because he wrote in such dense prose. The perception has likely resulted in many educators not appreciating fully how Dewey currently does and potentially can inform their practices.

Ask teacher candidates what they know about Dewey, and they almost invariably respond with something like, "Learning by doing." In one respect, Deweyan philosophy has become a cliché. What many current and future educators do not realize is that Dewey has given us much more. He specified effective ways to arrange and sequence the curriculum, how to connect content to students' prior knowledge, guidelines to provide quality learning experiences, methods for developing intelligence, and much more.

He also clearly articulated the critical importance of teachers, which bolstered respect for the profession. Likewise, he analyzed the importance of subject matter as processes including the arts, social studies, and sciences. When the reader of Dewey is able to transcend the obfuscations, what emerges is a clear picture of what it means to educate the whole child. In fact, some of the most robust and current research today validates Dewey's contributions.

This book is not about attacking the No Child Left Behind law nor is it about discrediting the Assessment and Accountability Movement. Like any law or reform, there are both healthy and deleterious elements depending on your perspective. What this book does is look at current issues, educational trends, and best practices research through the lens of Deweyan philosophy, which offers insights into educating the whole child. We strongly encourage the readers of this book also to read Dewey's primary writings. Perhaps start by picking up the spare treatise *Experience and Education* (1938), and then find a quiet place to savor the logic and powerful prose.

Part One

FUNDAMENTAL ISSUES IN EDUCATING THE WHOLE CHILD

Chapter One

Creating a Curriculum for Teaching the Whole Child

No doubt some of the repulsiveness of purely abstract intellectual studies to many children is simply the reflex of the fact that the things—the
facts and truths—presented to them have been isolated from their human
context.

—Dewey (1913, pp. 86–87)

In the past half century, education reform in the United States has been predicated on the notion that graduating students often lack the skills necessary for
competing economically in contemporary society. Further, since the 1980s,
standards-based reforms have transformed classroom pedagogy and practice.
With the passage of the No Child Left Behind Act of 2001, high-stakes testing has become a ubiquitous feature of public school children's daily rituals.

Reform advocates argue that testing leads to greater alignment of the curriculum with teaching and learning, teacher and student accountability, and
in some cases, a preservation of our cultural heritage. Opponents contend
that testing results in prolific cheating, higher dropout rates, and a narrowing
curriculum with emphases on teaching to the test. Moreover, some evidence
suggests that a singular focus on passing the test at all costs leads to neglect in
other areas including attending to students' spiritual and ethical needs as well
as developing abilities to collaborate with others, communicate effectively,
and innovatively solve problems.

Nearly a century ago, Dewey proposed a philosophy of education addressing the needs of the whole student. He provided insights into the development of intelligence, the importance of socially useful skills, and the healthy
growth of the individual. In the context of high-stakes testing and best practices, his insights may be more prescient than ever.

Focus Questions

1. What does teaching to the "whole" child mean to you?
2. What do you know about the No Child Left Behind Act of 2001?
3. How has high-stakes testing affected students, teachers, administrators, and parents?
4. What is the ideal way to promote the healthy growth of each student?

———∞∞∞———

Perhaps no individual defined learning in the modern age more succinctly than John Dewey. Dewey—the teacher, philosopher, and pragmatist— offered education a philosophical foundation for educating the whole child. Over his lifetime, he was a prolific author and education reformist who contributed insights into learning as well as the basic functioning of the human condition, which later became manifested in the progressive movement.

He came of age while the United States went through profound changes: mending from a vicious civil war, transforming from a rural to urban society, and perhaps most importantly, immersing in the great Industrial Revolution, which resulted in myriad consequences for education.

Despite the fact that universal education was a widely accepted belief by the end of the nineteenth century, in practice, few high-school-age children were actually graduated from high school (Null, 2007). The shift from an agricultural economy to one based on manufacturing restructured lives while millions of immigrants entered the country to work in the new economy and their children assimilated into the schools (Weiss, DeFalco, & Weiss, 2005).

Moreover, schools became a battleground over the type and transmittal of knowledge. On one side were the traditionalists, who favored a continuation of a liberal arts education centered on the learning of Latin, Greek, philosophy, and mathematics as the core courses, and pedagogy based on rote memorization and recitation. On the other side emerged the progressives, who sought to tear down authoritarian structures and replace them with the free flow of ideas.

Dewey's teachings attempted to bridge these positions by placing learning in the context of the environment with an examination of human nature. By rejecting these divisive dualisms, Dewey was able to transcend the debate and elevate the needs of the whole child above the fray. Today, the remnants of earlier cultural struggles continue, but in a different context. With standards-based accountability and high-stakes testing, educators face many new challenges. Perhaps, more than ever, it is time to revisit Dewey's ideas.

THE GREAT PHILOSOPHER

John Dewey dedicated his life to spanning the abyss between philosophy and the nascent field of psychology (Alexander, 2006). He was born on October 20, 1859, and lived to the ripe old age of 92 years before passing on June 1, 1952. Growing up in a deeply religious and conservative family, he studied a classical liberal arts curriculum at Oil City High School in Oil City, Pennsylvania. Upon graduating, Dewey attended the University of Vermont in 1879 where he studied classical languages, mathematics, and ancient history.

He returned to his high school alma mater where he taught science for two years, an endeavor for which he showed little interest. All the while, he pursued his interests in philosophy. Shortly thereafter, he borrowed two thousand dollars from his aunt to attend graduate school at Johns Hopkins University, where he was deeply influenced by the ideas of Hegel (Stallones, 2006).

Dewey embraced Hegelianism because the philosophy reconciled competing notions into a unitary whole. In this way, Dewey was able to neatly package his piety and moral upbringing into a coherent understanding of the modern world without divorcing himself from his religious past (Stallones, 2006). Perhaps more importantly, the unifying concepts later served as the basis for a new kind of educational philosophy premised on context, which eventually became known as American pragmatism.

To an American pragmatist, the ultimate goal is serving "the purposes of action" (Kivinen & Ristela, 2003, p. 364). In this way, learning is an active process. Dewey viewed learning as the experience gained from the control over actions and the resulting consequences, which was the "formation of habits of action" (p. 365). In other words, Dewey focused on the transactions between the person and the environment.

From these ideas derived an epistemology that described knowledge as a culmination of experiences in which individuals shaped their destinies with others. Likewise, education provided the real-world ability to solve problems as long as one discovered reality in context (Sutinen, 2008; Trifonas & Ghiraldelli Jr., 2004). Later, constructivist theorists such as Piaget, Vygotsky, and Kuhn extrapolated these concepts to include cognitive structures and mental representations (Hung, 2002; Prawat, 1998). Dewey viewed these actions as the instruments for the development of the whole child, including the development of intelligence.

What Dewey offered us was a general theory of intelligence that was not dependent on a specific subject, but rather spoke to the *process* of education. According to Sternberg (2008), psychological theories about learning and pedagogy are important for five reasons: (1) they provide a scientific foundation for discovering how individuals comprehend, feel, and take action; (2)

they provide detailed descriptions about what effective instruction and/or practice look like; (3) they can provide specific detail for appropriate assessments; (4) they are falsifiable by further evidence; and (5) they can be tested by putting them into practice.

Other examples include Gardner's theory of multiple intelligences and Sternberg's theory of successful intelligence. The general theories of intelligence are supported by empirical research, which suggests that a general intelligence is hierarchically supported by more specific abilities. This may be particularly important in a high-stakes testing environment because promoting higher-order thinking and success in contemporary society may involve more than training children to perform well in narrowly tested curriculum areas. Dewey recognized that subject matter transcended unidimensional purposes (Dewey, 1913, 1938).

Rather than following the dictum that specific subject areas such as Latin and mathematics enhance intelligence, Dewey believed that subject matters served intelligence by providing student interest. Further, the desired result was an *attitude* for learning, not a transfer of intelligence that is measured specifically on tests. As Gibboney (2006, p. 170) eloquently posited, "What is transferred when a student learns something that is truly important is intangible and immeasurable by tests."

Moreover, evidence suggests that students can perform well on retention tests, meaning tests of recall, but many struggle with transfer tests, where applications of previous knowledge are applied to new situations (Mayer, 1998). As we shall see later, Dewey's conceptualization of intelligence underscores a skills-based approach to learning supported by interest theory.

HISTORY OF STANDARDS-BASED EDUCATION

Education reform movements in the United States have historically been associated with the problems and successes of the American economy (Cuban, 2001). Following the publication of *A Nation at Risk* in 1983 and the perceived inability of American students and workers to compete internationally, the standards-based education reform movement catapulted to the forefront of educational policy in the conservative politics of the time.

Rather than using the traditional norm-referenced measures of comparing student achievement with a sample from peers, the new outcomes-based measures were established by comparing performance on clearly articulated objectives. Student performance was measured empirically using criterion-referenced tests, which specifically align with desired outcomes. For example, if the criterion was for the student to solve an algebraic equation with one variable, then an appropriate assessment would be to solve for x, in $3x +$ $12 = 18$. Throughout the 1980s and 1990s, standards-based reform eventually gained bipartisan support.

Goals 2000: Education America Act of 1994

Standards-based education contained four key components: high expectations that all children could be academically successful; a curriculum that speci- fied the knowledge and skills to be learned; criterion-based assessments that aligned to the curriculum; and the inclusion of some high-stakes assessment such as the passing of a test to be promoted to the next grade level, graduate from high school, or to pursue a particular academic track (Superfine, 2005).

The standards curriculum originated from political discussions, which identified the knowledge and skills required for the modern workplace. On March 31, 1994, Congress legislated some of the first comprehensive standards-based outcomes in Goals 2000: Education America Act and laid the groundwork for identifying rigorous standards, measuring student progress, and providing the resources to achieve the standards.

Goals 2000 was a reauthorization of the Elementary and Secondary Act (ESEA) of 1965 and provided the funds for states to identify and enact their own standards, accountability, and assessment systems. Title I of ESEA provided states with billions of dollars to educate low-income and high-risk students. The federal government conditioned the receipt of Title I funds on each state's completion of a standards-based assessment system.

Goals 2000 articulated eight national goals to be reached by the year 2000: (1) all children will begin school ready to learn; (2) the graduation rate will reach a minimum of 90 percent; (3) all students will achieve at the desired competency levels before leaving grades 4, 8, and 12 in the subject areas and develop critical-thinking skills to become effective citizens and productive employees; and (4) teachers will have acquired the knowledge and skills to be effective through professional development opportunities.

The remaining goals were (5) U.S. students will rank number one in the world in mathematics and science; (6) all adults will develop the critical- thinking skills to become effective citizens and productive employees; (7) schools will offer a disciplined environment free from drugs, alcohol, vio- lence, and weapons; and (8) schools and parents will form partnerships to nurture the growth of children (North Central Regional Educational Labora- tory, 2004b).

Unfortunately, by all practical measures, none of the goals were achieved, most likely because of the political opposition to the accountability mecha- nisms and lack of federal enforcement. By the end of 1996, Goals 2000 had lost potency, and legislators were reluctant to continue (Superfine, 2005). In 2002, the No Child Left Behind Act (NCLB) replaced Goals 2000. NCLB became the most ambitious attempt to promote standards-based reform.

No Child Left Behind Act of 2001

Like Goals 2000, NCLB emerged from the reauthorization of ESEA. Likewise, NCLB contained provisions and incentives for states to enact standards and accountability systems. However, NCLB also extended the reach of federal statutes in education like never before in the nation's history. In order to receive continued Title I funding, states had to use assessments to measure "adequate yearly progress" as defined by the states themselves. In the event that progress was not achieved, NCLB prescribed sanctions such as restructuring schools, supplemental services for at-risk students, and allowing parents alternative public school choices (Superfine, 2005).

NCLB outlined four key provisions, based on student testing, scientifically based research, teacher quality, and public school choice. Students were required to be tested in reading and math every year in grades 3 through 8 as well as at least one time in high school. Further, school districts were required to publish the results by school and, most importantly, disaggregate the results based on ethnicity, race, gender, English as a second language, disability status, socioeconomic status, and migrant status when the numbers of individuals were statistically significant (Education Trust, 2003).

Scientifically based research (SBR) provided the guidelines for effective practice and pedagogy. NCLB specifically detailed SBR to include large, empirical, quantitative studies with control groups; data collection across a variety of valid and reliable measures; rigorous analysis; replicable results; and a peer-review process (North Central Regional Educational Laboratory, 2004a).

Teacher quality required that all teachers have earned a bachelor's degree, passed a certification test, and demonstrated subject-matter expertise (Kaplan & Owings, 2002). Parents were able to enroll their children in other designated public schools if the target schools were deemed dangerous or the test scores indicated that the school was failing to make adequate yearly progress (Ashford, 2003; U.S. Department of Education, 2002a). All the while, NCLB has ignited passions from advocates and critics alike.

NCLB proponents claim that the legislation reforms education by providing greater alignment among curriculum, pedagogy, and practice. Conservative ideologues view education in a perilous state after a half century of decay. Dougherty (2007) asserts that "education in the name of progress emphasized experience at the expense of the inherited," meaning that we have forsaken the "truths" of Western European ancestry for a process devoid of a meaningful liberal arts curriculum (p. 3).

While deep philosophical, moral, and ethical differences exist, both sides agree that the legislation has succeeded in highlighting the experiences of traditionally underrepresented and at-risk children. However, the critics question at what cost. Critics of standards-based reform, and particularly NCLB, cite a litany of problems and issues.

Apple (2007) posits that the dominant conservative supporters co-opted progressive language to cloak controversial measures, including changing definitions to suit their own needs. He also questions true funding levels as well as the arbitrary nature of standardized test scores. While some conservative critics lament the loss of local control, it is the unintended consequences that Apple examines related to the label of "failing public schools."

Perhaps one of the great ironies is Apple's contention that parents home-school kids as one possible outcome of failing public schools. Schools are deemed failing if they neglect to make adequate yearly progress, a highly arbitrary measure. In general, home-schooled children fall under little or no accountability—and anyone can teach them—which completely undermines the NCLB tenet of high teacher quality! Another component is the push for private-school vouchers, which places a blind faith in the capitalist notion of free markets and ignores the social and cultural effects of education while stressing only the managerial aspects.

Other objections to high-stakes testing include the inherent corruption that has economic, social, ethical, and curricular consequences. Nichols and Berliner (2007) point out that high-stakes testing leads to widespread cheating by students, teachers, and administrators; increased dropout rates for at-risk students; the diverting of scarce resources to "bubble" students, meaning those on the edge of passing; and a narrowing of the curriculum with an emphasis on teaching to the test.

Moreover, as Shapiro (2008) contends, a singular focus on justifying education on the grounds of global competitiveness ignores the other important facets of human existence including spiritual needs, creativity, emotional considerations, ethical behavior, and intellectual curiosity. The modern world also demands the ability to work with others toward common goals, the capacity for innovative problem solving, and effective communication skills. It seems that we have lost our way. It may be time to return to the philosophy of John Dewey to educate the whole child.

The current cultural wars over the control of knowledge, teaching, and learning are a manifestation of earlier battles. When John Dewey published his seminal work, *Experience and Education*, in 1938, a cultural war had been raging over the conduct of schooling in the context of the Great Depression.

The traditionalists advocated an authoritarian structure that emphasized rote memorization and recitation.

Progressive thinkers staked out an opposing claim to promote the reduction of barriers and the free flow of ideas. Dewey dismissed both of these extremes and developed a commonsense learning philosophy grounded in the realities of learning environments and human nature. He identified three fundamental aspects of curriculum to educate the whole child: the development of intelligence, the acquisition of socially useful skills, and the healthy growth of the individual. By examining best practices in light of Dewey's curriculum, it may be possible to educate the whole student in an atmosphere of high-stakes testing.

THE DEVELOPMENT OF INTELLIGENCE

Dewey viewed the development of intelligence as a manifestation of human nature, specifically the desire for freedom. Although most people juxtapose freedom with physical movement and constraint, Dewey (1938) defined "freedom of intelligence" as the most lasting freedom of "observation and judgment" that the student finds "intrinsically worth while" (p. 61). Therefore, the main impetus for the development of intelligence is the cultivation of motivation.

Motivation

In their influential report, *The Silent Epidemic: Perspectives of High School Dropouts*, Bridgeland, DiJulio, and Morison (2006) reported that nearly one-third of all high-school age children drop out of school. Likewise, about one-half of all Native Americans, Hispanics, and Blacks do not graduate with their classes. When asked to characterize their experiences, 69 percent of the respondents remarked that they "were not motivated or inspired to work hard" in school (p. iii).

Moreover, the focus groups sharply indicated that educators failed to make school interesting, and many felt "a lack of connection to the school environment" (p. 4). Dewey (1913) argued vigorously in *Interest and Effort in Education* that students who learn based on interest are more motivated than students who work by effort alone. Using anecdotal logic, Dewey reasoned that there were two types of interest: one that sprang from the proclivities of the student and the other as a result of the context. In other words, there are individual and situational interests. The nexus of these interests sparks motivation to learn.

In a high-stakes testing environment, the motivation for individual learning occurs in a unidimensional framework of one size fits all. The assumption is that all students are ideal and rational test takers who are motivated by the consequences of the tests such as advancing to the next grade or meeting graduation requirements (Amrein & Berliner, 2003; Clarke et al., 2003).

Yet, research suggests that motivation involves many complexities that go far beyond punishments and rewards. These complexities include individual differences and school-level conditions (Sloane & Kelly, 2003). In the past decade, researchers reported a spate of studies related to social motivation and academic achievement on different populations and individuals (Anderman & Kaplan, 2008). There are several foci to this research including social motives, relationships, and students' perceptions of acceptance or belongingness in a school context.

Because high-stakes testing is a summative event in the lives of public-school children, recent research has attempted to address individuals' beliefs in an achievement setting (Ryan, Ryan, Arbuthnot, & Samuels, 2007). Characteristics of motivational theory related to setting include achievement goals, value, self-concept, self-efficacy, test anxiety, and cognitive processes. Achievement goals are the most studied phenomenon related to motivation and encompass the paradigm for viewing individuals' beliefs about the factors that influence performance and ways of thinking about achievement.

There are two dimensions to goals, definitions and valence, where valence is "a subjective measure that relates the chances of an Agent being able to fulfill its goals given a particular environment situation, its internal state and its set capabilities" (Oliveira & Sarmento, 2002, p. 3). Therefore, the two dimensions on two measures results in four student goal orientations: mastery-approach goals, mastery-avoid goals, performance-approach goals, and performance-avoid goals.

The four student goal orientations originate from distinct student purposes. A mastery-approach goal occurs when a student concentrates on achieving mastery on a particular task with the ultimate goal of success. The student is cognizant of the knowledge and skills necessary for completing a challenging task.

Likewise, a mastery-avoid goal happens when a student focuses on avoiding misunderstandings, committing errors, and failing relative to previous performances. In the performance-approach condition, the student is concerned with appearing smart and competent to others and in comparison with other students. Similar to mastery-avoid goals, performance-avoid goals reflect a student's desire to avoid misunderstandings and failure, but are motivated by the avoidance of appearing dumb or incompetent to others (Ryan et al., 2007).

Another measure of student motivation concerns value, which involves student interest, perceived utility, and importance. According to Ryan, Ryan, Arbuthnot, and Samuels (2007), interest refers to intrinsic motivation (e.g., satisfaction, enjoyment, and attraction of challenges), utility is the usefulness of the task for future benefit, and importance is a measure of how task performance reinforces elements of identity.

Therefore, students may find value in high-stakes testing for a variety of reasons. Moreover, the reasons are often contingent on student views of competence of self and within specific domains as well as notions of effectiveness of producing desirable outcomes.

Recent studies of academic achievement motivation can be categorized by individuals' domain-general self-concept, domain-specific self-concept, and self-efficacy. Domain-general self-concept refers to individuals' beliefs about their achievement abilities in general (e.g., ability to do well in school). In addition, individuals also hold ability beliefs related to specific areas of the curriculum such as social studies and mathematics.

When a student evaluates her value and competence, she develops notions of her ability to succeed in achieving specific outcomes, referred to as self-efficacy. Self-efficacy is an organic process that is constantly evolving as the student gains additional experience. Self-efficacy also serves as the determinant to whether a student continues to try or simply gives up (Ryan et al., 2007). Another consideration is test anxiety.

While earlier considerations focused on whether students wanted to achieve success on tests with goals and value, and whether they had the perceived ability to actually perform well on the tests with self-concept and self-efficacy, another area is performance while taking the test. Negative feelings and fears during testing times contribute to test anxiety, which encompasses emotionality and worry components.

Emotionality refers to physical reactions to testing such as sweating, nervousness, and rapid heart rates. On the other hand, worry involves cognitive processes such as negative thoughts about failure and distracting ideas, which may interfere with concentration. The latter also may indicate differences in cognitive processes related to high-stakes test taking.

Cognitive processing can be organized into three types: cognitive disorganization, deep processing, and surface processing. While cognitive disorganization indicates distracting thoughts perhaps caused by test anxiety, deep processing involves higher-order thinking and the assimilation and accommodation of new information into mental schemas. Surface processing, on the other hand, involves lower-order thinking skills such as memory and recall. Further, individual differences allow motivational researchers to study composite characteristics of various populations.

Motivation Related to Different Populations

While individual differences can explain much of the variance in motivation related to high-stakes testing, other areas include research related to specific populations. In light of the high attrition rates for Hispanic, Black, and Native American high school students, some researchers have sought to examine motivation among these groups and others.

In examining the motivational power of high-stakes tests, Clarke, Shore, Rhoades, Abrams, Miao, and Li (2003) noted a variety of positive, negative, and neutral effects on pedagogy and practice across a wide variety of schools in three states. Specifically, the researchers concluded that high-achieving and suburban students were most likely to be motivated by the high-stakes exams, while low-achieving, minority, and elementary students in urban districts were most negatively affected, resulting in demoralization. These differences were supported by other studies as well.

Koth, Bradshaw, and Leaf (2008) reported that much of the variance in achievement motivation occurred at the classroom level as opposed to a schoolwide level. In elementary grades, boys and minority students exhibited lower levels of motivation than did Caucasian children. The study sought to explain motivational patterns with school climate factors.

The researchers surmised that in order to enhance motivation, school officials should target individuals with negative attitudes and institute programs to improve relationships between teachers and students as well as student groupings within classrooms. Additional studies have sought to examine the relationship between motivation and belongingness in schools.

Motivation and Belongingness

Recently, researchers have documented the effects of belongingness or interpersonal relationships on academic motivation. Despite a wide variety of foci, two major themes emerge from the research, social motives and social relationships. As noted earlier, boys and minority students generally show lower levels of motivation at the elementary level than Caucasian children. Further, social motives are inherently part of achievement goals as student performance during testing is often moderated by consideration of others' perceptions. Social relationship research examines student interactions with various partners (Anderman & Kaplan, 2008).

Current studies on social relationships and academic motivation include student-teacher relationships, student-student relationships, and a more general perception of student acceptance, belongingness, and identity within the school environment, particularly with adolescents because motivation sharply decreases as students transition from middle to high schools. Moreover, expectations and the quality of relationships affect the levels of adaptive motivation (Nelson & Debacker, 2008).

Overall, students who perceive that they are valued and respected in school display attributes associated with increased motivation (Nelson & Debacker, 2008; Nichols, 2008; Patrick, Mantzicopoulos, Samarapungavan, & French, 2008). The attributes and quality of student-to-student relationships serve as a predictor for individual motivation, both good and bad, with students who report being respected and valued also indicating increased mastery and self-efficacy as well as a performance-approach and responsibility disposition to goals (Nelson & Debacker, 2008). In total, if students have strong, positive social relationships with teachers and peers, they exhibit enhanced motivation to do well in school.

Differentiation of Instruction

A second element Dewey (1938) addressed for the development of intelligence involves teacher pedagogy that is based on understanding "the capacities and needs" of the "individuals" and using this understanding to institute instruction "for individuality of experience" (p. 58). Teachers are expected to provide appropriate experiences through various types of instruction.

Because of time constraints as well as other pressures related to high-stakes testing, teachers sometimes believe that they must choose between teaching basic skills and providing students meaningful opportunities to engage in challenging and deep work, something Newmann, Bryk, and Nagaoka (2001) called "a false dichotomy" (p. 2). While teaching basic skills is important, research suggests that differentiating instruction can reach more learners, result in deeper learning, enhance motivation, and increase test scores (Balfanz, Legters, & Jordan, 2004; Langer, 2002; Newmann et al., 2001).

In one major study, researchers examined the effectiveness of an experimental intervention composed of active-learning strategies and extended instruction in reading and mathematics in low socioeconomic high schools in two large urban school districts. Prior to the study, most of the participants tested below grade level.

School officials conceived the experimental programs as a way to accelerate learning for poorly prepared students in the ninth grade. The students received extended instruction in math and English, including several research-based courses "to overcome poor prior preparation and succeed in standards-based high school courses" (Balfanz, Legters, & Jordan, 2004, pp. 8–9).

The interventions embodied multiple instructional approaches. The reading and English interventions included four general strategies to promote student fluency and comprehension. The strategies included think-aloud and read-aloud, comprehension strategies related to various genres of literature, small cooperative learning groups, and choice reading and writing times.

Moreover, the targeted plays and novels contained content of high interest to teenagers, and the staff prepared discussion guides to aid with context and vocabulary. The math curriculum in the experimental schools embodied real-world connections and follow-up learning activities allowing students to share ideas and use hands-on approaches. Students worked with partners, engaged in whole-class discovery, and received a variety of individual and small-group instruction and activities.

Additionally, each lesson ended with a metacognitive exercise for students to reflect on the day's learning. At the control schools, the students also received a similar amount of time devoted to math and reading instruction. Further, the students' socioeconomic status (SES), prior achievement levels, age, and attendance were similar to the experimental schools. One major difference was that all the control teachers placed a heavy emphasis on preparing for the state tests and a didactic skills-based approach to learning.

The results of the study strongly indicated that students in the experimental groups—those who received a variety of research-based differentiated instructional strategies—outperformed their control-group peers significantly in math and reading when controlling for gender, age, prior achievement, and attendance. Furthermore, all students benefited from the intervention, regardless of prior achievement.

The results also suggested that learning can be accelerated for those students who are behind in grade level and that the strategies are powerful because the implementation occurred with several setbacks. Likewise, in each school, only a handful of teachers emerged as strong practitioners, suggesting that greater gains may be realized with better implementation and training. Another positive outcome emerged from the results of a survey, which intimated that many teachers and students enjoyed and perceived value from the courses.

Implications of the study included a call for pretesting students to diagnose deficiencies for differentiated instructional solutions. Overall, the study supported the notion that research-based differentiated instructional strategies can promote student learning and testing outcomes. Another large literacy study affirmed these conclusions.

In her book *Effective Literacy Instruction: Building Successful Reading and Writing Programs*, Langer (2002) reported on the results of a five-year study to characterize the literacy practices of teachers in schools where the students scored significantly higher on standardized tests (i.e., *effective* schools) than their peers at similar schools (i.e., *typical* schools).

The researchers conducted the study in four states at schools with similar student populations, mostly in urban settings with culturally diverse students. Using the results of high-stakes literacy tests, investigators were able to isolate behaviors that occurred in classrooms where the students scored well, compared to demographically similar classrooms where the students performed typically.

Langer and her research team discovered that effective schools nurtured supportive environments. These schools overtly focused on improving student achievement while promoting teacher professional development. At the same time, administrators and other school officials enhanced teacher empowerment with professional instructional activities. The school environment fostered strong commitments to teaching, supported a caring atmosphere toward students and colleagues, and promoted learning "as a normal part of life" (p. 41). Because school climate was closely related to teacher success, she reported several findings related to effective literacy instruction across the middle and high schools.

A major finding related to teacher approaches to skill instruction. In effective schools, teachers instructed using "*separated, simulated*, and *integrated* activities" (p. 14). Separated instruction referred to the process where teachers focused on isolated skills and knowledge, usually by directly showing the students how to do something. Simulated instruction involved applying rules and concepts to a specific area of English language arts. And integrated instruction occurred when students used the skills and knowledge in a purposeful activity.

For example, in effective schools a teacher may explain the steps of paragraph construction to students by illustrating the various parts including the use of topic sentences (separated), and the students may practice writing paragraphs in workbooks (simulated), and perhaps the next day the students may write a letter to a friend drawing on the experience from the previous day (integrated).

In typical schools (i.e., schools where similar students scored expectedly on the tests), teachers used one dominant approach to skill instruction, rather than using all three in a near-equal fashion, which suggested that teachers often failed to differentiate their instructional strategies. Besides advocating a focus on the needs of the individual learners, Dewey (1913, 1938/2008) also articulated an emphasis on inquiry.

Inquiry-based Learning

Inquiry-based learning refers to a range of student-centered pedagogical strategies involving independent investigation of a problem or issue that may contain more than one solution (Barrow, 2006; O'Steen, 2008). In describing the sequence and scope for the arrangement of curricula, Dewey (1938) identified a third way to promote the development of intelligence.

He asserted that "problems are the stimulus of thinking" and that teachers are responsible for organizing content so that instruction "arouses in the learner an active quest for information and the production of new ideas" (p. 79). Through systematic inquiry, students examine problems, and in the process, they create solutions and new forms of knowledge, infusing content knowledge into their interests and experiences.

A paucity of research exists to guide teachers to use inquiry in a high-stakes testing environment. According to Amrein and Berliner (2002a), affluent students in high-performing schools have more opportunities for inquiry learning than poorer students in other schools because the teachers spend more time teaching the tested skills, despite the evidence that lower-achieving students benefit from hands-on activities.

One qualitative study focused on 12 preservice science teachers and concluded that some schools failed to offer significant opportunities for inquiry-based learning. Other schools promoted a holistic view of education and streamlined their curricula to provide time for active learning strategies such as inquiry learning because teachers and school administrators collaborated to provide optimal conditions for hands-on activities (Eick, 2002).

Today, inquiry-based learning is firmly grounded in constructivist pedagogy and occurs across domains and disciplines. Theorists believe that inquiry learning operates within the following contexts:

1. Initial analysis of the problem and activation of prior knowledge through small-group discussion.
2. Elaboration on prior knowledge and active processing of new information.
3. Restructuring of knowledge and active processing of new information.
4. Social knowledge construction.
5. Learning in context.
6. Stimulation of curiosity related to presentation of a relevant problem. (Igo, Moore, Ramsey, & Ricketts, 2008, p. 54)

In addition, much of the research on the effectiveness of inquiry occurred in the sciences.

A recent meta-analysis examined the effects of K–12 science pedagogical strategies on student achievement (Schroeder, Scott, Tolson, Huang, & Lee, 2007). The researchers analyzed hundreds of studies conducted in the United States from 1980 through 2004, ending with 61 studies that met the inclusion requirements of experimental or quasi-experimental design. Inquiry strategies indicated "a strong effect" (p. 1452) over traditional types of teaching such as lecture and teacher-led activities. Moreover, more recent studies suggest that inquiry-based learning results in statistically significant achievement gains for diverse student populations in particular (Lynch, Kuipers, Pyke, & Szesze, 2005; Tal, Krajcik, & Blumenfeld, 2006).

Reflection

A fourth means of developing individual intelligence is through reflection. Dewey (1938) explained reflection as the process of "thinking" with the added "postponement of immediate action" involving the "self-control" of "impulses" (p. 64). In this schema, intelligence operates as the agent of self-control. Reflection allows learners to regulate, monitor, and control their thinking.

In an effort to understand the role of *executive functions*, specifically the regulation of control over thinking and actions, on high-poverty students' performance on high-stakes tests, Waber, Gerber, Turcios, Wagner, and Forbes (2006) conducted a study on a group of 92 fifth graders because "high-stakes achievement testing bears a clear and systematic relationship to their neurobehavioral characteristics, especially executive functioning" (p. 472).

The researchers reported a high correlation between teacher reports of executive function, performance on a psychometric test of executive function, and achievement test scores. More telling, the students performed in the normal range for basic functioning such as memory tasks and processing speeds, which suggests that metacognition plays an important role in the day-to-day functioning of students as well as performance on standardized achievement tests. Metacognition signifies awareness or self-monitoring of reflections and learning.

Furthermore, the study suggested that metacognition played a larger role for performance on English language arts tests than on mathematics exams. The research strongly supported the notion that children from poorer households benefited from targeted metacognitive strategies in schools.

In *effective* schools, Langer (2002) noted that *effective* teachers utilized metacognition in their pedagogy. Furthermore, these exemplary educators also promoted student metacognition by creating nurturing and intimate environments for pupils to reflect on their accomplishments using strategies such as reader-response theory and portfolios. For instance, students created portfolios in one classroom where they reflected on what they had learned and commented on their weaknesses. These portfolios served as springboards for improvement in the proceeding semester.

SOCIALLY USEFUL SKILLS

The development of intelligence depends on the continuity and quality of the experiences. Dewey (1938) said that all experiences were social in nature. Therefore, to navigate toward the "experiences that are worth while" educationally, students must develop socially useful skills (p. 40). Students gain experiences from "the nature of the work done as a social enterprise," which also functions as "the primary source of social control" that gives each student "an opportunity to contribute something" (p. 56). Dewey maintained that teachers should provide social experiences to cultivate socially useful skills.

Evidence from large-scale studies suggests that social skills play an integral part in student achievement on standardized tests (Langer, 2002; Newmann et al., 2001; Smith, Lee, & Newmann, 2001). In a three-year study that examined more than 400 classrooms in 19 Chicago elementary schools with high-poverty students, a research team determined that students with teachers who exposed them to demanding assignments scored considerably higher on standardized math and reading tests.

HEALTHY GROWTH

The third fundamental aspect of curriculum relates to the healthy growth of the individual. Dewey (1938) explicitly acknowledged the role of the curriculum in context, particularly regarding "subject matter . . . in an organization which is free . . . because it is in accord with the growth of experience itself" (pp. 81–82).

Experience originates from the interaction of "needs, desires, purposes, and capacities to create" (p. 44). Hence, students thrive within a broader curriculum in which intelligence—manifested through motivation and reflection and expertly guided with differentiated instructional strategies, including inquiry-based learning—can be exercised to overcome perceived difficulties.

A Narrow Curriculum and Teaching to the Test

Teaching to the test and narrowing the curriculum are widely reported consequences of high-stakes testing. According to Jerald (2006a), "item teachers" teach disaggregated bits of information that are most likely to appear on the test, leading to a narrow curriculum. On the other hand, "curriculum teachers" take into account the full breadth of skills and knowledge associated with a domain (p. 2). Moreover, item teachers tend to substitute the test for the curriculum, resulting in instructional materials that mimic test items such as similar questions or a limited amount of tested vocabulary words.

In order to teach to the test, schools and districts have reduced the scope of the curriculum by eliminating time teachers spend on nontested areas, including nonacademic time spent on lunch, recess, and naps for younger children (Nichols & Berliner, 2007). Additionally, academic areas such as music, art, foreign language, the social studies, and other areas are sometimes neglected because in many states these content areas are not tested. These issues are explored in greater detail in chapter 3.

Authentic Learning

The healthy growth of the individual also depends on the quality of the educational experience. Dewey envisioned curricula in which the items "fall within the scope of ordinary life-experiences" making the subject matter relevant and interesting to the learner, something educators refer to as "authentic" today (p. 73).

In the Chicago schools study, Newmann and his associates (2001) examined thousands of classroom assignments for elements of authentic intellectual work (AIW). The researchers coined the term AIW based on the notion that adults developed mastery when they engaged effectively in complex tasks. Further, the types of tasks that teachers often asked students to perform were quite different from demands placed in the real world of adults. They defined AIW by three main characteristics: the construction of knowledge, disciplined inquiry, and added value beyond school.

The three attributes of AIW, according to the researchers, defined what it meant for adults to function in modern society. Adults are expected to construct knowledge in order to solve "complex problems that are often novel or unique" based on a process of drawing on prior knowledge to devise solutions (Newmann et al., 2001, p. 15). In order for the solutions to be sufficient, adults have to acquire a foundation of basic skills and understanding in previous knowledge.

Likewise, the ability to use that knowledge to promote deep understanding is another characteristic of disciplined inquiry. And, as mentioned earlier, adults across a wide array of occupations engage in elaborated communication during the course of their work and often report the outcomes. In sum, disciplined inquiry is the development of a prior knowledge base, the application of that knowledge base in unique ways to promote deep understanding on specific tasks, and the ability to use complex communication both during the process and after to report the results.

AIW has broad applications beyond the school environment, which inherently gives value and meaning to the task. Examples of this type of work in school include investing hypothetical money in the stock market to learn mathematical fractions or writing letters to politicians to enhance writing skills and civic engagement. The researchers reported that students who received challenging assignments scored substantially higher on standardized reading and math tests, more than 20 percent above the national average.

In contrast, those students in classrooms with less challenging work scored "25 percent less than the national average in reading and 22 percent less in mathematics" (Newmann et al., 2001, p. 23). Moreover, further investigation revealed that high-quality assignments benefited all students, although low achievers benefited more in mathematics while high achievers benefited more in reading.

Attitudes about Learning

A final consideration of the healthy growth of the individual is his or her attitudes about learning. Dewey (1938) stated that the most important attitude is the "desire to go on learning" (p. 48). Yet, by several accounts, the pressure of high-stakes testing creates negative attitudes toward learning (Gulek, 2003; Jerald, 2006a; Nichols & Berliner, 2007).

In a literature review of best practices for preparing students for standardized tests, Gulek (2003) pointed out that while some people believe that high-stakes testing leads to greater alignment of the curriculum with instruction, many studies indicated a growing consensus that high-stakes testing led to negative attitudes toward learning and increased test anxiety. The anxiety appears to affect students differently. In general, non-White female students experience more test anxiety than males and White students. Test anxiety often leads to cognitive interference, which adversely impacts student test performance. Similarly, test anxiety also stymies a student's ability to study meaningfully.

Suggested strategies for reducing test anxiety include the following:

1. Introduce and provide examples of test questions to the students to enhance confidence—a little test preparation provides maximum benefit.
2. Provide positive affirmations of students' abilities.
3. Offer coping strategies for dealing with stress while acknowledging that some stress is beneficial for alertness.
4. Allow students to take breaks during long tests with opportunities for stretching to relieve stress. (Gulek, 2003)

Further, test anxiety begins in the elementary grades and intensifies as the student advances through high school. Few students seek services, perhaps

because of embarrassment; therefore, teacher referrals may be critical in identifying and aiding those students. Teachers can reduce anxiety by teaching
time management and incorporating a variety of active-learning strategies to
reach all learners. Teachers can also integrate key words and practice careful
reading during test times (Ross & Driscoll, 2006).

CONCLUSION

In contemporary society, education reform rests on the assumption that we
must prepare children for twenty-first-century jobs, and the only way to
achieve this is to articulate the standards and skills, then test some of them at
various intervals throughout their publicly educated lives.

As Shapiro (2008) conjectured, "Where is the concern for our children's
emotional life, intellectual curiosity, creativity, ethical awareness, and spiritual development?" (p. 21). Similarly, one can argue that there is a disconcert-
ing lack of concern for the unacceptable attrition rates of minority students.
Educational research suggests that these concerns can be addressed by invok-
ing best practices.

Some of the large-scale studies offer encouraging results (Langer, 2002;
Newmann et al., 2001; Smith et al., 2001). We can provide *all* children a
quality education without resorting to didactic teaching and drill-and-kill
practice. In fact, the scenario is much more complicated than it appears on
the surface.

When we use Dewey's philosophy as a paradigm to examine best practices,
we see that everything from school climate, teacher instructional choices, and
student dispositions offers a complex interplay that can enhance or attenuate
student achievement on high-stakes tests—or perhaps influence whether a
student remains in school.

Moreover, all of these factors may symbiotically and exponentially affect
the others. It is not hard to imagine how powerful a force motivation is and
how selecting the right instructional strategies and combining them with
authentic intellectual tasks can lead to success in other areas, such as the development of peer collaboration skills and heightened reflection. According
to the research, these students perform better on standardized tests and derive
more satisfaction from school (Balfanz et al., 2004).

Discussion Questions

1. In what ways did Dewey's early life contribute to his philosophy of education?

2. How has the role of the federal government evolved during the standards-based reform movement?
3. What are the major provisions of the No Child Left Behind Act of 2001? Are all the provisions attainable? Why?
4. Articulate arguments *for* and *against* high-stakes testing. Where do you stand on the issue?
5. According to Dewey, what does it mean to educate the *whole* child?
6. What role does motivation play in high-stakes testing? How does research support or refute this role?
7. What does differentiated instruction look like? How does research inform us about the effectiveness of differentiated instruction?
8. What is the purpose of reflection? What are some specific ways for teachers to use reflection in the classroom?
9. In great detail, describe an assignment that contains authentic intellectual work (AIW). What are the requisite parts? According to the research, AIW is a powerful instructional strategy. Why?
10. Discuss the role of the teacher in promoting the healthy growth of the individual child. Other than those issues addressed in this chapter, what else is important?

Further Reflection

1. Today, we often hear of "cultural wars" being fought over the curriculum. How are today's battles *similar* and *different* from the issues dividing the traditionalists and progressives in Dewey's time?
2. Reflect on a time when you either witnessed or engaged in an effective lesson. What made it effective? In what ways did it address the needs of the whole student?
3. What content areas does your state test? What types of test questions are on the examinations? Why does this matter?

Chapter Two

Changing Demographics: Promoting the New Democracy, Education, and the Whole Child

The power of the public schools to assimilate different races to our own institutions, through the education given to the younger generation, is doubtless one of the most remarkable exhibitions of vitality that the world has ever seen.

—Dewey (1976d, p. 85)

The structure of repression in the personality thus had its source, according to Dewey, in undemocratic forms of social organization; democracy extended would witness the achievement of wholeness in people, the end of repression.

—Feuer (1959, p. 567)

In the first decades of the twentieth century, profound population shifts dramatically altered the American landscape as millions of immigrants flooded into towns and cities primarily from eastern and southern Europe. While many conservative and reactionary forces viewed these influxes as threats to the status quo and way of life, Dewey embraced these changes by arguing that all citizens benefited from coming into contact with diverse individuals because these encounters informed and enriched personal experiences as long as there was mutual listening and respect.

Because schools were smaller communities imitating larger structures, they served a unique capacity for assimilating immigrants while evolving to meet the needs of all citizens because the modern industrial world broke down traditional forms of authority such as the family and church. Therefore, Dewey asserted that schools should become more democratic in a political sense and, at the same time, serve higher moral and intellectual purposes. In the end, students' exposure to other viewpoints enhanced the inquiry process and the development of intelligence exercised through socially useful skills, which ultimately led to the healthy growth of each individual. Of course, democracy as a social and political institution also benefited because citizens freely associated as a public to identify and solve common problems.

Today, we also are experiencing massive immigration flows into the United States, presenting many problems and opportunities, particularly in education. While NCLB targets English language learners (ELLs) with additional resources, it fails to address some of the pressing underlying conditions such as the effects of undocumented immigrant status as well as the lack of flow of services from the federal to the state and local levels. Moreover, ELL students are increasingly showing up in states where services and expertise are underdeveloped, and they are often concentrated in low-performing schools. One indication of the severity of the challenge is the high dropout rates associated with immigrant populations. Therefore, teaching to the whole ELL student is not only good for individuals, but is also necessary for sustaining democracy in an aging, pluralistic society.

Focus Questions

1. How does democracy relate to teaching and learning?
2. Who are the new immigrants in your community?
3. How do immigration patterns of 100 years ago compare and contrast with immigration today?
4. In what ways do all students benefit from supporting diversity in the schools?

--- ∞ ---

In the early decades of the twentieth century, global population shifts transformed the landscape of the United States. During this epoch, millions of European immigrants, together with smaller numbers from around the world, flooded the towns and cities in search of jobs and new ways of life. As often happens with such abrupt changes, the concerned citizens of the United States engaged in vigorous debates about the effects of immigration on jobs and political and social institutions.

Of course, schools were not immune to these debates, and it was not surprising that Dewey would comment during these turbulent times. According to Eisele (1975), between 1902 and 1927, Dewey was to write about immigrants at least a dozen times. Throughout these early years, persons obtaining legal permanent resident status exceeded one million, not to be reached again until the latter part of the century. In his writings and speeches, Dewey staunchly supported the rights and roles of immigrants in American society.

Even more importantly, Dewey's educational philosophy valued the diversity of perspectives resulting from the cultural encounters, which enriched the experiences of those engaged in learning. However, in the 1970s, a revisionist view emerged challenging Dewey's commitment to immigrant rights and issues.

In spite of this reinterpretation, nearly all of Dewey's pronouncements, writings, and acts pointed to the essential benefits of embracing diverse national, ethnic, and social perspectives in strengthening democracy and education, providing lessons relevant for today. The new democracy is about welcoming students from all walks of life and places, because in the end, every student benefits from others' lived experiences. As a consequence, schools, according to Dewey, must constantly evolve to meet the changing needs of students and society.

DEWEY AND THE IMMIGRANTS

The American manufacturing juggernaut steamed full-speed ahead in the first decade of the twentieth century, and millions of immigrants, primarily from southern and western Europe, were beckoned to the shores of America in search of jobs, more freedom, and a higher standard of living. Between 1900 and 1909, the U.S. government granted over 8.2 million individuals legal permanent status with 92 percent of the new arrivals originating from Europe.

In the next decade, 1910–1919, the numbers decreased to 6.3 million persons followed by another drop to a total of nearly 4.3 million in the third decade from 1920 to 1929, representing a nearly 50 percent decrease from the high of the first decade. Stoked by growing nativist sentiments, the weariness of World War I, the perception of the war as a European problem, and the impending Great Depression, the political winds shifted to an isolationist stance by the end of the 1920s resulting in a steep drop-off in immigration into the United States.

By the fourth decade of the 1930s, fewer than 700,000 immigrants were granted legal permanent status (Department of Homeland Security, 2009). These changes reflected the perception of an immigration problem to which Dewey responded as a staunch supporter of inclusion.

Many of Dewey's ideas were profoundly shaped by his establishment of the laboratory school at the University of Chicago and his close personal friendship with Jane Addams. In the atmosphere of late nineteenth-century Chicago, Dewey embraced a culture that had rebounded from the repressive

policies following the violent uprising of the Haymarket affair, an 1886 pro-
test that resulted in the deaths of eight police officers and countless civilians,
to become the most socially progressive in the nation (Feuer, 1959).

Addams founded Hull House, part of the settlement house movement, in
Chicago in 1899 for the impoverished and homesick immigrants who flocked
to the burgeoning city. In Addams, Dewey discovered a like soul who was
unwaveringly committed to bringing democracy to the downtrodden and
achieving practical goals through social legislation.

In an introductory essay commemorating the republication of her book
Peace and Bread in Time of War, Dewey (1945) exclaimed, "In nothing is
Miss Addams' book more timely than in its sense of the positive values contributed by our immigrant populations" (p. xvi). In fact, Dewey's philosophy
supported the influx of diverse groups as a mechanism for bolstering democracy and education.

VALUING DIVERSITY IN
DEMOCRACY AND EDUCATION

Dewey essentially altered the definition of democracy by describing active
connections among democracy, citizenship, and diversity (Karier, 1975). He
argued that progression into the modern world was characterized by the specialization of labor based on Darwin's evolutionary principles. Initially, the
family or tribe passed on the requisite knowledge to the young.

Subsequently, with the rise of the great city-states and empires of antiq-
uity, Western knowledge became codified in the schools of ancient Greece
and Rome. And following the collapse of the Roman Empire in the Middle
Ages, the church assumed the primary role of formally educating individuals
as part of the spiritual realm on Earth and as preparation for the hereafter. In
order for modern citizens to survive and flourish, the state had to assume the
complex task of educating youth because of the explosion in knowledge into
domains and disciplines.

With the rise of the modern states, individuals demanded and exercised
more political freedoms bringing different classes and varieties of peoples
together like never before. In a complex democratic society, Dewey argued,
citizenship was transformed from a purely political process to one that included the right of individuals to freely associate in order to solve problems
both in and out of the political arena. Schools, he asserted further, should be
reformed to reflect these new modern realities.

The traditional liberal arts curriculum of the late nineteenth century promoted the transmission of knowledge through memorization and recitation

and emanated from an intellectual perspective with emphases on classical languages and the humanities, not particularly useful to the masses who labored during the Industrial Revolution. Moreover, the great advances in technology—particularly transportation—that allowed for "[t]he intermingling in the school of youth of different races, differing religions, and unlike customs creates for all a new and broader environment" (Dewey, 1938, p. 21).

While the larger public wrestled with problems related to the swift demographic changes of towns and cities, Dewey advocated the assimilative role of schools as a solution. He rejected the notion of American society as a melting pot and the Americanization of immigrants, instead establishing a culturally pluralistic position, something Westbrook (1991) attributed to Dewey's desire "to build an ethnic and racial democracy to be a model for international politics" (p. 212).

As part of this model, Dewey recognized that a cultural balance must be maintained between the ethnic heritage of the immigrants and societal harmony. To that end, he declared:

> Indeed wise observers in both New York and Chicago have recently sounded a note of alarm. They have called attention to the fact that in some respects the children are too rapidly, I will not say Americanized, but too rapidly denationalized. They lose the positive and conservative value of their own native traditions, their native music, art, and literature. (Dewey, 1976d, p. 85)

Dewey lamented the loss of the "positive and conservative value" of heritage that newly arrived immigrants brought to the shores of America because these traditions enriched the experiences of all around as long as there was interaction and mutual respect, which later led him to proclaim an oft-repeated aphorism, "The point is to see to it that the hyphen connects instead of separates. And this means at least that our public schools shall teach each factor to respect every other, and shall take pains to enlighten all as to the great past contributions of every strain in our composite make-up" (Dewey, 1918, p. 286).

School served the purpose of assimilating the immigrant children into American society, and native children benefited mutually from the exposure to diverse perspectives resulting in a strengthening of democracy as a political process, and equally important, as an inquiry mechanism for learning, which he described in some detail.

Dewey viewed the school as an organic entity, which evolved with the needs of a modern democratic society. In a speech delivered to the National Council of Education in Minneapolis, Dewey (1976d) outlined four factors supporting schools as social centers. First, he discussed how transportation innovations and the rapid dissemination of information and ideas brought people together from around the world. Recognizing the dangers of the global displacement of masses of individuals, he viewed schools as one of "the various ways in which social and intellectual intercourse may be promoted, and employs them systematically, not only to counteract dangers which these same agencies are bringing with them, but so as to make them positive causes in raising the whole level of life" (Dewey, 1976d, p. 85).

Second, he recognized that in the modern world, traditional familial and social controls diminished with the increasing opportunities for forming associations with others. In a world of factories and time clocks, parents exerted less influence over their children than in isolated agrarian societies and medieval towns. At the same time that familial social bonds weakened, the traditional power of the church to morally guide citizens also eroded.

Schools, according to Dewey, could provide the discipline and structure resulting from the power vacuum. In a 1916 speech before the National Education Association, Dewey asserted that schools protected democracy in moral and intellectual ways by "subordinating a local, provincial, sectarian, and partisan spirit of mind to aims and interests which are common to all men and women of the country . . . which form the mind and morals of the community" (Dewey, 1918, p. 284).

Further, he noted that society must provide other agencies as well for the continued support of the older generations and those who completed their short stints in the schools. At the turn of the century, the average American completed about five grades.

Third, Dewey acknowledged the increasingly interconnected world of ideas that related to daily living. In effect, a traditional, intellectual, liberal arts curriculum was divorced from most people's reality in modern times: a reality of specialized labor and applied science. In former times, most workers were part of a whole system either in making things like in a guild, or in growing things through an agricultural cycle. Dewey saw schools as a way to make individuals whole again, so "that they are instructed in the scientific foundation and social bearings of the things they see about them, and of the activities in which they are themselves engaging" (Dewey, 1976d, p. 89).

And fourth, Dewey pointed out that modern times demand continuous learning because of rapidly changing conditions. New problems sprouted and new ideas were exchanged at rates that defied previous generations. The school served the function of bringing people and ideas together into a community whose members communicated with each other and practiced mutual respect in the pursuit of common and shared purposes.

Because schools were smaller communities nested within the larger societal structures, children benefited from the same democratic freedoms as adults. They engaged collaboratively through work and play in the pursuit of common purposes while concomitantly establishing links to the community beyond school boundaries. Dewey posited that democracy and education were joined together by the communication of disparate individuals genuinely engaged in a respectful give-and-take of ideas and words. In the process, they developed common bonds and experiences.

Further, within Dewey's central idea of the growth of intelligence exercised through inquiry experiences (see chapter 5 for a detailed analysis), coming in contact with diverse perspectives enriched learning. As Pring (2007) noted:

> Democracy is a deep and active communication between individuals. It welcomes and sustains diversity of experience and background. It reflects the constant attempt to break down the barriers that inhibit communication—those of social class, racial stereotyping, or selective schooling. Any such separateness impoverishes the experience of all. It blocks off the experiences of others from which one's own experience would be enriched. (p. 119)

Given the centrality of diversity to Dewey's philosophical foundation, it is necessary to briefly examine the Polish study of World War I, and the resultant revisionist history of the 1970s, which severely questioned Dewey's commitment to immigrants and democracy.

THE POLISH STUDY AND THE QUESTIONING OF DEWEY'S COMMITMENT TO DEMOCRACY

In 1975, reflecting a resurgence of interest in Dewey, the *History of Education Quarterly* devoted an entire issue to him. The special publication ignited a firestorm of controversy as two sides coalesced into competing camps around the issue of Dewey's commitment to democracy about an event that came to be known as the "Polish question" (Westbrook, 1991, p. 212).

During World War I, Dewey abandoned isolationism and articulated an interventionist stance, arguing that the effects of globalization necessitated that the United States intervene in the affairs of Europe and provide a model for a culturally pluralistic society. This also marked the beginning of Dewey's foray into politics and international affairs.

Dewey's critics contended that he abandoned his scientific empiricism for intervention that recklessly tied democracy to the use of force. The criticism reemerged in the 1970s among education historians in relation to a study Dewey conducted during the war examining Polish immigrant politics in the United States (Westbrook, 1991).

While teaching a philosophy seminar at Columbia University around 1917, Dewey encountered a student with substantial means who proposed to finance a study of Philadelphia's Polish community. The study evolved into a political investigation centered on competing factions vying for public support in assuming control of a newly independent Poland as proposed by President Woodrow Wilson.

Dewey and the other investigators viewed this as an opportunity to apply Dewey's democratic philosophy in the real world. Two leading factions emerged in the conflict, a conservative organization, which supported a restoration of the monarchy, and the other a liberal group, which proposed the creation of a liberal democracy. During the war, the Allied governments conferred semirecognition on the conservative faction because it identified with czarist Russia, a nation that supported the Allies in the war effort.

When a bill surfaced in Congress that would recognize the conservative faction as the official Polish government-in-exile, Dewey vigorously objected in published articles and speeches. Dewey attempted to pressure the government to prevent the conservatives from meeting in Detroit in August 1918 and urged the forming of a commission to investigate his claims. In doing so, "Dewey was not simply calling for policies to guarantee a freer circulation of information on Polish affairs but was recommending that the American government take an active, indeed a controlling, role in Polish-American politics" (Westbrook, 1991, p. 219).

Therefore, the entire episode provided an ironic moment in the life of John Dewey by illustrating how someone so committed to democracy was willing to abandon democratic means in order to advance his own ideals. As Westbrook (1991) succinctly stated, "Dewey here called for manipulation to end manipulation" (p. 221). It appeared that Dewey could not resist the temptation to align Deweyan democracy with Wilsonian idealism, and nearly 60 years later, he was again the subject of intense speculation.

Clearly, prior to the publication of the special *History of Education Quarterly* issue, tension simmered among educational historians about Dewey's commitment to immigrants and democracy. The ensuing arguments appeared in the form of claims, counterclaims, and rebuttals over the next year and a half.

Despite all the ironies associated with Dewey's Polish study, the compendium of evidence—a long lifetime of democratic devotion—indicates that Dewey valued immigrants and the strengthening of democracy. Similar to a hundred years ago, today we find ourselves at a similar crossroads, embracing the vibrant diversity of new waves of immigrants and sorting out the role of schools.

A BRIEF OVERVIEW OF U.S. IMMIGRATION LAWS

Immigration laws in the United States emanated from perceived problems, often based on underlying racial ideologies. Before the 1880s, there were no laws restricting immigration, but with the passage of a law in 1885, restrictions were placed on Chinese immigrants largely because of pressure exerted by dismayed Californians. Later, in 1917, laws were enacted to completely deny all immigrants from East Asia into the United States together with anyone deemed illiterate (Capps, 2007).

As America became increasingly isolationist following World War I, restrictions were also placed on immigrants arriving from Europe. Laws passed in the 1920s were directed mainly at new arrivals from eastern and southern Europe through a mechanism that required immigration quotas to correspond to 1890 ethnic distributions. By postdating the standard, Congress was able to severely limit the total number of immigrants from these regions. These quotas were reaffirmed in 1952 with the passage of the Immigration and Nationality Act (Capps, 2007).

Beginning in the 1960s, immigration laws were liberalized reflecting a changing awareness of discriminatory practices. The policy of setting quotas on national origins was abandoned in favor of treating all immigrants equally. In 1976, countries of the Western Hemisphere were also included in this major policy shift.

Congress passed the Immigration Reform Control Act of 1986 (IRCA), which completely transformed the old system with two new reforms. First, it granted legal status to about 1.7 million undocumented immigrants who had been residing in the United States for at least five years. Second, it also provided legal status to about 1 million undocumented agricultural workers. And third, it punished employers who knowingly hired undocumented workers (Capps, 2007).

In 1990, Congress again passed immigration laws, which boosted the flows of immigrants into the country by about 40 percent. With an emphasis on increasing numbers for those seeking employment and those from previously underrepresented countries, the number of work visas tripled and a special diversity category was implemented. The intent was to admit more immigrants from Europe, but the result was increased flows from Asia and Africa. Since the 1990 law, the government has enacted legislation affecting the legality of immigration including immigration and welfare reform laws in 1996 and the USA PATRIOT Act of 2002.

The net effect today has been massive flows of both documented and undocumented immigrants. Of a total foreign-born population in 2005 of about 37 million people, 10.5 million (28 percent) are legal permanent residents, 11.1 million (30 percent) are unauthorized immigrants, 11.5 million (31 percent) are naturalized citizens, 2.6 million (7 percent) are refugees and asylees, and 1.3 million (3 percent) are legal temporary residents (Capps, 2007; Monger & Rytina, 2009).

As the name suggests, legal permanent residents are allowed to permanently reside in the United States and are usually sponsored by family members or employers. Unauthorized immigrants, on the other hand, may have entered the country illegally—such as large numbers crossing the Mexican-American border—remain after their temporary visas expire, or breach the rules of their entry. After living in the United States for at least five years, legal permanent residents can typically qualify to become naturalized citizens. If they marry a citizen, the wait is reduced to three years. At that time they must pass a citizenship test in English and endure rigorous background checks.

Before they can enter the United States, refugees must apply for legal entry demonstrating a real threat of persecution. Asylees, likewise, must also establish persecution, but they have already entered the United States and may have violated the terms of a temporary visa or entered illegally. After one year, they may seek legal permanent resident status. Every year, large numbers of foreign tourists, workers, and students enter and qualify as legal temporary residents. Overall, current immigration flows are at historic peaks (Capps, 2007), which mirrors earlier patterns of a century ago.

CURRENT U.S. IMMIGRANT SETTLEMENT PATTERNS

Exactly 75 years separates the two years when persons obtaining legal immigrant status in the United States topped 1 million. In 1914, the figure was 1,218,480 and in 1989 it nearly doubled from the previous year to end at 1,090,172 persons. Through most of the 1990s the numbers continued to be substantial, but hovered below the million-person mark.

In the 2000s, individuals seeking legal resident status surged once again, reflecting uncertain world events and quests for jobs. The foreign-born population of the United States crested in 1910 to about 15 percent of the total population, although in 2005 it reached a similar height of about 12 percent of the total (Capps, 2007).

The U.S. Department of Homeland Security reported that the new permanent residents were born in about 200 different countries (Monger & Rytina, 2009). Like nearly 100 years ago, massive immigration has changed the landscape of the United States. In addition, three distinctions characterize the current immigrant populations: how they entered the United States, where they settled, and their socioeconomic status.

What clearly distinguish current immigrant settlement patterns from earlier ones are the large number of immigrants entering the United States illegally, the new ethnic distributions in the non-California West, the Midwest, and the Southeast, and typical immigrant profiles. The Center on Labor, Human Services and Population at the Urban Institute estimates that in the United States today there are nearly as many undocumented immigrants as documented ones (Capps, 2007). Further, the dispersal of immigrants across new regions of the United States and the characteristics of the immigrants present many challenges for educators and society.

Between 1990 and 2008, the estimated number of unauthorized immigrants residing in the United States exploded from 3.5 million to 11.9 million. Of these immigrants, about three-fourths are Hispanic and about 59 percent, or 7 million, are from Mexico. Combined with the regions of Central America, Asia, South America, and the Caribbean, these places account for over 90 percent of the total U.S. immigrant population.

After Mexico, the leading countries of origin for undocumented persons are China, the Philippines, and India. Furthermore, today, unauthorized immigrants represent about 4 percent of the total population and 5.4 percent of the labor force (Capps, 2007; Hoefer, Rytina, & Baker, 2009; Passel & Cohn, 2009).

Before the 1990s, a vast majority of immigrants settled in just six states: California, Texas, Florida, Illinois, New Jersey, and New York. In total numbers, many immigrants still settle in those states, but the acceleration into the other regions has been dramatic. For example, from 2000 to 2005, South Carolina experienced the fastest growth in immigrant populations.

Throughout the 1990s, North Carolina held the distinction. With the exception of just a few northern Rocky Mountain states, Arizona, Louisiana, and some rustbelt states of the northern Midwest and Atlantic regions, nearly all the other continental states experienced rapid increases, with 20 states actually exceeding the growth rate of the big six. The issue for many of these states is that they started with a relatively small base of immigrants, which amplifies immigrant surges.

Unlike the big six, they have not developed the expertise or resources to deal with the diverse influxes, particularly with regard to social and school services. The political backlash has been immense with many longtime residents supporting immigration reform that would restrict immigrants' entry, and in some cases, their benefits and rights (Capps, 2007; Passel & Cohn, 2009).

Other characteristics distinguishing the immigrants settling the new growth areas from established settlements are their age and legal and socioeconomic status. Compared to the two-thirds of the immigrant population settled in the lower-growth, big six states, they tend to be younger in age, and contain larger numbers of unauthorized entries and poorer, non-English speakers with lower levels of educational attainment. All this adds up to increased strains on limited school resources in areas ill-equipped and unrehearsed in servicing these populations. When the data are analyzed further, additional challenges abound (Capps, 2007; Passel & Cohn, 2009).

When we look at the big picture, a pattern emerges in the early 2000s, where immigrants in substantial numbers, both documented and undocumented, fulfill an economic need to work low-paying and menial jobs. In turn, rapid demographic changes and the cost of providing services, particularly to children, has skyrocketed producing anxiety and conflict.

The implications for education and democracy are numerous. In 2008, 5.5 million children had at least one undocumented parent, even though 73 percent of the kids were themselves U.S.-born citizens. Undocumented parents are less likely to become involved in the schools because of their fear of arrest and deportation.

Moreover, about two-thirds of all limited English proficiency (LEP) students are not first-generation immigrants; rather, they are born in the United States and reside in homes where another language is spoken. Furthermore, recent trends indicate that LEP students are increasingly concentrated in handfuls of schools in both the well-established immigrant enclaves as well as some of the new gateway communities. These schools contain a high concentration of poor, minority students and tend to have less-qualified teachers than low-LEP schools (Capps, 2007; Passel & Cohn, 2009).

As Capps (2007) concluded, "This concentration means that children are not just attending schools that are economically and ethnically segregated, but also linguistically isolated" (p. 199). Of course, linguistic isolation is also a characteristic of the home (Covington Clarkson, 2008). Given this combination of factors—high poverty, community conflict, minority and immigrant concentration in low-performing schools with less-qualified teachers, and linguistic isolation—many immigrant children are at risk for school failure.

Another factor increasing the odds of school failure among many immigrant children is the interruption in formal education. Among the increasing waves of immigrant students, many of them are classified as students with interrupted formal education or SIFE.

According to the Office of English Language Learners of the New York City Department of Education (NYC DOE), SIFE differ from other English language learners because they are older than typical students in the grades they are placed, tend to fall two or more years below grade level in math and reading, are unfamiliar with the sociocultural aspects of U.S. schools, and are illiterate or exhibit little literacy in their native languages. Moreover, many of the students struggle to earn a living while in school (DeCapua, Smathers, & Tang, 2007; Medina, 2009; Santos, 2007).

New York State is one of the only states to actually address SIFE. Being one of the big six states, it also has an extensive history of adapting to meet the needs of diverse and nontraditional students. In the 2005–2006 school year, approximately 13.4 percent or 18,900 of the entire ELL population in New York City was diagnosed as SIFE (DeCapua et al., 2007).

Further, many of the SIFE tend to enter New York City schools in the eighth, ninth, and tenth grades, and the largest contingent (12.5 percent) is concentrated in District 79, which is a unique citywide program of over 300 alternative schools and programs serving over 20,000 school-age students and 50,000 adult learners. In 2003, the NYC DOE launched a program specifically targeted at this population because little was understood about the students' attributes and needs.

In addition, only 45 percent of all SIFE who entered the system in middle school ever exited from an ELL program; for those entering at the high school level, an even more abysmal 15 percent were ever able to leave ELL services. Many of these students failed in a standards-based, high-stakes testing environment leading to prolific dropout rates and few graduating as program completers.

With a mandate from NCLB, the NYC DOE committed new resources in the form of personnel, programs, and data collection, yet the spending is spread evenly across the entire ELL population, meaning extra funds are not spent directly on SIFE. Not surprisingly, most of these programs are concentrated on increasing achievement in English language arts and math. Working with the City University of New York (CUNY), the DOE is currently evaluating the effectiveness of the program (Medina, 2009; Santos, 2007).

NO CHILD LEFT BEHIND AND
THE NEW IMMIGRANTS

Title III of the No Child Left Behind Act of 2001, also called, "Language Instruction for Limited English Proficient and Immigrant Students," addresses needs and strategies for the burgeoning immigrant student population to meet state standards. With an initial grant amount of $650 million in 2002, the legislation empowers state agencies to ensure that all ELL teachers are certified in English and any other program languages to provide high-quality oral and written instruction. While districts and schools are free to select a curriculum and resources, the methods must be based on proven scientific research. Moreover, at least 95 percent of the grants must be directed to the local level (U.S. Department of Education, 2002b).

One of the main objectives of the legislation is to increase ELL students' English proficiency by promoting achievement on high-stakes tests. All ELL students are required to participate in the same assessments as all other students.

Title I and Title III of NCLB also require that schools measure English proficiency in ELL students from kindergarten through grade 12.

During their first year of enrollment, ELL students are exempt from taking the English language arts (ELA)/reading assessment at the discretion of the local education agencies (LEAs). The LEAs may also allow the students to take the ELA/reading assessments in their native languages from three to five additional years. Schools may provide other accommodations as well, such as extra time and bilingual dictionaries.

However, schools must meet the 95 percent testing requirement for adequate yearly progress (AYP) purposes. Further, schools are required to disaggregate the data based on socioeconomic status, gender, ethnicity, and home language. If the ELL students collectively fail to meet the required achievement targets, the school faces onerous sanctions (see chapter 1).

In addition, failing schools are required to provide students with private tutoring (Jacobson, 2006). NCLB also requires that the schools involve parents by notifying them that their child requires specialized language instruction and that, when available, they have the right to select the type of program. Parents also have the right to remove children from these programs (Capps, 2007; U.S. Department of Education, 2002a).

PROBLEMS ASSOCIATED WITH NO CHILD LEFT BEHIND AND IMMIGRANT STUDENTS

Despite the emphasis on improving the performance of ELL students, NCLB, according to its critics, either causes schools to channel adolescent students into adult programs, does not go far enough in identifying problems, or fails to address fundamental needs. Adolescent ELL students may be denied the services and opportunities provided to their peers.

Likewise, the reporting requirements of NCLB are problematic because they fail to capture specific immigrant populations that may be small in number. Additionally, the legislation does not address the true problems underlying school failure because the federal government does not provide funds to *integrate* the students and their families into the schools and communities.

One unintended effect of NCLB on adolescent ELL students is the pressure they face to enroll in adult literacy courses rather than in public high schools. Because schools are required to test ELL students after one year in the system, administrators are reluctant to welcome immigrants into their schools because of failure to achieve adequate yearly progress. In addition, schools are under intense pressure to cut costs in these lean economic times, and immigrant students are often viewed as a drain on valuable resources (Rance-Roney, 2009).

When immigrant students are welcomed into our nation's public schools, one of the main criticisms of the NCLB reporting requirements is that the data disaggregation fails to capture small immigrant populations spread across schools in a district. While NCLB requires the reporting of LEP students, it also requires only five main categories for reporting ethnic group identification: African/African American, American Indian, Asian/Asian American, Hispanic, and White.

Therefore, unless immigrant students from a particular region settle in one school in significant numbers, their uniqueness and needs go unreported. For instance, immigrants from particular regions or countries of the world may number fewer than 20 in a school and are often reported within other subgroups that come from places with different languages, cultures, and ethnicities.

A student from a sub-Saharan African country such as Zambia will be wholly different from a student from Egypt, but they will often be placed together in the same subgroup. Another criticism is that even if the subgroups are fairly representative one year, they may not be the next because of rapidly changing immigration patterns.

As Covington Clarkson (2008) reports, "[T]he ELL category is not sufficient to report the diverse groups of immigrant students, their reasons for immigrating, their previous experience with formal education, and the resulting challenges that are faced in the classroom and the communities" (p. 24). In other words, reporting does not require vital data that may be critical for addressing fundamental needs.

The problems associated with the reporting function of NCLB belie even greater challenges with the integration of families and students into the schools and communities. NCLB, and the federal government as a whole, does little to nothing to support the integration of immigrant families. The burden falls on states, municipalities, and local schools, which, in most cases, have neither the expertise nor adequate funding.

The reality is that in the United States today, there is a critical mass of authorized and unauthorized immigrants who have children. About three-fourths of the children are natural-born citizens and are entitled to all the rights and privileges of citizenship. Further, undocumented students are entitled to a free, public education. Yet, the parents are reticent to fully assert these rights because of their own fear of arrest and deportation.

One consequence is that parents do not get involved with the schools. Another consequence is that a general perception emerges at the local level that immigrants exhaust limited resources, producing a xenophobic reaction as it did in California in 1994 when the voters approved Proposition 187, which sharply curtailed immigrants from using health care, public education, and other government services; a federal court later ruled the proposition unconstitutional (Morse & Ludovina, 1999).

The failure to integrate families into the schools and communities means that many of the neediest students are not able to take advantage of available resources. Because immigrant students are concentrated in high-poverty areas, many attend schools that fail to make adequate yearly progress for two years in a row.

In these cases, students are entitled to receive free private tutoring as part of the substantial 20 percent of Title I money given to schools for transportation. A significant percentage of states do not evaluate the quality of the tutoring programs, and few students actually take advantage of the service. According to the Center on Education Policy, only 18 percent of eligible students actually enroll in free tutoring. The center also estimates this percentage to be lower for immigrant students because parents are concerned about exposing their unauthorized status (Jacobson, 2006).

Contrary to public opinion at the local level, several studies in the 1990s concluded that immigrants contributed more to society than the cost of providing governmental services because they were reluctant to use the services and, while most immigrants worked jobs and overpaid taxes, they were also reluctant to file tax returns to collect refunds.

However, the perception at the local level is quite different because while tax receipts may flow copiously to the federal government producing a net surplus in unclaimed money, at the state and local levels that may not be the case. The government provides limited grant assistance to the schools through the English language provisions of NCLB, but a substantial burden falls on local municipalities to fund the schools and other social services.

By failing to address fundamental needs and the integration of immigrants into society, we are in danger of creating a permanent underclass of our fastest-growing population in an aging society, which can only portend bad long-term outcomes for democracy. Likewise, by failing to address the needs and fears of unauthorized immigrants, we are preventing them from using one of their greatest assets in ensuring their children's academic success, specifically the full support of families.

DEWEY, PARENTS, AND FAMILIES

In his laboratory school at the University of Chicago, Dewey recognized the importance of parental involvement for reforming education to make it more democratic. At the turn of the nineteenth century, American students studying subjects of interest, working with others on common projects, and moving around the classroom (and the outdoors!) at will were radical ideas.

Parents formed an association to be part of the process and to offer defense of these reform measures. Teachers were also invited to attend these meetings. By the 1930s, it became acceptable and mainstream for parents and teachers to inform the educational process. Before that time, administrators held authoritative sway over the daily rituals of education, mimicking the authoritative traditional structure of classroom schooling.

Dewey's school-parent association was charged with two purposes: First, the association discussed pedagogical and learning theories and how best to implement them at the school. Second, the parents participated in guiding school activities. Of particular interest to Dewey was the idea that the cooperation students engaged in at home was also carried over into the activities of the school. In other words, he was aligning the communal life in the home sphere with the development of a school community based on democratic principles of free associations with others.

In Dewey's time, the school matriculated White middle- and upper-class children, meaning that these democratic reforms were highly limited in scope. Further, it was not until the civil rights reform era of the 1960s that schools also embarked on various missions to involve high-poverty and minority parents (Tanner, 1997).

Legally recognizing undocumented immigrants, together with supporting and educating families, may be the key for breaking the vicious cycle of nonparental involvement and unacceptably high failure rates. One successful group of immigrants, studied in the 1970s and 1980s, may offer insights on approaching current challenges.

"THE BOAT PEOPLE"

In 1981, Caplan, Choy, and Whitmore conducted a major study to document the economic achievement of Indochinese refugees and asylees. The study included three groups of refugees: a group of Chinese Vietnamese, Laotians, and Vietnamese, who collectively became known as the boat people. Most of the immigrants had endured brutal conditions in fleeing political upheavals, residing in refugee camps, and numerous violent acts such as rape and torture.

During the course of the study, the researchers were astounded by the abundance of news articles praising the academic achievement of the immigrant children, in fact, so much so that they decided to expand the scope of their investigation to include a formal inquiry. The news reports piqued the investigators' curiosity because the students had lost anywhere from one to three years of formal schooling and were linguistically isolated in the home.

The parents, likewise, were poorly educated and had primarily settled in large urban areas with other poor, minority families. The children attended schools that were in many ways below average, and yet, they excelled. In other words, these immigrant children experienced many of the same hardships and challenges faced by immigrant students and second- or third-generation arrivals as today. However, the outcomes were quite different and eventually led to the publication of a book titled *Children of the Boat People* (1991).

The investigators honed in on data from the 1984 school year. When they examined the immigrant pupils' grade point averages, the mean was 3.05. Most surprisingly, about 47 percent of the students earned an A in math. In order to establish the reliability of the grades in these low-performing schools, they next looked at standardized test scores.

The test scores indicated that the Indochinese students performed as well or better than the national average in spelling, language and reading, and math. The researchers studied demographic factors to explain the students' academic success. The results of a questionnaire indicated that the three diverse immigrant groups coalesced around six cultural factors: a cultural foundation that respected authority and tradition, family-based achievement and loyalty, hard work and sacrifice, the family seeking a new balance in society, self-reliance and pride, and coping and integration.

All of these factors added up to family units keenly concentrated on growth and achievement. For example, even though the parents tended to have little formal education and spoke little or no English, they viewed their roles as facilitators of homework and prepared a proper environment for the entire family to engage in study nearly every evening. In fact, the researchers stated, "Nowhere is the commitment to the children's education more evident than in the pooling of family resources for purposes of homework" (Caplan et al., 1991, p. 124).

TEACHING TO THE WHOLE ELL STUDENT

Many ELL immigrant students come to the United States under duress and may experience psychological and social challenges. The students have been displaced from familiar surroundings and are expected to succeed academically with little knowledge of the English language and American culture. These students may experience a culture shock evident by a silent stage as they attempt to learn and absorb all that swirls around them.

Additionally, the students may experience feelings of isolation, helplessness, exhaustion, and resistance to adapt to the new culture (DeCapua et al., 2007; Taylor, 2004). Current best practices related to ELL instruction for immigrant students recognize the complexity of individual student experiences by valuing and respecting those experiences and targeting interactive strategies to educate the whole child. Much like the culturally pluralistic position Dewey articulated nearly one hundred years ago, ELL best practices acknowledge that *all* students benefit when immigrant experiences are valued, respected, and shared.

Leveraging Existing Skills and Knowledge

Unlike the recent past when immigrant, minority students were viewed as a monolithic group who showed up at schools with a deficit of skills, today educators recognize that individuals exhibit significant differences even within the same linguistic and cultural backgrounds. The students are constantly interacting with different subgroups within and outside of the home resulting in complex patterns of language use and cultural exchanges.

Often the skills and knowledge that these students bring to the schools are incongruent with the standards-based learning and outcomes expected for their age and life experiences. Therefore, educators must first develop an understanding of the unique characteristics of each ELL student and then bridge the gap by building an instructional plan based on historical, cultural, and linguistic considerations (Genesee & Harper, 2008; Taylor, 2004).

Using the immigrant student's first language as a tool for learning English literacy has emerged as an effective instructional practice. Compounding the challenge is the fact that many students may be illiterate or partially literate in their native tongues. A special panel investigating literacy development in these populations concluded that enhancing literacy in the first language will aid ELL students in learning English.

For example, many of the cognates between Spanish and English are similar, such as "terminar" in Spanish and "to terminate" in English. The panel also recognized that oral proficiency in native languages can also be used as a way to produce, discriminate, segment, and enhance English vocabulary. When combined with reading in the first language, students develop strategies for English spelling, writing, and reading comprehension (August & Shanahan, 2006).

When students are literate in their primary languages, teachers can furnish them with specific, academic content in those languages. Teachers can also prepare special course guides using simplified English with emphases on the discipline's academic vocabulary, allowing students to develop the critical background knowledge. Likewise, students can consult bilingual dictionaries (Villegas & Lucas, 2007).

Developing an Authentic and Useful Curriculum

As mentioned earlier, the fastest growing school populations are fueled by first-generation immigrants and sometimes their children and grandchildren who grow up in circumstances where they develop insufficient English skills to succeed in school. Because of these vast demographic changes in certain schools, there is a need to transform traditional attitudes and pedagogy to reflect these circumstances.

Developing an authentic and useful curriculum to serve these students in a standards-based education may include embracing a whole-school reform effort as well as new and effective instructional techniques such as culturally responsive teaching, sheltered instruction, and cluster models. In the process, classrooms reflect the reality of complex ecological systems.

In addition to using the student's first language and engaging in bilingual instruction, culturally responsive teaching means that administrators and teachers embrace students' backgrounds and create a nurturing environment for all to learn. Howard (2007) contends that reforming newly diverse schools is the only way to face the reality of change. He suggests that administrators and teachers should transition through a series of five professional development phases to create the conditions necessary for student success.

In the initial phases, administrators and teachers embark on efforts to build trust, develop ways to engage students' personal culture, and confront social hegemony and social inequities. In the last two phases, they work on changing instructional practices and engaging the whole school community in efforts to better serve these immigrant populations. In the first phase of building trust, administrators and teachers acknowledge that most of them are from White, middle-class backgrounds and that recognizing these differences with the immigrant students can result in identifying problems and solutions.

The assumptions include the recognition that inequities and injustices are mainly the result of misunderstandings and misconceptions and not intentional discrimination, educators from all backgrounds and cultures should contribute to the discussions, and also that White educators and their backgrounds are part of the complex interactions that occur in a school setting. The resulting agreements should identify real challenges and reject the notion of a color-blind society. This will allow educators to form strong relationships with students from different cultures and backgrounds.

The second phase attempts to build on the challenges identified in the first phase by promoting cultural bridges between educators and students.

Educators acknowledge the at-risk immigrant populations and the multitude of research, that indicates student academic performance is strongly related to the quality of educator-to-student relationships. Therefore, educators enhance their own cultural competence, with a goal of developing trust with the students, providing a safe and secure learning environment, and holding high expectations that all students can learn. Moreover, developing this competence exposes educators to the inherent inequities entrenched in the system.

In phase three, educators confront mainstream cultural and social dominance and construct narratives to inspire all for change. By engaging in historical and sociocultural conversations about power and privilege, "[s]chool leaders and teachers engage in lively conversation about race, class, gender, sexual orientation, immigration, and other dimensions of diversity and social dominance" (Howard, 2007, p. 19). Through these sometimes brave and controversial measures, schools and districts can focus on equity issues related to minority underrepresentation in honors and gifted classes as well as studying other schoolwide problems.

Phase four focuses on culturally responsive classroom teaching. Educators draw on their cultural competence to develop real and nurturing relationships with the students. They also attempt to infuse the curriculum with elements from individual students' lives and cultures. An example would be Banks and Banks's (2007) four levels of multicultural curriculum integration. In the first level, named the contributions approach, teachers focus on discrete cultural elements such as specific heroes or special days. For instance, as part of Black history month, students may learn about Martin Luther King Jr.

In the second level, aptly titled the additive approach, teachers may add an entire theme or unit into a lesson or lessons without changing the basic structure of the curriculum. For example, students may learn about Harriet Tubman and also read a book about the Underground Railroad.

In the highest two levels, titled the transformation and social action approaches, the teacher transforms the curriculum to challenge students to view themes, issues, and concepts from multiple perspectives, and to identify social challenges and take measures to solve problems respectively. An example of the transformation approach is to view the Civil War from the viewpoints of a variety of White and Black perspectives in both the North and South, such as free Black women in the North and White women in the South.

In the highest level of social action, students in a science class may study how pollution affects certain populations in a city; for example, students may examine where the best and cleanest playgrounds are located and who lives adjacent to them. Integrating the curriculum means infusing elements from the students' personal lives as well as studying social topics and challenges from the view of underrepresented groups.

Phase four also means that teachers and administrators maintain high expectations for student success while explicitly showing respect for each student's ability to learn and adapting new and effective pedagogy for individualized instruction. A major, research-based strategy called sheltered instruction, also known as Specifically Designed Academic Instruction (SDAIE), approaches ELL instruction using a whole-language approach, rather than a focus on sentence structures and grammar.

Further, SDAIE embraces current research about learning English while studying in the content areas, so students can develop both general English skills and academic vocabulary in authentic ways (August & Shanahan, 2006; Genesee & Harper, 2008; Rance-Roney, 2009). According to Hansen-Thomas (2008), teachers are already familiar with some of the elements and should be trained in the rest, which include,

• Use of cooperative learning activities with appropriately designed heterogeneous grouping of students
• A focus on academic language as well as key content vocabulary
• Judicious use of ELL's first language as a tool to provide comprehensibility
• Use of hands-on activities using authentic materials, demonstrations, and modeling
• Explicit teaching and implementation of learning strategies (p. 166)

Initially used in self-contained ELL classrooms, the strategy is now recommended for all inclusive classrooms. Moreover, schools with large immigrant student populations could also enhance ELL pupil learning by creating classrooms with compositions of one-quarter to one-third ELL students and the remaining being native-English speakers, known as the cluster model.

In the Deweyan spirit, clusters are really small communities of diverse students developing mutual understanding and respect. For late-adolescent students, schools should also focus on academic core classes rather than electives and consider extended school hours and days including weekends, summers, and an additional year of high school (Rance-Roney, 2009).

The last phase of reforming traditional schools to effectively embrace and serve their immigrant populations is promoting the involvement of all the stakeholders. What often happens in areas with large influxes of foreign populations is the phenomenon of White flight, where light-skinned people often flee urban surroundings when darker-skinned individuals move into the area. Those who stay—including school faculty and staff—are often confused, frustrated, and upset by the changes.

The challenge is to bring all of the school community members together to create a welcoming and inclusive learning environment. Howard (2007) describes how East Ramapo Central School District in New York, just outside New York City, was able to embark on a broad-based diversity initiative that touched every member of the district from teachers and administrators to secretaries and bus drivers.

The sessions and forums resulted in authentic exchanges and better learning as evidenced by significantly higher student test scores across the board as well as decreasing margins between White students and students of color. Furthermore, the community forums invited the participation of parents.

Getting Immigrant Parents Involved

As the children who emigrated from Southeast Asia illustrate, parental support is one of the key tenets for immigrant student academic success. Likewise, finding a solution for parental reluctance because of unauthorized immigration status is a major barrier for participation requiring a political solution. Even when that hurdle is removed, "schools underestimate and underutilize parents' interest, motivation, and potential contributions" (August & Shanahan, 2006, p. 7).

A model for school and immigrant parent partnerships emerged in Annandale High School in the Washington, D.C., area beginning in 2004. According to Sobel and Kuglar (2007), building an immigrant parent leadership organization included the following elements:

- Holding parent leadership classes—in English and Spanish—to empower parents to become leaders in their own families, schools, and communities
- Offering programs for parents from specific ethnic groups, held in Spanish, Korean, and Vietnamese
- Guiding teachers in action research to increase their understanding of parents from other cultures and their skill at developing partnerships with parents
- Opening a parent resource center (p. 63)

The school participants and parents learned several lessons from this program. First, immigrant parents had trouble understanding the voluminous amount of information sent out in mass mailings. They required personal attention and support. Second, related to information overload, many parents did not speak or comprehend English well; therefore the school maintained parent translator liaisons.

Third, immigrants often came from countries where parental involvement was not welcome in the schools. Therefore, the leadership meetings were vital in promoting parental empowerment. Fourth, those parents with the time and inclination to become leaders in the school took the initiative to enhance peer networks or start projects of interest to them. Fifth, the school provided planning and programming that was specific to the needs of each cultural group.

For example, the school officials quickly realized that parents responded more effectively to unique, individual pamphlets for each group rather than creating one pamphlet with multiple translations. Sixth, when organizing programs and parents, smaller bodies of individuals were more effective than larger ones because they offered more personal intimacy. Personal relationships also developed within groups, and parents often organized phone trees.

And seventh, a parent resource center was established in the school so parents could feel welcome, seek information, and have access to the Internet. The Annandale initiative can provide a model for all schools experiencing demographic changes from surging immigrant populations.

CONCLUSION

The interconnections among immigration, schooling, and democracy presents a classic problem that Dewey addressed a century ago and requires at least one other philosophical consideration, specifically Dewey's idea of public. In *The Public and Its Problems* (1927/1954), Dewey alleged an entity called a public existed under a democratic form of government, which allowed all willing participants to freely and equally come forward.

Publics were collections of individuals who transcended joint associations and formed moral communities that united together in a process of identifying problems, engaging in reflection, and proposing common solutions. The solutions benefited no particular interest over another, but rather enriched society as a whole.

Clearly today, the sheer volume of undocumented immigrants and their children present a societal problem that must be solved by the public. So far, most of the national debate concerning immigrants has been situated in the political arena, rather than the moral communities that are "emotionally, intellectually, and consciously sustained" (Dewey, 1927/1954, p. 151).

The current political climate fails to address the needs of the whole student by dismissing a key factor in promoting the healthy growth of individuals, which is the tenuous connections parents and families have to society because of their undocumented status. Furthermore, because most of the new immigrants and ELL students are minority students, understanding their perspectives are crucial for gauging the success of NCLB.

In terms of opinions, minority students and parents tend to be more dissatisfied with their local educational institutions' curriculum and standards than do White students and parents. When corroborated with teacher surveys that report low morale and classroom discipline problems in minority schools, Hispanic and Black stakeholders express "very serious" concerns about drugs, alcohol abuse, violence, overcrowding, dropout rates, and low achievement (Wadsworth & Remaley, 2007).

Discussion Questions

1. How does the concept of diversity fit into Dewey's system of ideas?
2. According to Dewey, what roles do schools play in a modern, democratic society?
3. Summarize the Polish study. Why was it controversial?
4. In what ways has U.S. immigration policy reflected world events and mainstream American attitudes?
5. Elaborate on how current immigration patterns are different from the past. In your opinion, which difference impacts education most? Why?
6. Why are many immigrant children at risk for academic failure?
7. How does NCLB affect ELL students? Does it go far enough? Why?
8. Describe the various challenges older ELL students face? What are the unintended effects of NCLB on this student demographic?
9. How does the success of "the boat people" inform us about the effectiveness of NCLB and current immigration policy?
10. Create a comprehensive list of strategies to teach the whole ELL student. How might non-ELL students in an inclusive classroom benefit as well? Would Dewey agree? Why or why not?

Further Reflection

1. Interview an immigrant family in your community. What types of dreams and aspirations do the parents have for their children? What challenges do they face in the community? How do they perceive their relationship with the schools?
2. If Dewey were alive today, what advice might he give to education officials at the federal, state, and local levels in addressing immigrant student issues?
3. As an educator, how would you change your current thinking or educational practices to be more inclusive of immigrant students?

Chapter Three

Subverting the Whole Child through Narrowing of the Curriculum and Teaching to the Test

Rich kids will study philosophy and art, music and history; their poor peers will fill in bubbles on test sheets.

—Finn Jr. and Ravitch (2008, p. 77)

Democracy will not be democracy until education makes it its chief concern to release distinctive aptitudes in art, thought and companionship.

—Dewey (1976b, p. 300)

The No Child Left Behind Act of 2001 mandates high-stakes tests in English language arts and mathematics, and in response, schools have increased instructional time and resources in those disciplines at the expense of other areas such as the social studies, arts, music, and physical education. In addition, teachers experience intense pressure to "teach to the test," meaning they often limit their instruction to the tested content and formats. Dewey tells us that the untested content areas are vitally important for breaking down the barriers between mind and method, something he referred to as dualisms. In effect, students are denied opportunities to make meaningful connections and fully utilize imagination to engage in quality experiences. In spite of these negative effects, teachers can choose to teach for meaning, and students from all walks of life can pass the tests by engaging in authentic intellectual work and a well-balanced curriculum.

Focus Questions

1. Why do we value English language arts and mathematics over the other subject areas?

2. Should there be high-stakes tests in all school subjects?
3. What does "teaching to the test" mean to you? Is it important for students to pass the tests at all costs? Why?

———∞∞∞———

One of the controversial effects of the No Child Left Behind Act of 2001 is how instructional time has been reallocated to the tested subjects at the expense of other areas, a situation often referred to as the narrowing of the curriculum. According to the Center on Public Education, in 2007 nearly two-thirds of 349 responding school districts reported that their elementary teachers have increased instructional time substantially in mathematics and English language arts since the passage of the law in January 2002.

Moreover, these increases in time directed at tested subjects come at the expense of other classes and activities such as social studies, science, physical education, art, music, and recess (Center on Education Policy, 2008). While some NCLB critics lament the loss of elective and nontested subject times, others applaud these results pointing to better alignment of the curriculum to state standards, more consistent classroom pedagogy, and higher test scores.

However, Dewey tells us that a narrowing curriculum deprives students of essential programs necessary for educating the whole student because of the unique roles each of the narrowed subjects has in providing a *process* to learning, which, in effect, breaks down dualistic barriers between a pre-scribed curriculum and the student's way of knowing. In addition to devoting more time to the tested subject areas, many teachers feel pressured to "teach to the test," meaning directing valuable curricular time and resources to prac-ticing items and formats equivalent to what is tested.

EMPIRICAL EVIDENCE

As discussed in chapter 1, many scholars point to the 1983 report *A Nation at Risk* as the major event launching the modern standards and accountability movement. The report also spawned a "back-to-the-basics" movement plac-ing emphases on the traditional education pillars of reading, writing, and arithmetic. With the twenty-first-century codification of these subject areas in NCLB, the testing of these subjects has driven curriculum and instructional reform.

The U.S. Department of Education (USDOE) discovered that slightly over half of the schools identified as needing improvement restructured their daily schedules to accommodate more time for English language arts (ELA) and math (Stullich, Eisner, & McCrary, 2007). Building on the USDOE study, a subsequent inquiry found that 62 percent of districts had increased instructional time for math and ELA since the 2001–2002 school year, while 20 percent of middle schools reported more time as well.

The amount of increased time was significant, with average increases of 47 percent more for ELA and 37 percent more for math, representing an average of 37 percent combined. At the same time, 44 percent of these districts reported decreases in time allotted to nontested subjects and other activities nearly commensurate with the time gained with ELA and math.

Specifically, the districts reported losses totaling about 145 minutes per week or about 30 minutes per day. In other words, activity time and instructional time of subjects such as social studies, science, and fine arts were reduced by about one-third in aggregate. Furthermore, the study also revealed that these cuts were more prevalent in schools cited for needing improvement. And, not surprisingly, these schools reported placing greater emphases on the content and skills encountered on the tests (Center on Education Policy, 2008).

Compared to districts with no schools identified for improvement, those districts with elementary schools needing improvement reported on average spending a substantial 183 minutes more per week on ELA and a comparatively smaller 86 minutes on math. In order to achieve these increases, districts have also reported average decreased times of 90 minutes for social studies, 94 minutes for science, 61 minutes for art and music, 57 minutes for physical education, and 60 minutes for recess.

One of the reasons that the reported increases do not match the decreases precisely is that some schools have integrated social studies and science into the reading and math times. At the high school level, the study also reported that graduation requirements drove student schedules.

In high school, about 27 percent of all districts directed low-performing students to additional math and ELA courses. The qualitative data also suggested that middle and high schools modified their schedules to accommodate intervention classes for these students either before, during, or after school. During school, these intervention classes often meant that struggling students were denied access to school elective courses.

A follow-up study focusing on three states—Rhode Island, Illinois, and Washington—corroborated the earlier findings and offered additional insights into classroom practices. In addition to the narrowing of the curriculum, educators from these states also reported that the alignment of curriculum to the standards had been mainly successful, teachers often concentrated on student test preparation, and that data derived from the high-stakes assessments were generally used for making broad policy decisions, rather than being used to inform instructional choices in the classroom (Center on Education Policy, 2009).

Overall, the researchers reported that most of the educators had success-fully aligned the curriculum with the standards. The researchers also observed teachers working collaboratively and witnessed curricular consistency among teachers at the same grade level, as well as better vertical integration between grades. In general, the investigators concluded that curriculum alignment was more successful when the curriculum was uniform across a district and the teachers supported the standards.

Moreover, the alignment was also more easily achieved in a traditional school environment than alternative formats such as schools and classrooms that focused on inquiry learning. In other words, ample evidence suggested that the tests promoted curriculum alignment, pedagogical consistency, and traditional teaching methods such as direct instruction (Center on Education Policy, 2009).

In some of the states—most notably Illinois—the state standards did not completely match the tests. In most instances, teachers reported teaching to the test rather than the standards. Teachers also stated that they engaged their students in practice drills of the tested skills. One school reported a compre-hensive approach to test preparation that involved every adult in the school.

From the first day of school, the students practiced tested skills and content in test formats. At the same time, teachers also described how they were in-hibited from instituting more creative approaches to pedagogy because of the tests. However, in Washington State, science teachers refused to relinquish an inquiry approach in favor of a traditional approach to teaching the tested skills. Most of the educators stated that teaching to the test reduced time for more meaningful activities.

In addition to the diminished amount of time because of emphases on tested content, teachers also indicated that they would like professional devel-opment using data to guide instructional choices in the classroom. Likewise, teachers in all three states believed that alternative measures should be used in addition to high-stakes tests in determining success. In Washington State, the educators spoke of the demoralizing effects on teachers and students of adequate yearly progress (AYP) requirements in high-needs and high-poverty schools without sufficient resources.

At the same time, teachers in Rhode Island pointed to a superficial curricu-lum, reduced teacher morale, and a failure to educate the whole child because of NCLB. Additionally, teachers in schools and classrooms with nontradi-tional approaches to instruction recounted how the current configuration of standards and accountability do not fit with other modes of teaching (Center on Education Policy, 2009).

WHY DEWEY WOULD NOT SUPPORT
THE NARROWING CURRICULUM

In *Democracy and Education* (1916/2007a), Dewey articulated in great detail his philosophical underpinnings for transforming traditional education based on rote memorization and recitation into a social enterprise reflective of the larger community where the teacher skillfully guided students through various activities based on inquiry and quality experiences.

Dewey essentially rewrote the rules of learning by asserting that subject matter and methods were not separate, in effect, arguing that traditional education resulted in dualisms between mind and body. Students, according to Dewey, were not empty vessels that educators plied with scraps of knowledge; rather, students created knowledge from within by their individual abilities to make infinite connections with others and the natural world.

In his system of ideas, the social studies, sciences, fine arts, and playtime were vital subjects for the growth of the whole child. In fact, he argued that all subject matter was social because it was conceived and transmitted to successive generations socially. Further, he asserted that curriculum should be selected based on promoting growth and improving present conditions for the greatest numbers of human beings, not just as a justification for preserving traditional power centers.

In a line that has proved to be prescient and relevant to the current controversy swirling around NCLB and the narrowing curriculum, Dewey stated, "The notion that the 'essentials' of elementary education are the three R's mechanically treated, is based upon ignorance of the essentials needed for realization of democratic ideals" (Dewey, 1916/2007a, p. 145). In other words, in so much as NCLB narrows the curriculum to the tested subjects at the expense of other essential subject matter, Dewey would have vigorously disagreed with the legislation.

Moreover, Dewey would have also disagreed with the stifling of creativity and denial of social means for learning the curriculum as teachers today feel intense pressure to engage in direct instruction of the tested skills. By reducing instruction in the social studies, sciences, arts, and limiting play and recreational time, NCLB stymies the growth of the whole child, and on a societal level, erodes democracy over time.

The Social Studies

For Dewey, the social sciences, which through later arrangements would become the social studies, served the function of avoiding dualisms between mind and body (among many others) by providing a means for continuous experiences. Although Dewey never expressed public support for the Committee on Social Studies report that was published the same year as *Democracy and Education* in 1916, convincing evidence suggests that the resulting subject matter and goals were formulated from Dewey's ideas (Fallace, 2009).

From the social sciences, which Dewey primarily recognized as geography and history, students learned about the development of social occupations, which provided the means for inquiry and scientific investigations. These occupations were active pursuits involving play and work, which Dewey viewed as similar, purposeful processes with means and ends. When children engaged in play, they did so for no other reason, and the means and ends bore direct connections to each other. On the other hand, when they engaged in work, they did so with other ends in mind.

The difference between the two is merely the amount of time that passed, not expressed in hours and minutes. Instead, when a remote end was in sight, then play transformed into work characterized by intellectual intensity and careful consideration of the means. The key to understanding the importance of work and play in social activities was "the context of perceived connections in which it is placed; the reach of imagination in realizing connections is inexhaustible" (Dewey, 1916/2007a, p. 156).

Dewey defined context as space and time, which in education terms, meant geography and history. Students learned *all* subject matter by forming connections between their daily lives and the progress of humankind. Teachers provided learning experiences that gave meaning to students' lives in the context of what had been done before—making individual lives harmonious and continuous with the past, and more importantly, making students aware of these connections. In this way, the past was also the present because the goal of education was growth. Dewey (1916/2007a) proclaimed,

> To "learn geography" is to gain in power to perceive the spatial, the natural, connections to an ordinary act; to "learn history" is essentially to gain in power to recognize its human connections. For what is called geography as a formulated study is simply the body of facts and principles which have been discovered in other men's experience about the natural medium in which we live, and in connection with which the particular acts of our life have an explanation. So history as a formulated study is but the body of known facts about the activities and sufferings of the social groups with which our own lives are continuous, and through reference to which our own customs and institutions are illuminated. (pp. 157–158)

Therefore, geography and history were complementary in that the former provided the natural context while history furnished the social perspective, resplendent with difficulties, opportunities, and potential. Dewey warned us that history without geography became a collection of dissociated facts and events much like geography found relevance in the curriculum in its relation to history.

Otherwise, geography too became a mundane list of miscellaneous data such as "the height of a mountain here, the course of a river there, the quantity of shingles produced in this town, the tonnage of the shipping in that, the boundary of a county, the capital of a state" (Dewey, 1916/2007a, p. 159). Dewey also told us that geography supplied a dose of imagination with its exploration of exotic places and people, and in the curriculum, it should begin with a young child's immediate surroundings.

As geography expanded beyond a young child's immediate environment, so too did the level of specialization into other content areas. Because humans were products of social relations, every subject area found relevance in history and geography. As Dewey (1916/2007a) explained,

> No other method is to be found unless it be constantly borne in mind that the educational center of gravity is in the cultural or humane aspects of the subject. From this center, any material becomes relevant in so far as it is needed to help appreciate the significance of human activities and relations. (pp. 159–160)

Hence, geography and history supplied the context for binding subject matters together—be it mathematics, science, languages, or anything else—into continuous experiences because it made conscious to the learner connections, which in the past were not evident, producing bits and pieces of information that did not appear relevant or interesting.

Dewey also informed us that the study of history should begin with the present, in the form of a vexing social issue or problem, which established a connection between the student's life and the past, or in other words, establishing the continuous aspect of the human experience. In America at the turn of the twentieth century (and perhaps yet today), industrial history provided the grand idea linking contemporary social life with the past seen through the development of inventions and innovations.

Further, it explained the development of social occupations and economic survival. For Dewey, economic history was the most important type of history because it was decidedly humanistic, meaning it explained the rise of personal liberties and the birth of modern democracy. In this sense, learning history became a moral imperative whereby every individual shared responsibility in cultivating and advancing social connections in endless cycles of growth. The most effective way to grow, according to Dewey, was when students engaged in inquiry, in which the scientific method was the most effective form.

The Sciences

If the social studies—specifically history and geography—provided the social foundation for creating a continuous and quality experience, science provided a link to social occupations as an ideal, and as a method, supplied the most effective form of inquiry. Deweyan philosophy was partly a reaction to the antidemocratic forces of traditional social arrangements and its vestiges such as feudalism—forces that not only denied individual freedoms, but also impeded general economic progress.

The Enlightenment unleashed rational ideas that articulated personal rights and promulgated the scientific method. From the scientific method came the great inventions and innovations that produced vast wealth, and, gradually, transformed social relationships. Occupations emanated from both the scientific and social, offering pathways to the past (i.e., how things were made from then to now) while reinforcing the value of mutual cooperation (i.e., stemming from the human need for earning a living).

This recognition led Dewey to declare, "Economic history is more human, more democratic, and hence more liberalizing than political history" (Dewey, 1916/2007a, p. 162). Further, in the same manner as the social sciences, Dewey argued that science was more than a narrow course of study.

Like he did with all subject matter, Dewey shattered the dualistic barrier between knowledge and method in science: "Science . . . signifies a realization of the logical implications of any knowledge" (Dewey, 1916/2007a, p. 164). And in its purest form, it resulted from a process of hypothesizing, observing, reflecting, and testing. When engaging in this process, science became a part of a young student's experience, not an abstract ideal represented as characters and symbols, something more appropriate at the college level rather than for a beginning learner.

Dewey referred to this approach as the "psychological method" because young learners were able to internalize direct experiences before moving on to the abstract. In fact, Dewey noted that only a small percentage of students actually became scientists; therefore memorizing the works of others was unnecessary drudgery. And, as if to drive the point home further, he also added that successful scientists were able to avoid the harm of the traditional system of memorization and recitation because of some personal fortitude. To Dewey, the important point was that science provided the most perfect form for carrying out social occupations.

As mentioned earlier, science, or more succinctly the scientific method, broke down traditional barriers to knowledge by shattering customs and traditions, which mainly preserved power for the hereditary elite. Additionally, science also changed society drastically, bringing people closer together in manufacturing, intellectual, and all types of pursuits as never before. Dewey (1916/2007a) stated,

Science taking effect in human activity has broken down physical barriers which formerly separated men; it has immensely widened the area of intercourse. It has brought about interdependence of interests on an enormous scale. It has brought with it an established conviction of the possibility of control of nature in the interests of mankind and thus has led men to look to the future, instead of the past. (p. 167)

Applying an experimental meaning of science—meaning the scientific method—to experiences meant that a person used her or his accumulated knowledge or past experiences to grow. The growing process involved a person reaching back into prior experiences and reflecting on what was useful to guide the current one. When individual experiences carried such great import that they formed commonalities with other experiences represented in the social realm, then social progress occurred.

All experiences were coincidental based on an individual's unique circumstances, and ephemeral, unless they were purposely translated into some abstract characters or symbols to be used by others at some later time. The abstractions served as tools for others to use in their experiences in an ebb and flow vacillating between generalization and abstraction. In this manner, the number of abstracted elements grew exponentially, represented as symbols waiting for others to latch onto, which eventually resulted in new scientific theories, inventions, and innovations.

Applied and experimental science resulted in social progress because the context of all human endeavors was the natural world in which humans socially interacted. Understanding the history of science, and indeed, the history of human struggles through a scientific lens, made one aware of the superstitions and impediments to progress. It also made science a tool for transcending custom and tradition, elevating the highest form of rational knowledge—the scientific method—above lower forms that served no other purpose but to keep power structures intact.

Therefore, science in a social context was a narrative of movement toward a democratic and industrial society. Dewey believed that effective teachers engaged students in learning through social occupations, especially at the elementary level, as well as provided multiple opportunities for students to logically test ideas, leading to higher levels of abstraction in secondary and higher education.

The Arts

In the sciences, when an experience yielded some insight or peculiarity it could be lost to the moment, stored in one's personal memory, or shared in a social sense by converting the experience into an abstract form of characters and symbols where it became a tool for others to use in their experiences.

Dewey stated, "All language, all symbols, are implements of an indirect experience, in technical language the experience which is procured by their means is 'mediated'" (Dewey, 1916/2007a, p. 173).

In order for society to advance, the volume of indirect experiences multiplied exponentially, yielding tools such as historical accounts, mathematical formulae, and scientific notations. However, Dewey warned of situations where the end became the symbols, and young children failed to establish enough direct experiences to utilize indirect experiences in the present.

Therefore, Dewey also talked about the importance of *quality* direct experiences, which served the purpose of facilitating "genuine situations in which personal participation brings home the import of the material and the problems which it conveys" (Dewey, 1916/2007a, p. 174), and from the teacher's perspective, provided a foundation for the layering of a subject matter's symbolic material. From the student's view, a quality experience involved an *appreciative* element, which moved a direct experience beyond an automatic or mechanical undergoing such as memorizing and reciting.

Dewey informed us that only imagination—in the sense of the word as the receptivity and absorption of the full range of activity—could free an experience from the mechanical undergoing. Individuals employed imagination to harness the symbols and language lurking in the background as tools, and then infused them into the direct activity, which in essence, expanded the value and meaning of the direct activity.

Just like history and geography provided the social context for learning, and science explained the emergence of social occupations and the purest form of inquiry through the scientific method, art, as an appreciative *process*, supplied the imagination to unlock "the educative value of manual activities and of laboratory exercises, as well as of play" (p. 176). Every work of art involved experiences from the perspective of the maker and the observer, which Dewey called the *artistic* and *aesthetic qualities* respectively.

If the process yielded a *product* that provided social value, then it was categorized as part of the industrial arts. Likewise, when the product led to enhanced aesthetic appeal and appreciation, then one referred to the product as the fine arts such as painting, literature, drawing, music, and sculpting.

When the fine arts became a vehicle for expanded understanding and enjoyment beyond the ordinary boundaries of experience, they allowed students to fully assimilate symbols and meanings, transcending the works themselves. They evoked emotions, brought disparate elements into unified wholes, and most importantly, made the experiences worthwhile.

In other words, the appreciative values of the arts embedded in all educative experiences unlocked a full quality experience. Dewey proclaimed, "They are not luxuries of education, but emphatic expressions of that which makes any education worth while" (Dewey, 1916/2007a, p. 177). As Smith (2005) noted, "The first step was defining everyday experiences in a way that revealed their inherently dramatic character." The second was claiming that, "whenever experience exhibits a certain organization and possesses certain qualities, it may be regarded as art" (p. 21).

Not surprisingly, in his seminal work *Art as Experience* (1934/2005), Dewey expanded the appreciative aspects of experience, and one of the consequences was a passionate discourse on democratic individualism because "all of us can experience the aesthetic quality of a finished project in which parts and whole are unified, and an internal problematic resolved" (Steiner, 2004, p. 43).

In sum, Dewey believed that the arts should be central to the curriculum because the aesthetic experience through the force of imagination offered a pathway for students to utilize *all* educative experiences to the maximum potential or as Dewey (1934/2005) said, "[T]he work of art has a unique *quality*, but that it is that of clarifying and concentrating meanings contained in scattered and weakened ways in the material of other experiences" (p. 87).

Play and Natural Development

Dewey recognized play as an essential part of a child's educative experience. All play promoted unity and coherence of thoughts. Through play, children also developed the ability to think abstractly. Children participated in make-believe exercises with toys to which Dewey (1910/2007b) expounded:

> In manipulating them, they are living not with physical things, but in the large world of meanings, natural and social, evoked by these things. So when children play horse, play store, play house or making calls, they are subordinating the physically present to the ideally signified. In this way, a world of meanings, a store of concepts (so fundamental to all intellectual achievement), is defined and built up. (p. 161)

In effect, as the immature child matured, her or his attitude about play evolved into an attitude about work. Dewey further explained the process as the child looked to reality for enhanced meanings. He explained, "There is not enough stimulus to call forth satisfactory mental response" (Dewey, 1910/2007b, p. 163), meaning a child's natural, innate curiosity demanded a more appropriate object.

The process evolved into work because work was the attitude of some sort of end in sight. For these reasons, Dewey cautioned in *The School and Society* (1899/2001) that the objects of play must be as real as possible, representative of the authentic world because play was a serious endeavor. If play turned into foolishness, then "dissipation and disintegration followed" (Dewey, 1910/2007b, p. 217).

In the same vein, Dewey also cautioned against work with too much emphasis on the result, because then it turned into "drudgery." The ideal mental state was one where a balance of play and work existed, inasmuch as the mind was freed from all prejudices and preconceived notions when engaged in activities with a clear end in sight.

Play could also be conceived of as part of natural development. In the beginning chapters of *Democracy and Education* (1916/2007a), Dewey presented the case for a child-centered philosophical approach to education. Expanding on Rousseau's notion of natural development, Dewey explained that good health and fortitude were essential for growth. He suggested that educators "Make health an aim; normal development cannot be had without regard to the vigor of the body—an obvious enough fact and yet one whose due recognition in practice would almost automatically revolutionize many of our educational practices" (pp. 88–89).

He continued with this recommendation: "In other words, the aim of following nature means, in the concrete, regard for the actual part played by use of the bodily organs in explorations, in handling of materials, in plays and games" (p. 89). For Dewey, the mind and body were akin to the curriculum and method, inseparable and connected along a continuum.

TEACHING TO THE TEST

As introduced in chapter 1, a documented effect of the NCLB legislation related to the narrowing of the curriculum is the phenomenon known as "teaching to the test." When teachers teach to the test, they devote copious amounts of class time and resources to preparing students for the high-stakes tests. In this sense, the narrowing of the curriculum is a possible outcome of the purposeful action of teaching to the test. While teaching to the test most often conjures negative connotations of NCLB, not all commentators agree.

In fact, some proponents believe that *teaching to the test* equates with *teaching to the curriculum* (Mathews, 2006; Phelps, 2006; Posner, 2004). If the curriculum reflects local standards formulated and embraced by the local citizenry, the thinking proceeds, then teachers have a moral and legal obligation to teach to the test in order to satisfy the will of the people. Critics, on the other hand, contend that the negative effects of teaching to the test far outweigh any perceived benefits.

In the past, standardized tests have served useful purposes in guiding practice and informing pedagogy. The assessments were either norm-referenced,
meaning they offered peer performance comparisons, or criterion-referenced,
defined as test-taker achievement against a specific standard or benchmark.
Historically, teachers have used them to determine a student's strengths and
weaknesses. When combined with accountability measures under NCLB
today, students, teachers, and administrators face intense pressure to achieve
passing results at any cost (Nichols & Berliner, 2007).

Proponents of teaching to the test believe that the practice results in the
alignment of the curriculum with standards, and consequently, results in
better teaching and learning. Since the 1980s, researchers have studied the
alignment process as a kind of negotiation, "[t]hat is, once the test that best
fits the curriculum is chosen, the practiced curriculum is adjusted further in
response to the test" (Shepard, 1990, p. 5).

However, this process is tempered by matter of degree, meaning "whether
particular instances of this practice are defensible depends on the breadth of
the test content and how extensively the tested objectives take over instruction" (p. 6). While critics of teaching to the test cite evidence of mindless
drill exercises and numbing practice sessions mimicking the test formats,
proponents argue that these instances are rare and isolated.

One proponent asserted, "Strong teachers usually raise a ruckus, administrators back down and everybody goes back to the traditional lesson reviews
that all good teachers use" (Mathews, 2006, p. A21). However, anecdotal
observations aside, critics posit that the tests are faulty gauges of student
knowledge and drive curriculum in deleterious ways.

One of the more thought-provoking critical responses to teaching to the test
appeared in a 2004 article in *Phi Delta Kappan*. The author speculated about
how the high-stakes tests led to superficial learning and reasoning. Because
of test costs and other limitations, test items lacked the complexity of difficult
problems encountered in the real world.

Using the example of a physicist friend who had partially solved a seemingly intractable problem, the author lamented the loss of deep learning in
real-world contexts. He conjectured that the type of simple problems found
on most high-stakes tests driving curriculum and instruction in schools was
precisely the kind that suited the application of technology. Hence, today,
high-stakes tests are directly responsible for creating a generation of thinkers
who can easily be replaced with automation (Posner, 2004).

In addition to the simplistic types of items found on many tests, another
problem with teaching to the test is finding an appropriate balance between
test preparation and teaching to the standards-based curriculum. Popham
(2001) distinguished instruction according to whether the teacher was using

the same or similar examples to items found on the tests versus the knowl-edge and skills found in the curriculum, which he respectively labeled *item-teaching* and *curriculum-teaching*.

To engage in item-teaching meant that the teacher would have to be famil-iar with what was on the assessment either by obtaining past copies of the exams or through nefarious means such as obtaining an actual exam copy through theft or bargain. For example, an actual exam question might say something like "A train travels from New York to Boston at 50 miles per hour and the distance between the two cities is 200 miles. How long will it take in hours to travel the distance?"

An item teacher might have students practice something like, "A car travels between Chicago and St. Louis at 60 miles per hour. The distance between the two cities is 300 miles. How long will it take in hours to travel the distance?" In this example, only the mode of transportation, cities, speed, and distances vary. The problem requires the exact same cognitive chal-lenges.

A curriculum teacher may institute a whole host of instructional strategies and practice exercises to address a curriculum standard such as "Students will be able to calculate distances and times using a variety of measuring systems." In this case, a curriculum teacher would provide a variety of rich learning experiences and enrichment exercises perhaps using metric system variables or asking for values related to time, speed, and distance. The dis-tinction between item-teaching and curriculum-teaching is important because the tests are intended to be a measure of mastery.

When students score well (or poorly) because of the item-teaching ap-proach, it is impossible to make accurate inferences about what the student has learned. For example, if a district curriculum mandates that all fourth graders master a list of 300 words, and the state English language arts exam contains 50 items related to the list, a student answering correctly 40 of the items would be assumed to have achieved 80 percent mastery of the curricu-lum—not just the 50 items.

However, if the teacher engages in item-teaching such as the distance-trav-eled example above, the student may not have learned the curriculum, only what is on the exam or something nearly indistinguishably similar. Therefore, item-teaching results in flawed data. In these cases, teachers may not have reliable information to guide future instructional needs, and the schools may misallocate resources. Unfortunately, it is nearly impossible to determine whether a teacher is engaging in these practices (Popham, 2001).

In addition to problems associated with this type of teaching, other prob-lems include the dumbing down of instruction and practice and the debase-ment of the teaching profession. As Nichols and Berliner (2007) reported,

We found numerous examples from schools across the country that had dedicated hours upon hours preparing students for the test—drilling, emphasizing rote memorization, teaching students how to take tests, reviewing over and over again the concepts that will be represented on the test, and giving multiple practice tests, all at the expense of other content, ideas, and curricula that may not be represented on the test. . . . No longer are we measuring real-world math or reading skills. Instead, it becomes a test of how well students memorized math content or how adept students are at filling in test-booklet bubbles. (p. 122)

For evidence, the authors cite New Hampshire as one state where the students spend some of the least amount of time on test preparation, where sixth and tenth grade students spend about 25 hours per year while third grade students spend about 18 hours. At the other end of the spectrum, a survey revealed that about 80 percent of the elementary teachers in North Carolina reported that they spent more than 20 percent of instructional time on exam preparation. The authors reserved judgment as to what was a sufficient amount of time.

Another consequence of teaching to the test is the denigration of the teaching profession. In some instances, teachers are reduced to script readers relegating instructional decisions to the test preparation companies. Moreover, some believe that judging teachers (and schools) based on the test performances of students is demoralizing to the profession:

It is one thing that teachers are being evaluated on the basis of student test scores but yet another to humiliate and devalue them by judging performance for which they are at most co-creators. They are clearly not solely responsible for that performance, but teachers and schools are judged as if they were. Do physicians get punished when their patients supersize their food portions and develop diabetes? Do dentists get punished if their patients will not brush after every meal? This peculiarity of the teaching profession adds to the anxiety teachers feel. (Nichols & Berliner, 2007, p. 151)

Teachers often feel frustrated and disillusioned with their profession because of the pressures to teach to the test, and students may not engage in deep learning even in the tested subjects.

Teaching to the test can retard skill development in the tested subject areas because teachers provide shortcuts to pass the assessments at all costs. Some studies reported instances where children were taught how to locate context clues from a reading passage, and then selected the correct response from a multiple choice list without engaging in any deep learning.

In another study, investigators questioned students as to how and why they selected the correct answers on a standardized test. Many of the students had difficulty in explaining the reading, and instead, used test-wise strategies to select correct answers. One concern was that these students would not be able to advance to higher level work such as the type of learning encountered in colleges and universities. Likewise, a major concern is that teaching to the tests means students are not participating in work that is authentic in real-world settings such as conducting science experiments, writing research papers, and preparing oral presentations (Volante, 2004).

When viewed through an economic lens, the effects of teaching to the test are less clear. In an article published in the *Quarterly Journal of Economics*, Lazear (2006) concluded that under certain conditions, namely when the costs of learning and testing were high, high-stakes tests maximized learning efficiency. By extension, the author also determined the conditions of whether a test with clear questions based on some prescribed guidelines (e.g., standards) known in advance or a test with randomly selected questions from a broad base of knowledge would be most appropriate. In other words, "What were the optimal conditions for teaching to the test?"

Using an equivalent problem of a speeding driver, the author defined the variables and conducted an economic analysis of the circumstances. The speeding driver metaphor assumed that a city had a limited amount of police officers to patrol the roads. The question was whether the city should provide the precise location of the patrol officers or randomly assign the officers to various locations unannounced in an effort to deter speeders.

If the city announced the location of the officers, then one possible outcome was that drivers would obey the legal speed limits only in those locations and speed on nonpatrolled roadways. On the other hand, if there were few officers relative to the amount of roadways, drivers may have gambled and sped on all roadways. Hence, when a city used fewer officers, it was more effective to announce the location to deter speeding at least in those areas. Using these principles, the author determined that the situation was equivalent to teaching to the test.

In a testing environment today, the curriculum is similar to the roadways in the speeding driver analogy. According to this logic, alerting students to what will be tested or randomly selecting questions from a large body of knowledge helps students decide whether to study a little for things they know will be on the test or study substantially in an effort to cover all possible topics and skills.

Limiting the scope of tested items increases the incentives for learning and studying. Therefore, those students who are motivated little by incentives would benefit from the limited amount of items. On the contrary, students with high motivation learn and prepare well when the incentives are spread across a larger curriculum.

In teaching to the test, teachers and students may ignore the nontested skills and knowledge. The equivalent proposition in the speeding driver problem is the city alerting the driver where the police were posted. This was a more efficient way to deter speeding when the city spent less money on enforcement because drivers obeyed the legal limits in the posted areas.

In terms of high-stakes testing, when the costs of learning are high, it is better to teach to the test because "announcing the questions concentrates incentives and induces at least some learning" (Lazear, 2006, p. 1046). Conversely, when learning costs are low, the exams should contain random items from a more expansive range of knowledge.

Besides the learning costs, another outcome of the analysis is the cost of testing. When the cost of testing is high, it is better to teach to the test because there are fewer questions, which results in low incentives for learning (i.e., motivation). Again, the opposite is true if the costs of testing are low as the author states, "Then the optimum is to announce nothing" (Lazear, 2006, p. 1047). So the question is: What makes a good test?

Many educators believe that a good test is one where students are not able to predict the answers, and the test items generalize to some broad content and skill area. According to the economic analysis, this may not always be the case. Students with low motivation as a result of a high cost of learning would learn nothing without well-defined tests, meaning some teaching to the test.

Students with high motivation and low costs of learning benefit more from random questions from a broader curriculum because they are willing and able to master a great amount of material. From this analysis, the author presents an interesting point: NCLB and high-stakes testing are primarily directed at low-performing schools because high-performing students in effective schools will most likely achieve passing levels. Further, the analysis also takes into consideration the efforts of the teacher.

Because NCLB also places emphases on highly qualified teachers, the economic model also assumes that teacher motivation is important. Because enforcement and monitoring mechanisms are inconsistent and variable across the nation, the model assumes that intrinsic motivation is the only impetus measure. In the final analysis, the researcher concludes that less-capable and less-motivated teachers benefit from well-defined items in teaching to the test. On the other hand, highly motivated and capable teachers instruct better when curriculum standards are less defined and wider in breadth.

However, this economic analysis is built on two major assumptions: One is a singular focus on outputs, meaning passing the high-stakes test at the lowest costs in motivation and abilities; and the second is the social value attached to English language arts and mathematics over the other subject areas. Dewey would disagree with these two assumptions. For the former, thirty years of evidence suggests that teachers can teach for understanding, *and* students can pass the tests. In the case of the latter and as explicated previously, Dewey explained how other subject areas such as the fine arts and history are vitally important to learning.

TEACHING FOR UNDERSTANDING UNDER NCLB

The narrowing of the curriculum to the tested subject areas and the teaching to the test comes with substantial costs to the future because determining which students pass on to the next grade level, the courses the students are allowed to enroll in during the academic year, and how the districts and schools allocate scarce resources hinge on the results of these actions.

Likewise, these actions mainly diminish the force and value of integrated, interdisciplinary knowledge. As discovered earlier, the tests and the curriculum instantiate a reciprocal process, and therefore, a good test may also result in best practices instruction. Only tests based on valid and reliable measures of the curriculum will yield useful data. Further, even in the absence of good tests to drive effective instruction, teachers can choose to follow best practices, and students can still achieve passing levels on the high-stakes tests; and as the evidence suggests, more students will stay in school and learn.

The Integrated Interdisciplinary Curriculum

The lynchpin of Deweyan philosophy is that human progress is marked by movement toward a unified whole through infinite points of individual growth. Growth is the gaining of knowledge in a recursive mode of new experiences and the reconstruction of existing experiences through deliberate reflection.

Moreover, the processes occur in a social and political context in the natural world. Given this mix of factors among individuals, social interactions, political institutions, and the natural world, the learner can only reap the full benefits of instruction when subjects are presented in an integrated and interdisciplinary fashion. Examples from science, art, and social studies can illustrate these concepts.

At the time of this writing, NCLB mandated that states develop high-stakes science tests by the 2005–2006 academic year, which were supposed to be implemented in the 2007–2008 period. While some states do administer these tests in accordance or exceeding the three required testing intervals during grades 3–5, 6–9, and 10–12, many states have chosen to defer implementation based on a clause requiring Congress to fund these initiatives.

However, as in the case of the sciences, the standards do not truly represent the interdisciplinary nature of knowledge as Dewey articulated, even though they mainly embrace inquiry activities. Rudolph (2005) laments how in the past half century science standards have evolved into engineering-type tasks, rather than true, pure, scientific inquiry. For example, much of the teaching and learning, together with many of the textbooks and curricular resources, promote students engaging in hands-on activities. Usually, students examine real-world problems and test solutions. On the surface, this seems to suggest the implementation of Deweyan quality learning experiences.

The problem, according to the author, is that the inquiry activities tend to fall on the side of a continuum marked by engineering tasks such as building boats. In this example, students then apply weights to the boats to see at what point they will fail to float. The students learn science doing engineering-type activities at the expense of intellectual goals grounded in the pure science of the natural world. He illustrates this point by using Project MUSE, where students build models of planets to account for night and day patterns based on theoretical considerations.

When science is presented as engineering tasks—which are often reflected in standards—students and the public generally view science "as an enterprise that has the ability to produce reliable, objective knowledge about the natural world through the rigorous application of its methods" (p. 806). Meaning, science in a vacuum, distinct and separate from any social, political, ideological, or any other type of context, produces truth, which is not to be challenged. In this isolated arena, science is not responsive to the wants and challenges of society, and as the author specifies,

> It seems clear, then, that presenting design/engineering-inquiry activities in the ideological trope of pure science has the potential to further disengage what some observers claim is already a politically-quiescent citizenry. . . . When complex technical issues of national importance come up for public debate— issues related to transportation policy, energy development, or communications technology—the likelihood is that the public, seeing the problem as primarily "scientific" and possessing all the characteristics of science in the abstract, might be inclined to defer to the experts. (Rudolph, 2005, p. 808)

The solution, according to the author, requires standards and instruction that reflect Dewey's instrumental pragmatism, where pure science becomes a tool for inquiry *with social ends in mind*. This would involve the injection of philosophy, history, sociology, and other subjects into the science curriculum. In effect, science and knowledge become democratized.

In its present form, NCLB does not mandate high-stakes tests in the arts and the social studies. Rather, the arts and some social studies subject areas are identified as core academic disciplines in the legislation. Although the law does not specify which art disciplines compose the core, in 1997, the National

Assessment of Educational Progress (NAEP) arts assessment was instituted with distinct assessments in the visual arts, theater, music, and dance.

Similarly, the law defines civics and government, geography, and history as core academic disciplines. The value of this designation means that whenever legislation targets the core, the arts and the listed social studies areas would be eligible for funding for technology, teacher training, or curricular enhancements (Arts Education Partnership, 2005).

In addition to the narrowing of the curriculum, much of the reported evidence indicates that NCLB has transformed the relationship between tested and nontested subjects in other ways. Perhaps the greatest change involves how teachers *use* the nontested subject areas such as the arts and social studies to teach ELA and mathematical skills and knowledge.

Professional organizations such as the National Council for the Social Studies (NCSS), while acknowledging the narrowing of the curriculum and teaching to the test, offers a position statement advocating for an integrative approach with all subject matter, which includes, "With a strong interdisciplinary curriculum, teachers find ways to promote children's competence in social sciences, literacy, mathematics, and other subjects within integrated learning experiences" (National Council for the Social Studies, 2009, para. 13).

Another example is the National Association for Music Education, which advocates music becoming a schoolwide resource for learning in other areas such as math, literacy, and history (Brown, 2009). Of course, both organizations carefully assert that their content areas should remain fixed in the core of academics. In effect, what many of the nontested subject area professional associations have done is offer defenses for the narrowing curriculum by providing evidence of student gains with an integrative approach to learning.

In the case of the arts, research suggests that students who participate in these content areas achieve myriad learning outcomes. The NAEP provided data showing how eighth graders involved with art classes achieved at higher levels in other subjects at school. Other research provided positive correlations between SAT scores and whether a student participated in art classes.

Some claim that the arts offer students tools for interpreting and communicating culture and personal expression. And still others claim that the decoding and coding processes found in reading and math can be developed or strengthened through arts education (Diket, 2003; Hetland & Winner, 2002; Winner, 1993).

Social studies teachers incorporate many of the reading skills into their instruction in response to high-stakes tests in literacy. In a metasynthesis analysis of 49 qualitative studies, Au (2007) confirmed the recursive relationship between tests and the curriculum and the narrowing to the tested subjects, teaching to the test where content is taught in an isolated fashion and learned in the tested formats, and teacher-centered pedagogy to cover the tested topics.

Further, he also discovered that in some instances, the social studies curriculum (i.e., time allotted by teachers for social studies instruction and practice) has actually expanded because of the focus on tested literacy skills. The metasynthesis also suggests what a good test may look like.

Good Tests

The metasynthesis also revealed another insight: some teachers engaged in more student-centered instruction and expanded their curriculum in the social studies in response to "good" high-stakes tests. In essence, these teachers developed more effective pedagogies in response to teaching literacy skills.

For example, in New York State, elementary students in the fifth grade are required to take a social studies examination in the beginning of the school year consisting of multiple choice and document-based questions (DBQs), which demand a whole host of higher-order literacy skills.

On the DBQs, students analyze primary source documents and respond to a writing prompt, synthesizing an answer with prior knowledge and effective writing. The study author concludes, "[I]t is possible that social studies represents a special case in relation to high-stakes testing and curricular control . . . [and] that test construction matters in terms of teachers' curricular responses to high-stakes tests" (Au, 2007, p. 264).

Why don't more states use better tests? The answer is cost. It costs more to produce, administer, and assess DBQ written responses than multiple choice formats. Reporting on a series of studies, Jerald (2006a) responded, "[T]he combination of accountability, the lack of a clear curriculum, and cheaper off-the-shelf tests is a recipe for bad teaching" (p. 2). While the problem may be linked to all tested subject matter in a particular state, it may be more acute in those states with a test in the social studies. To make matters even less clear, there may be differences between elementary social studies versus the middle and high school levels.

Elementary teachers devalue social studies in relation to math and ELA, but middle and high school teachers face the daunting task of covering a broad and deep curriculum resulting in teacher-centered instruction and "'just the facts' content coverage" (Vogler & Virtue, 2007, p. 56). For cash-starved states, the best alternative has been ready-made tests that are easily evaluated. However, if these tests are contributing to teacher-centered instruction, teaching to the test, and a narrowing curriculum, then the quality of the data is in doubt.

Why Data Matter

While there have been many calls for the use of high-stakes assessment data to drive resource allocation and curricular choices, they are mainly used to make decisions at the district or school levels, not in the classroom (Center on Education Policy, 2009; Jerald, 2006b). Perhaps one of the explanations is a question of validity, meaning that the tests may not be measuring what they are supposed to be measuring.

Nichols and Berliner (2007) discuss four types of validity: content, construct, criterion, and consequential. Content validity simply means that the content of the tests should be reflective of the larger curriculum standards with representative questions from across the tested curriculum. For construct validity, the test should also represent the abstract representations of knowledge unique to a discipline.

For example, experts would determine what higher-order thinking skills in a history course might look like and assess them with a DBQ-type test. With criterion validity, a test contains predictive power to some measure such as semester grades or overall grade point average (GPA), offering data for guiding student placement and teacher instructional choices. When teachers or school officials act on the data, the tests provide consequential validity.

The problem with teaching to the test is that the resultant data can distort all four validities. For example, if teachers spend too much time on test preparation—especially teaching the test items—they engage the students in drill-and-practice exercises and rote memorization. In this case, we cannot have confidence that the answers to the test items represent that domain of learning nor that the test items themselves are now accurate representations, indicating breaches in content and construct validities.

Of course, the predictive power of the data is compromised together with any actions that are taken based on the data; therefore, criterion and consequential validities are also suspect. This may explain why teachers either do not have access to the data or choose not to act on it because they rely on their own expertise instead of some flawed output.

Choosing to Teach for Understanding

Despite all of the misconceptions and flawed policies related to NCLB, teachers can still choose to teach for understanding. As explained in great detail in chapter 1, some large-scale studies in the 1990s indicated that when students were given assignments involving authentic intellectual work (AIW), standardized test achievement increased independent of income and other factors (Newmann, Bryk, & Nagaoka, 2001; Scheurman & Newmann, 1998; Smith, Lee, & Newmann, 2001). Furthermore and also explained in chapter 1, students in high-poverty schools scored better when teachers taught skills using separate, simulated, and integrated activities (Langer, 2002).

Teachers can deliberately avoid teaching to the test by promoting deep, sustained learning. They can prepare students for the high-stakes exams by employing a variety of pedagogical strategies. McTighe, Seif, and Wiggins (2004) recommend five heuristics as follows:

- Understanding big ideas in content is central to the work of students.
- Students can only find and make meaning when they are asked to inquire, think at high levels, and solve problems.
- Students should be expected to apply knowledge and skills in meaningful tasks within authentic contexts.
- Teachers should regularly use thought-provoking, engaging, and interactive instructional strategies.
- Students need opportunities to revise their assignments using clear examples of success work, known criteria, and timely feedback. (p. 27)

Additionally, districts can help teachers recognize teaching to the test and promote effective instruction for meaning.

Schools and districts should actively train staff to identify situations suggesting teaching to the test. One idea is to offer a variety of mandatory and volunteer in-service trainings for both teachers and administrators. Teachers could learn about effective test preparation that does not drive instruction in harmful ways. Administrators, in addition to helping with the training processes, also can learn to effectively use the data in their decision making and identify dubious results.

Of course, there should be frequent examinations of the curriculum and tests to ensure alignment and accuracy. Moreover, teachers should institute a variety of traditional and alternative assessments to guide practice and pedagogy (Center on Education Policy, 2007; Volante, 2004).

CONCLUSION

A one-year study involving English language learners in New York City illustrated an extreme example of how teachers felt pressured to teach to the test. The teachers across the schools knowingly abandoned effective learning strategies utilizing multilingual instruction to focus on native-language-only test preparation because the students could take the exam in their first languages (Menken, 2006). Thus, the tests completely subverted a goal of learning effective language instruction in English.

Likewise, the example showcased the recursive relationship of how instruction and testing affected each other sometimes in harmful ways. While not everyone agrees that teaching to the test is a bad thing, the mere term invites confusion, and therefore, it may be more appropriate to say that one is teaching to the tested items or teaching to the curricular aims and goals (Popham, 2004).

Recently, advocates for the science curriculum have succeeded in adopting science tests in many of the states as well as procuring substantial resources. The America Competes Act of 2007 significantly increased funding for science, technology, education, and math (STEM). When combined with NCLB, the legislation places a premium on a small skill set, further intensifying the narrowing curriculum.

The justification for these bills—and indeed the impetus for all modern educational reform movements—has been the loss of American economic prowess because of poor learning in the sciences and the three traditional subjects of reading, writing, and arithmetic. As Finn and Ravitch (2008) succinctly conclude,

> The STEM-winders mean well . . . [b]ut these enthusiasts don't understand that what makes Americans competitive on a shrinking, globalizing planet isn't outgunning Asians at technical skills. Rather, it's our people's creativity, versatility, imagination, restlessness, energy, ambition, and problem-solving prowess. (p. 74)

Dewey would agree with that observation. He would also advocate a return to teaching to the whole curriculum in a meaningful way.

Discussion Questions

1. Describe the types of evidence that the authors cite for a narrowing curriculum. What are the evident patterns?
2. What are the differences in the narrowing curriculum among the lower, middle, and upper grades? What explains these differences?
3. According to Dewey, what was the purpose of the social studies, especially history and geography?
4. According to Dewey, what was the purpose of the sciences?
5. According to Dewey, what was the purpose of the arts?
6. In Deweyan philosophy, why are play and work important? How are they different?
7. Describe the recursive process between instruction and high-stakes tests. When can this be a positive process?

8. What can teachers do to teach for understanding? Is it possible to teach to the test and teach for understanding? Why?
9. What happens to the resulting data when teachers teach to the test?
10. What assumptions do we inherently make when we narrow the curriculum?

Further Reflection

1. Think about the high-stakes tests in your state; what can be done to improve their effectiveness?
2. Suggest ways that teachers in your school or a school you attended can avoid the narrowing curriculum and teaching to the test.
3. Does NCLB affect America's competitiveness? Locate recent articles to support or refute this claim.

Chapter Four

Critiquing Scientific Dogmatism in Education with Implications for Current Supervisory and Administrative Practice within a Standards-based Environment

When people place uncritical faith in scientific research methodologies to discover truth, and in rational discourse to articulate their vision of the good, they ultimately limit the intelligence and free will of the moral agent by denying the possible fallibility of scientific or rational method. Rationality, on this account, becomes a dogmatic caricature of science and logic. Rather than understanding them as tools to serve ends greater than themselves, . . . [they] are transformed into objects of worship and devotion. . . . When taken to an extreme, . . . [they] can become dogmatic.

—Alexander (2001, p. 135, basing his views on Michael Polanyi, 1964)

Drawing on historical research, this chapter draws attention to Dewey's often neglected but no less brilliant work published in 1929, *The Sources of a Science of Education.* Dewey's critique of efforts in his day to seek "quick fixes" to practical educational and curricular issues by employing premature scientific investigations and findings has relevance not only from a historical perspective, but can provide a lens from which to understand current supervisory practice common in many schools. The chapter examines Dewey's work by examining the rise of efforts toward a "science of supervision" starting in the 1920s and 1930s, and continuing through the 1940s.

Dewey and some others harshly criticized attempts to emphasize a definitive "science of education," paying little attention to the artistic side of the field, without mindful attention to the exigencies of scientific discovery. Efforts to quantify and categorize teaching practices in dogmatic ways were criticized by Dewey. Administrators and supervisors who tried to apply the "science of teaching" to a "science of supervision" were similarly criticized. Current standards-based supervisory practices (e.g., walk-throughs) can be viewed as another historical instance of the proclivity of some educators to apply arbitrary standards and unproven supervisory strategies. Through examination of Dewey's critique of scientific dogmatism in his day implications can be drawn to ways educators today misuse science in order to promulgate spurious notions of "best practices" and "research-based findings" that provide fodder for the accountability movement, and thus, influence the narrowing of the curriculum.

Focus Questions

1. Undoubtedly, you have been affected, to some degree, by NCLB, standards-based education, and increased accountability measures. How have the aforementioned affected your practice in or experience with supervision and/or administration?
2. How is supervision practiced in your school?
3. What sorts of "research-based" practices are advocated by educational leaders in your school or district?
4. As you read this chapter, what lesson(s) might you learn about how best to approach instructional improvement in your school or district?

—❦—

Arguably, the most egregious deficiency in education, and particularly in regard to the field of supervision, is its ahistoricism (Alfonso & Firth, 1990; Bolin & Panaritis, 1992; Glanz, 1995; Pajak, 1993a). Educators, laypeople, policy makers, and other politicians often neglect to consider historical antecedents in promulgating and implementing ideas and programs.

The past is viewed, at best, as an interesting exercise in nostalgia but with few lessons to inform and shape current practice. They eschew Ernst Cassirer's (1953) astute observation that the past, present, and future form an "undifferentiated unity and an indiscriminate whole" (p. 8). Fredrich Kummel (1966) explains this notion of temporality as a historical process "in which the past never assumes a final shape, nor the future ever shuts its doors."

He continues, "Their essential interdependency also means, however, that there can be no progress without a retreat into the past in search of a deeper foundation" (p. 50). To think historically requires a realization that past generations might have encountered equally intractable problems and might have considered ways to confront these issues.

To think historically encourages the art of reflection and, at the same time, demands forbearance. To think historically means to ask these, among other questions: How have significant ideas, events, and people influenced or informed current practice? How are our advocated theories and prevailing practices connected to the past? and What might we learn from the past to shape current policy and practice?

The current and continuous clarion cries for increased accountability, implementation of high-stakes testing within a standards-driven educational environment, viewed historically, is not new, albeit its form and emphases might vary from past practices. The national movement toward standards-based education with its emphasis of raising standards and promoting uniformity of curricular offerings to raise academic achievement began with efforts by the 1892 Committee of Ten that sought to establish new curriculum standards for high school students so that all students would receive a high-quality academic curriculum (Kliebard, 1987).

Later, in 1918, standards were reinforced through the efforts of the Commission on the Reorganization of Secondary Education (Krug, 1964), the College Entrance Examination Board (formed in the 1890s), the Scholastic Aptitude Test (the first SAT was administered in 1926), and the American College Testing Program (established in 1959). The passage of the National Defense Education Act (NDEA), which poured millions of dollars into mathematics, sciences, and engineering, similarly sought to raise levels of student achievement (Ravitch, 1995).

With continually declining SAT scores and a host of social, economic, political, and educational challenges in the 1960s and 1970s, the report *A Nation at Risk: The Imperative for Educational Reform* was published by the National Commission on Excellence in Education in 1983. Many asserted that schools had lowered their standards too much and that American students were not competitive with their international counterparts.

The spate of national and state reports continued through the 1980s, each advocating fundamental educational change (e.g., Carnegie Forum on Education and the Economy, 1986; the Holmes Report, 1986). The Education Summit held in 1989 by then President George Bush and state governors led eventually to the signing of Goals 2000 on March 31, 1994, which proclaimed, in part, that by the year 2000 "U.S. students will be first in the world in science and mathematics achievement" and "Every school will be free of drugs and violence and will offer a disciplined environment conducive to learning."

Standards in education were buttressed in 1991, when the U.S. Congress established the National Council on Educational Standards and Testing (NCEST) that encouraged educators and politicians to translate somewhat vague national goals into content curriculum standards. NCEST recommended that educators establish specific standards in specific subject areas. The National Council of Teachers of Mathematics (NCTM) led the way by publishing standards that quickly influenced textbook companies and testing agencies.

Continuing in the tradition of standards-based education, President George W. Bush signed into law the No Child Left Behind (NCLB) Act of 2001, a reauthorization of the Elementary and Secondary Education Act of 1965. Four basic principles were evident: stronger accountability for results, increased flexibility and local control, expanded options for parents, and *an emphasis on teaching methods that presumably have been proven to work* (italics added).

Educators and policy makers currently involved in grappling with seemingly contentious and intractable problems and issues need to consider their proposals and resolutions as part of a historical continuum. To examine the past in a nuanced, mindful, and reflective manner might reveal subtleties or approaches that have relevance and potency to shape current and future policy and practice.

From another frame, such historical inquiry might unmask current efforts to address urgent problems as little more than failed or unproven nostrums. Extant proposals that rely on questionable practices of the past might not only serve to revisit past educational transgressions, but might exacerbate and sustain the very problems they meant to resolve.

This chapter highlights a particular aspect of the latter goal of NCLB, as stated above in italics, regarding the employment of educational methods that have been "proven to work." The chapter does not focus on specific curricular programs in reading, mathematics, or the language arts, but it does imply the overall presumption that such programs are premised and founded on scientific grounds. More pointedly and fundamentally, the very nature of science as applied to education may need scrutiny.

The specific analysis of this chapter, however, focuses on supervisory practice that has mirrored, in many ways, more general developments described above in regard to education and curriculum (see, e.g., Glanz, 1992). Furthermore, although examination of science in relation to education and curriculum has been undertaken (see, e.g., Kliebard, 1987), little, if any, attention has been paid to this topic in the field of supervision.

Therefore, the nature of scientific inquiry itself is examined in this chapter in regard, specifically and narrowly, to supervisory theories and practices that have gained attention and legitimacy amid the prevailing standards-based educational environment. Although the focus here is on the science of supervision, the implications of such analyses for education and curriculum, specifically, are relevant.

We will examine possible antecedents for present-day proclivities to implement supervisory programs and apply theories or practices that have not undergone empirical or scientific scrutiny. We will also point out that Dewey's work may help us place current supervisory efforts in a sounder, more "scientific" frame.

WHY DEWEY?

Have you ever read John Dewey's (1929) often neglected work titled *The Sources of a Science of Education*? This 77-page essay is remarkable in several ways. First, it represents a concise yet strident critique of educational practice in the early decades of the twentieth century. Chastising educators who seek to apply preliminary yet unproven scientific findings to immediately solve urgent practical problems in schools, Dewey charts an intellectually cogent path for establishing a scientific base to education, teaching, and curriculum.

A second reason why Dewey's work is so important is because it influenced some educators in his day to address difficult problems facing schools. Ever-increasing administrative and organizational demands of the newly established school bureaucracy necessitated, for instance, better means of facilities management, operational governance, curriculum development, and teacher training. Educators looked to science to help provide some answers and guidelines for practice. Dewey's admonitions are intellectually engaging and historically relevant.

Third, highlighting Dewey's arguments sheds light on a nearly forgotten period in American educational history, and serves as a guidepost to help current educators find an appropriate and reasonable balance between the art and science of teaching. And finally, Dewey's work can perhaps serve as an intellectual anchor to address current supervisory practices within the standards-based environment.

HISTORICAL PERSPECTIVE AND FRAMEWORK

There is no extant research in the field of supervision that examines this topic (i.e., supervision, John Dewey, and the science of supervision). Some authorities have tangentially addressed some of these issues (e.g., Tomlinson, 1997). A few dissertations have as well (Arlington, 1972; Button, 1961; Glanz, 1977). These doctoral dissertations were general treatments but not in-depth analyses (Glanz, 1998). What follows then is a historical perspective forming the core of the analysis.

Unprecedented growth precipitated by the Industrial Revolution characterized the second half of the nineteenth century. During this period, schoolmen, specifically superintendents, began shaping schools in large cities into organized networks. In the battle that ensued to reorganize the nation's schools, sources of authority and responsibility in education were permanently transformed (Tyack, 1974).

By the end of the nineteenth century, reformers concerned with undermining inefficiency and corruption transformed schools into streamlined, central administrative bureaucracies with superintendents as supervisors in charge. Supervision, during this struggle, became an important tool by which the superintendent legitimized his existence in the school system (Glanz, 1991). Supervision, therefore, was a function that superintendents performed to oversee schools more efficiently.

Supervision can best be viewed as an inspectional function during this period. The practice of supervision by inspection was indeed compatible with the emerging bureaucratic school system with its assumption that expertise was concentrated in the upper echelons of the hierarchy. Many teachers perceived supervision as inspectional, rather than a helping or improvement function.

Numerous technological advances greatly influenced American education after 1900. As a result of the work of Frederick Winslow Taylor (1911), who published a book titled *The Principles of Scientific Management*, "efficiency" became the watchword of the day. Taylor's book stressed scientific management and efficiency in the workplace.

The worker, according to Taylor, was merely a cog in the business machinery, and the main purpose of management was to promote the efficiency of the worker. Within a relatively short period of time, *Taylorism* and *efficiency* became household words and ultimately had a profound impact on administrative and supervisory practices in schools.

Franklin Bobbitt (1913), a professor at the University of Chicago, tried to apply the ideas that Taylor espoused to the "problems of educational management and supervision." Bobbitt firmly held that management, direction, and supervision of schools were necessary to achieve "organizational goals." Bobbitt maintained that supervision was an essential function "to coordinate school affairs. . . . Supervisory members must co-ordinate the labors of all, . . . find the best methods of work, and enforce the use of these methods on the part of the workers" (pp. 76, 78).

The employment of scientific principles in supervision, said Bobbitt, is a necessity for the continued progress of the school system. Many supervisors, including principals, were eager to adopt Bobbitt's ideas of scientific management for use in schools. Just as "supervision as inspection" reflected the "emergence of bureaucracy" in education, so too "supervision as social efficiency" was largely influenced by scientific management in education. It is within this context that Dewey's work emerged.

The movement to alter supervisory theory and practice to more democratic and improvement foci, while at the same time minimizing the evaluative function, occurred in the 1920s as a direct result of growing opposition to autocratic supervisory methods. Influenced in large measure by Dewey's (1929) theories of democratic and scientific thinking as well as by Hosic's (1920) ideas of democratic supervision, supervisors attempted to apply scientific methods and cooperative problem-solving approaches to educational problems (Pajak, 1993b). Dewey's work in particular served as the intellectual impetus to marshal opposition against emerging attempts to apply social efficiency to educational problems.

Examination of the literature indicates, however, that the momentum of social efficiency with its crude and ill-conceived application of science to solve educational problems gained rather than lessened as a result of Dewey's work. Although in the 1930s and 1940s educators believed that autocratic supervisory practices were no longer viable, they urged for more scientific approaches to supervisory practice in schools.

In much earlier times, supervision was conducted by means of checklist-type rating cards. The early attempts to apply science via rating cards were now losing favor. Burton (1930), a prolific writer in supervision, explained that the use of "rating schemes from our prescientific days, . . . would be wholly inadequate today." Although Burton recognized the usefulness of rating in some instances, he believed that "it is desirable and rapidly becoming possible to have more objectively determined items by means of which to evaluate the teacher's procedure" (p. 405).

One of the foremost proponents of science in education and supervision was A. S. Barr (1931). He stated emphatically that the application of scientific principles "is a part of a general movement to place supervision on a professional basis." Barr stated in precise terms what the supervisor needed to know:

> Supervisors must have the ability to analyze teaching situations and to locate the probable causes for poor work with a certain degree of expertness; they must have the ability to use an array of data-gathering devices peculiar to the field of supervision itself; they must possess certain constructive skills for the development of new means, methods, and materials of instruction; they must know how teachers learn to teach; they must have the ability to teach teachers how to teach; and they must be able to evaluate. In short, they must possess training in both the science of instructing pupils and the science of instructing teachers. Both are included in the science of supervision. (pp. x, xi)

Barr said the supervisor should first formulate objectives, followed by measurement surveys to determine the instructional status of schools.

Then, probable causes of poor work should be explored through the use of tests, rating scales, and observational instruments. The results of supervision, continued Barr, must be measured. Most important, according to Barr, the methods of science should be applied to the study and practice of supervision. More concretely, Barr (1925) asserted that a scientific analysis of teaching is a necessary part of the training of a supervisor: "How can the scientific knowledge of the teaching process be brought to bear upon the study and improvement of teaching?"

Barr contended that teaching could be broken down into its component parts, and that each part had to be studied scientifically. If good teaching procedures could be isolated, thought Barr, then specific standards could be established to guide the supervisor in judging the quality of instruction. He based his scientific approach to supervision "upon the success of the professional student of education in breaking up this complex mass into its innumerable elements and to study each objectively" (pp. 360, 363).

In a later work titled *Supervision: Democratic Leadership in the Improvement of Learning*, Barr, Burton, and Brueckner (1947) explained the task of a supervisor as fivefold:

1. Determine the objectives of the lesson.
2. Survey the classroom learning environment.
3. Search for the causes of unsatisfactory pupil achievement.
4. Train teachers to improve instruction.
5. Measure the results of supervision.

Apparently, Barr did not envision a contradiction between a scientific supervisory approach to teaching and democracy.

He was not alone. Many shared his view. William A. Smith (1934) in an article titled "Dictatorship and Democracy in Education from a Teacher's Viewpoint," in *School and Society*, asked, "Will the schools prepare for the efficiency of an autocrat in government or will they prepare for the less efficient, more complicated, and idealistic democracy?" His answer was typical among many of his contemporaries: "Efficiency and democracy should not be viewed as competing ideas, but rather as one entity" (p. 614). Schools, he thought, could be efficient democracies utilizing scientific technologies.

Some astute people at the time, however, realized an inherent ambiguity in this quest. Jesse H. Newlon, famed former superintendent in Denver, Colorado, and later professor of education at Teachers College, Columbia University, claimed that a reconciliation "between cooperation and dictatorship" was impossible. He argued that it was not feasible to require "obedience to constituted authority," and at the same time, encourage "teacher participation and freedom." Newlon (1934) explained:

> Almost all writers on the subject emphasize the importance of the authority of the principal. The advantages of a co-operative type of supervisory relationship

are stressed by most of the writers, but the practice which they advocate often seems inconsistent with these doctrines. Burton, for example, says, "Democracy has implicitly in it the idea of delegated authority and of obedience to properly constituted expert leadership." Burton has really stated the crux of the whole problem, *but he does not make clear* [italics added] how obedience to expert authority is to be reconciled with genuine teacher participation in the formulation of policies and freedom to exercise professional judgment in carrying out these policies. (pp. 188, 196)

Courtis (1928) summed up this view succinctly: "Can you supervise me scientifically and respect my personality? I'm afraid not" (p. 339).

Lucio and McNeil (1969), popular authors of a major textbook on supervision, explained the difficulty of advocating a scientific approach to supervision that aimed to inspect teachers. They said, "[T]eachers were regarded as instruments that should be closely supervised to insure that they mechanically carried out the methods of procedure determined by administrative and special supervisors" (p. 3).

Equally oppressive, they thought, were scientific methods that sought to quantify, explain, and predict with precision teaching behaviors in the classroom that would best promote student learning. Such presumed certainty of supervisory methods was unrealistic and misguided. For these supervisors, teaching was a science, not an art, through which application of a prescribed set of behaviors would yield teaching success and thus student achievement.

Another noted personality of the time who influenced the idea of scientific supervision was Charles H. Judd. In an address before the National Association of Secondary School Principals, Judd (1920) stated that "teachers must be supervised in a fashion which is at once direct and scientific." Judd criticized the manner in which supervisors were chosen without adequate training in the science of education.

In the future, he said, "[t]hey will be selected because they are equipped by mental capacities and by careful scientific study for administrative and managerial functions." Judd further urged that "both the non-supervisory attitude and the attitude of excessive supervision ought to be replaced by scientific method of determining whether classroom work is efficient or not" (p. 31).

E. E. Lewis, a superintendent in Rockford, Illinois, interestingly, yet curiously, compared the science of child intelligence to the work of supervisors in measuring teacher performance. Lewis (1923) described three ways of measuring pupil accomplishment: through personal opinion, comparison with other pupils, and by standard units of accomplishment. Dismissing the first two rather quickly, Lewis favored IQ testing. "It is much fairer and far more accurate to measure the general intelligence of a child in terms of an IQ than it is to measure in terms of 'bright,' 'average,' or 'dull.'" Furthermore, continued Lewis, "an IQ means practically the same thing anywhere the child may happen to go, while 'bright,' 'average,' or 'dull' may change meaning when used by the same person a half hour later."

Lewis also emphasized the importance of fair and just scientific comparison between teachers. "Let us give this new movement in education our heartiest support and in time we will really have a science and a technique of measurement that will be a substitute for inaccurate opinion and comparison" (pp. 43, 146).

One of the earliest objectors to the use of scientific supervision was a professor of education at Ohio State University named Orville G. Brim. In an article titled "Changing and Conflicting Conceptions of Supervision," Brim (1930) acknowledged "the rapid growth of scientific supervision." He labeled the application of science to the work of supervisors as "inspectorial, a fact-finding process." He claimed that use of "diagnostic tests" and recording teacher behaviors in "numerical form" had the "quality of authority, of finality."

Decrying such an application of science to the work of supervision, Brim stated emphatically and with a tinge of sarcasm:

> This belief in the reliability of the findings of scientific investigations, the belief that the standard established should become the universal practice, has tended to make the scientific supervisor more autocratic than his predecessor, the inspector, for the scientific supervisor thinks he has the authority of "facts" spelled in capital letters. (p. 133)

While others joined Brim in his condemnation of the injudicious application of science to supervisory practice, the impetus for their criticisms can be found in the groundbreaking work of John Dewey (1916/2007a, 1929).

Dewey (1916/2007a) believed that the future of civilization depended "upon the widening spread and deepening hold of the scientific habit of mind; and that the problem of problems in our education is therefore to discover how to mature and make effective this scientific habit." Dewey held that

> [s]cience must have something to say about what we do, and not merely about how we may do it most easily and economically. . . . When our schools truly become laboratories of knowledge-making, not mills fitted out with information-hoppers, there will no longer be need to discuss the place of science in education. . . . The problem of educational use of science is to create an intelligence pregnant with belief in the possibility of the direction of human affairs by itself. . . . The method of science engrained through education in habit means emancipation from rule of thumb. (pp. 167, 168)

Dewey asserted that science, to have any lasting effect in schools, must be grounded in the "lived experience" of the members of each school.

Science is experience becoming rational. The effect of science is thus to change man's idea of the nature and inherent possibilities of experience. By the same token it changes the idea and the operation of reason. Instead of being something beyond experience, remote, aloof, concerned with a sublime region that has nothing to do with the experienced facts of life, it is found indigenous in-experience: the factor by which past experiences are purified and rendered into tools for discovery and advance. (p. 228)

Dewey, in sum, believed that scientific theory was related to practice "as the agency of its expansion and its direction to new possibilities" (p. 228).

Dewey's (1929) most scathing critique of existing scientific practices in the schools, as well as the most lucid exposition of his ideas on scientific inquiry, was set forth in his sometimes read, but not understood, volume *The Sources of a Science of Education*. In response to the question "Is there a science of education? . . . Can there be a science of education?" Dewey replied that while scientific and systematic investigation sheds light on a range of facts by enabling "us to understand them better and to control them more intelligently, less haphazardly and with less routine," our current utilization of science in schools is inadequate and misdirected.

Dewey denounced the current practice of science in education. There is "a strong tendency to identify teaching ability with use of procedures that yield immediately successful results, success being measured by such things as order in the classroom, correct recitations by pupils in assigned lessons, passing of examinations, promotion of pupils to a higher grade, etc." Educators, charged Dewey, "want recipes for classroom success." This view of "science is antagonistic to education as an art," declared Dewey.

Dewey claimed the use of rating schemes was not an "enhancement of science in education," but a detraction from the true aims of science. "Such attempts, even when made unconsciously and with laudable intent to tender education more scientific," he said, "defeat their own purpose and create reactions against the very concept of educational science."

Dewey concluded his little book with a recapitulation and final admonition. The only way, said Dewey, to create a science of education is to involve oneself in the "educational act itself." The intense interaction between practitioner and pupil will in and of itself yield "scientific formulations." "Education is by its nature an endless circle or spiral, . . . in its very process it sets more problems to be further studied, which then react into the educative process to change it still further, and thus demand more thought, more science, and so on, in everlasting sequence."

Dewey warned that to ignore the value of "experimentation and discovery" will lead to a mistaken conception of the "true meaning of scientific inquiry." Science based on experimentation, said Dewey, is emancipatory and purposeful.

Dewey's ideas of science as applied to educational practice did not receive wide acceptance. Supervisors, in particular, did not adopt Dewey's model of scientific inquiry. Much of his writing, especially about the science of education, was technical and enigmatic in its presentation. As a result, confusion and misinterpretation of Dewey's views prevailed.

Given the fact that there was much misunderstanding, it was not surprising that supervisors did not adopt Dewey's ideas. More significantly, supervisors eschewed his ideas about science because they were more interested in definite, ready-made prescriptions. Dewey's admonitions to avoid definitive scientific formulations in favor of gradual experimentation of ideas in the classroom did not find favor among supervisors.

Supervisors desperately wanted instant solutions to the problems they faced in schools. Rating schemes, for example, were appealing to supervisors because they could, it was thought, accurately assess the performance of teachers' work. Their ideas backfired as teacher opposition to rating schemes and misuse of science grew in intensity (Hill, 1918; Rousmaniere, 1992).

Although Dewey's ideas did not hold sway in most schools, proposals were proffered that aligned with Dewey's scientific formulations. Throughout the 1930s–1950s, the idea that supervision involves improving instruction based on classroom observation gained momentum (see, e.g., Burton & Brueckner, 1955). Supervision as a means of improving instruction through observation was also reinforced by the use of "stenographic reports," which were the brainchild of Romiett Stevens, a professor at Teachers College, Columbia University.

Stevens thought that the best way to improve instruction was to record verbatim accounts of actual lessons "without criticism or comment." Stevens's stenographic account was "the first major systematic study of classroom behavior" (Hoetker & Ahlbrand, 1969). Dewey, we surmise, would have applauded Stevens's stenographic accounts because they were descriptive, not prescriptive. Stevens's work needs greater attention because it laid the groundwork for much of the descriptive, nonjudgmental approaches of supervision that were advocated from the 1970s till this day.

As supervision matured in theory throughout the 1950s and beyond, emphasis was placed on participative and collegial functions of supervision. Invented by Morris Cogan (1973) at Harvard University, clinical supervision was conceived as a "vehicle for developing professionally responsible teachers who were capable of analyzing their own performance" with an "emphasis on reflective problem solving" (Pajak, 2000, p. 5). Goldhammer (1969), one of the early proponents of clinical supervision and a student of Cogan, stated that the model for clinical supervision was "motivated, primarily, by contemporary views of weaknesses that commonly exist in educational practice" (p. 1).

The premise of clinical supervision was that a prescribed, formal process of collaboration between teacher and supervisor could improve teaching. The literature of clinical supervision has been replete with concepts of collegiality, collaboration, assistance, and improvement of instruction. Bolin and Panaritis (1992) explained that clinical supervision "appealed to many educators" because of its "emphasis on 'collegiality'" (p. 35).

Clinical supervision favored collaborative practice over inspectional, faultfinding supervision. Supervision as a science seemed to take a backseat to more simply engaging teachers in meaningful conversations about their practice in the classroom. Prescriptive measures of supervision were not advocated. It should be noted, though, that as is usual practice in education and supervision, in particular, a disconnect between advocated theory and everyday practice in schools existed.

Many schools, despite advocacy for collaboration, incorporated traditional forms of inspectional supervision. Such practices focused on observation usually for evaluation wherein a supervisor observes a teacher (a preconference might have occurred) and then writes up a formal evaluation for the teacher's file (a postconference may or may not have occurred). Supervision of this sort was reminiscent of impressionistic and evaluative supervisory practices throughout the early twentieth century.

Criticism leveled at the educational bureaucracy continued through the 1980s and had consequences for school supervision (Firth & Eiken, 1982). Throughout this period educators continued to consider alternative methods of supervision. In the early 1980s, developmental supervision, in which varied levels of teaching abilities were acknowledged, gained attention (Glickman, 1981).

By the end of the decade transformational leadership, which advocated that supervisors serve as change agents, became popular (e.g., Liethwood & Jantzi, 1990). Other writers in the 1990s advanced alternative approaches known as "culturally responsive" supervision (e.g., Bowers & Flinders, 1991). Teacher empowerment (e.g., Darling-Hammond & Goodwin, 1993) gained attention as a viable means for teachers to become active participants in decision-making processes in schools.

Peer supervision (e.g., Willerman, McNeely, & Koffman, 1991) appeared in the literature as an alternative to traditional supervision by "professionally trained supervisors," as did cognitive coaching (Costa & Garmston, 1994). Other collegiality and democratic supervisory methods continued to receive notice (e.g., Ovando, 1995, 2000; Ovando & Harris, 1992; Smyth, 1991).

The publication of *Supervision in Transition* (1992) by the Association for Supervision and Curriculum Development (ASCD) marked a refinement in the changing conception of supervision as a democratic enterprise. Glickman, editor of the yearbook, clearly set the tone by stating emphatically that the very term "supervision" connoted a distasteful, even "disgusting" metaphor for school improvement.

Instead of even using the words *supervision* or *supervisor*, educators, or what Glickman called "risk-taking practitioners," were more comfortable with terms such as "instructional leadership" and "instructional leader." The transition that Glickman and the authors of this comprehensive account of supervision envisioned was one that valued collegiality. Supervision, in the words of Sergiovanni (1992), was viewed as "professional and moral."

Other models and conceptions of supervision emerged in an attempt to extend democratic methods in order to disassociate it from bureaucratic and inspectional supervision. Clinical, developmental, transformational, among other models of supervision, then, had a common bond in that they emerged to counter the ill effects of supervision's bureaucratic legacy.

During today's high-stakes accountability NCLB era, directive approaches to supervision are commonplace (Marshall, 2003; Sullivan, Shulman, & Glanz, 2005). One such practice is known as the walk-through promulgated by Downey, Steffy, English, Frase, and Poston Jr. (2004) in a volume titled *The Three-Minute Classroom Walk-Through*. Such practices find justification within a standards-based educational milieu.

They also find legitimacy given the overall pejorative legacy of the supervision field. "Walk-through," conceived as a democratic process involving teachers, is used primarily as a monitoring tool (Roberts & Pruitt, 2003). Such a supervisory practice is aligned with attempts to discover a science of teaching.

The Institute of Education Science, sponsored by the U.S. Department of Education, discussed in the Implications section of this chapter below, has identified "research-based" findings of sound educational practices for "implementation" in schools and classrooms. Supervision has become a monitoring instrument to ensure that such practices are employed (Sullivan, 2006).

Very few empirical studies exist on the effectiveness of walk-throughs. Jane David (2007), in reviewing extant research, explains that walk-throughs, "also called learning walks, quick visits, and data walks," are "touted as a systematic way to gather helpful data on instructional practices" (p. 81). In explaining the idea behind the concept, she says principals, for example, might "want to know whether teachers are able to put into practice their recent training on quick-writes and pair-shares" (p. 81).

Sullivan (2006) explains that walk-throughs "shed light on an approach to classroom observation that can become monitoring couched in the language of teacher growth and reflective practice" (p. 2). Sullivan cites the following characteristics of walk-throughs as evidence of their monitoring function:

1. Unannounced—in authentic reflective practice and supervision, teachers or teachers and supervisor conduct a planning conference to decide on a focus of observation. Much of the learning can take place before a classroom visit so that the observer sees improving or improved practice. Also, planning gives the teacher the opportunity to discuss his or her perceived needs rather than leaving it to an unannounced visitor. Unannounced visits eliminate the role of the teacher in initiating and reflecting on what will be observed.
2. Brief (two–three minutes)—reflective practice involves observation as well as feedback. What kind of meaningful learning or teaching can be observed in two to three minutes, even if the observations are repeated several times before a discussion takes place?
3. No checklist of teaching practices to look for—apparently an improvement on a checklist, however authentic, reflective supervision has one focus. Multiple foci do not result in improved instruction, only confusion for the teacher.
4. Focus on professional growth—how can one address real professional growth based on two- to three-minute observations?
5. Ultimately lead to reflective conversation—reflective conversation is well nigh impossible when the teacher has had no say in the observation process and is presented with feedback from an authority. Reflective conversation has to be developed together, and in this case is based on one-sided information. (p. 2)

Sullivan expounds on her critique of the walk-through, especially the Downey et al. model, but concludes by saying, "The real danger of the "Three-Minute Classroom Walk-Through" is that it provides a justification for the worst sins of the 'snoopervisor'" (p. 3).

David (2007) reviewing the little research available on walk-throughs explains that according to one study "administrators find walk-throughs more useful than do teachers (who rarely receive individual feedback)" (p. 81). David points out "significant risks" with such practices. She says when a climate of trust and improvement is not secured in a school, then walk-throughs are perceived "as compliance checks, increasing distrust and tension" (p. 82).

David, in her article, seems to suggest, however, that walk-throughs if appropriately implemented can play "a constructive role" in instructional improvement (p. 82). She advocates proper training for observers and adequate communication of the purposes of walk-throughs, and recommends that they not merely be used to monitor implementation of some schoolwide practice. David and others seem to not understand that walk-throughs and similar approaches are likely to be viewed as inspectional because they resemble checklist approaches of the past. Shortcuts and quick fixes, expedient and efficient as they are, are not conducive to classroom and school improvement.

IMPLICATIONS FOR CURRENT
SUPERVISORY PRACTICE

Dewey criticized educators of his day for attempting to discover ready-made recipes for teaching success without fully understanding the nature of scientific inquiry. What can we learn about supervisory practice today from Dewey's critique of scientific dogmatism? This chapter has challenged readers to consider past efforts to reach a science of supervision in light of current practices.

Certainly, circumstances today, in light of NCLB and its concomitant high-stakes testing influence and vigorous accountability issues, are not precisely what educators during the first half of the previous century confronted. However, educators of yesteryear did confront seemingly intractable problems of their own that are similar to criticism of supervisory practices today.

Declining test scores, teacher qualification issues, lack of adequate supervision, insufficient attention to instructional exigencies faced by teachers, and lack of research into instructional and supervisory practices characterize both eras. Educators in Dewey's day realized these problems and looked to science for a cure-all. Dewey's vociferous attack was not necessarily about their attempt to study education scientifically. His critique centered on a twofold problem.

First, he lamented their impatience for quick solutions. "Learning to wait," Dewey (1929) explained, "is one of the important things that scientific method teaches" (p. 42). Dewey criticized educators who looked to science to provide ready-made answers.

Second, and not an unrelated point, when science, he said, did yield some valuable (or in today's lingo, "research-based") findings, even then, a deliberate, tentative, and inquiring stance must be taken. He explained the title of his book on this point, which is crucial to understanding Dewey's perspective:

> The net conclusion of our discussion is that the final reality of educational science is not found in books, nor in experimental laboratories, nor in the classrooms where it is taught, but in the minds of those engaged in the educative act.

But they are not *educational* [italics in original] science short of this point. They are psychology, sociology, statistics, or whatever. . . . This is the point upon which my whole discussion turns. We must distinguish between the *sources of educational science* [italics in original] and scientific content. We are in constant danger of confusing the two; we tend to suppose that certain results, *because they are scientific, are already educational science* [emphasis ours]. Enlightenment, clarity and progress can come about only as we remember that such results are *sources* [italics in original] to be used, through the medium of the minds of educators, to make educational functions more intelligent. (pp. 32–33)

Surveying the scientific dimensions of supervision, Killian and Post (1998) document the historic proclivity to cling to theories of scientific management in education and their impact on supervisory practice. Citing Sergiovanni and Starratt's noted text *Supervision: A Redefinition*, Killian and Post explain that as long as society values a technical-rational approach that emphasizes scientific discoveries as paramount, scientific conceptions of supervision are inevitable.

They explain, "[C]laiming that supervision and teaching are applied sciences lends respect to those fields, and that trying to use research to identify the 'one best practice' is attractive." Sergiovanni and Starratt, according to Killian and Post, state that "teaching and learning are too complex to be captured simply. In the real world of teaching, none of the assumptions hold up very well and the related practices portray an unrealistic view of teaching and supervision" (p. 1051).

A more realistic view is aligned with Dewey's notions of the tentativeness of science in education and its exploratory nature. Killian and Post cite a variety of "problems that plague applications of scientific management to supervisory practice," including, among others, "rushed implementation" (p. 1051). "Failure to establish an adequate research base in advance of implementation results," Killian and Post argue, "in . . . catastrophic" outcomes (p. 1052).

They offer this concluding note: scientific supervision, stemming from the days of Taylor and Bobbitt, "continues to be a major competing force in supervision." Citing Sergiovanni and Starratt once more, they say that we seem to prefer the exact answer to a wrong question rather than an approximate answer to the right question. Killian and Post end, "The important issue thus becomes, not so much whether the legacy of scientific management will endure, but whether our predilection for the most simplistic of its forms can be tempered by some lessons learned about its failures" (p. 1052).

As we were writing this section of the chapter we came across a website called Doing What Works put out by the U.S. Department of Education (dww

.ed.gov/index.cfm?). Hit play on the video "Quality of Teaching," and here's what it says, in part:

> I am a teacher. I am an assistant superintendent. I provide assistance to schools and district. I needed help and found it here. Welcome to the Doing What Works web site sponsored by the U.S. Department of Education (and the Institute of Education Science). This site is designed to support NCLB by helping educators to use research-based practices in their schools and classrooms. . . . We don't have all the answers when it comes to understanding how students learn best. But we do know some things that are likely to make a difference. . . . The site provides research-based practices and examples of implementation tools. Will it help me meet the goals of NCLB? The NCLB Act of 2001 was passed to ensure that all of our children get a quality education. It holds schools accountable for helping all students read and do math and science at grade level by the year 2014.

What would strike Dewey about this statement? Well, he might applaud the part that states "We don't have all the answers when it comes to understanding how students learn best." Yet, what he would find most troubling, it seems to us, is some of the text that follows:

> But we do know some things that are likely to make a difference. . . . The site provides research-based practices and examples of implementation tools. Will it help me meet the goals of NCLB? The NCLB Act of 2001 was passed to ensure that all of our children get a quality education. It holds schools accountable for helping all students read and do math and science at grade level by the year 2014.

Allow us to break down each of these key sentences. "But we do know some things that are likely to make a difference." Fair enough. Science can indeed yield some useful information to inform classroom teaching practice. But Dewey cautioned us to avoid using "scientific discoveries" as inevitably applicable in all situations. Context is key. Now for the next sentence, "The site provides research-based practices and examples of implementation tools."

Harmless enough, or maybe a foreboding of what is to come? One can only presume that the "research-based" findings are indeed of sound methodology and have appropriate applicability (generalizability). Even if these "research-based" findings were sound, the second phrase, "and examples of implementation tools," might imply a prescriptive nature without fully understanding or appreciating the unique social, economic, and educational circumstances of a particular school or classroom.

Then, the sentence "It holds schools accountable for helping all students read and do math and science at grade level by the year 2014" is perhaps most troublesome. If it were not for the track record of NCLB and its uncompromising meting out of punishments to schools and districts that have not met their AYP objectives, the sentence might serve as a lofty goal, for after all, who's against accountability and not in favor of every child reading and doing math?

The incongruity, it appears to us, is in the fact that the statement states plainly that research has yielded "some" findings that are "likely" to make a difference. Such tentativeness is laudable until the accountability issue is raised. Dewey, we think, would lament the premise that schools, writ large, would be held accountable when facts have not been established for all situations under all conditions, not that such a goal is even possible.

Dewey would be more deliberate and consider the unique circumstances and challenges of each school. Implementation of findings by this Institute of Education Science (notice the title, rather than using "Research," a more tentative and exploratory term, the word "Science" is not too subtly attached to "education").

Operating under the aegis of science, NCLB and its adherents attempt to apply science rigorously and prescriptively. Dewey, it seems to us, would be in the forefront to challenge such an application of science to education and schooling. Unfortunately, if history is any indicator, his ideas and voice would be muted.

Interestingly, Edward Pajak, respected professor of supervision and currently chair of education at Johns Hopkins University, in an e-mail correspondence (2007), agreed that "the field of supervision doesn't seem to have much of a memory, which is true of education generally."

He also concurred that "Dewey's influence on thinking in our field has been significant, but largely forgotten." As regards a "science of supervision," he said, "I think you're correct that we're now looking for scientific 'answers,' instead of employing the scientific process to the work of educators, which is what Dewey really proposed."

Regarding the NCLB website mentioned above, it is interesting to note that several educators have supported the use of research-based findings based on "sound science" for adoption in schools. Robert J. Marzano's (2007) work readily comes to mind.

In his *The Art and Science of Teaching: A Comprehensive Framework for Effective Instruction*, he presents a "model for ensuring quality teaching that balances the necessity of research-based data with the equally vital need to understand the strengths and weaknesses of individual students" (p. 4). Under the guise of "interventions that work," Marzano's work attempts to provide legitimacy for "scientific work" in education, teaching, and consequently, in supervision.

In another e-mail correspondence, but this time with James Popham (2007), prominent professor emeritus at UCLA and noted scholar and author on assessment, I queried him about Marzano's work. Popham stated, "I have immense respect for him [Marzano] and his efforts. But we think it is always necessary to toss in a caveat or two when offering 'research-based' guidance regarding a phenomenon as multivariate as education."

Popham claims that deriving findings "from empirical research in our field is probability-guided actions." He continues, "Even 'sound science,' at the very best, will only allow teachers to say, 'If I use this research-supported tactic, it is *more likely* that my students will achieve the curricular aim I have in mind for them than if I did not use this research-supported tactic—but I can't be *certain* that it will work.'"

CONCLUSION

So, what can we learn from Dewey's understanding of science and how might such an understanding inform current and, perhaps, future supervisory practice? The field of supervision needs to redefine, reculture, or, even, refind itself (see English, 2007, who makes a similar argument about educational administration, albeit for different reasons).

We think we need to find a more appropriate and reasonable balance between the art and science of teaching. In order for us to have a science of supervision, or education for that matter, we need to continue research to establish a "solid base" for teaching practice. Extant research findings, verified time and time again in differing contexts, it seems to us, are critical for establishing such a base.

Continued research will provide us a deeper, more thorough understanding of good teaching practice. Supervision, it seems to us, can benefit profoundly from such a teaching research base to inform work with teachers. But in the end, a science of education is not what we should be looking for. Rather, as Dewey has admonished, we need to look for the "sources" of a science of education. In that light our work is much more nuanced, tentative, less dogmatic and prescriptive.

For Dewey, even expressed in his later works (Dewey, 1938), inquiry should be viewed as "thoughts-in-progress" so as to eschew misunderstandings and outright errors. Supervision, thus, becomes a process of engaging teachers in an artful, in-depth, and continuous dialogue or conversation about what is transpiring in the classroom. That is the lesson we think Dewey would advocate.

On this very point, Dewey (1929) said that education is unlike physics, chemistry, or biology. "Just because educational science has no such achievement of laws to fall back upon, it is in a tentative and inchoate state. . . . To treat them as scientific rather than as philosophic is to conceal from view their hypothetical character and to freeze them into *rigid dogmas* [italics added] that hamper instead of assisting actual inquiry" (p. 55).

Discussion Questions

1. Contrast the descriptions of the history of supervision described in this chapter with your experiences. Do your experiences affirm or contradict this history? Explain.
2. Is it possible to be at once scientific, yet professional? Explain why or why not.
3. How has Dewey's work, as described in this chapter, helped you better understand education as it is practiced today?
4. Discuss your experience with walk-throughs. Is such "supervision" helpful? Explain why or why not.
5. React to the criticisms discussed about walk-throughs. Do you agree or disagree with them? Explain.
6. How do you see "scientific dogmatism" played out in your school or district?
7. What might John Dewey say if he visited your school or district? Why? Explain.
8. What impact might the scientific dogmatism manifested in supervision and administration affect curriculum in your school or district?
9. What might an ideal supervisory program look like?
10. What else strikes you about the ideas highlighted in this chapter?

Further Reflection

1. Interview a supervisor or administrator. Ask "How has your practice of supervision changed since NCLB?"; "What 'research-based' practices or theories are most important in your work?"; and "What complaints do you have about your job?" Record the responses in some way. Then, discuss how his or her responses connect in any way to the ideas you read about in this chapter.
2. If you had the power and authority to change educational practices, what changes would you make, and why? How might John Dewey react to such changes? Explain.
3. What are the curricular implications of Dewey's critique? What lesson(s) might you glean from Dewey in your day-to-day practice in a school or district?

Chapter Five

Implementing Inquiry,
Holistic Learning through Technology

> Industry has ceased to be essentially an empirical, rule-of-thumb proce-
> dure, handed down by custom. Its technique is now technological: that
> is to say, based upon machinery resulting from discoveries in mathemat-
> ics, physics, chemistry, bacteriology, etc. The economic revolution has
> stimulated science by setting problems for solution, by producing greater
> intellectual respect for mechanical appliances.
>
> —Dewey (1916/2007a, p. 231)

Despite the investment of tens of billions of dollars in equipping schools with
computer and related technologies over the past three decades, technology
has failed to live up to its promise of transforming educational pedagogy and
practice. Since the 1990s, teachers have primarily used technology to communicate through e-mail and locate supplemental curricular material. At the
same time, students have persistently engaged in low-level uses including
writing with word processors, searching for information on the Internet, and
gaining access for reward or free time.

A paucity of research suggests that when technology is infused into the
curriculum to promote higher-order thinking in authentic and productive
ways, such as when students create technological products such as presentations, interest and achievement increase, particularly on high-stakes tests.
Moreover, there is strong evidence that using technology in this manner
benefits low socioeconomic status populations, but teachers and administrators mainly direct these students to drill-and-practice tutorials in preparation
for the tests. Further, some studies suggest that teachers are less willing to
integrate technology into the curriculum because of the effects of high-stakes
tests. By placing technology use in Dewey's pragmatic instrumentalism, we
can better understand both the successes and failures of current technology

practices. Dewey's philosophy provides the tools for analyzing educative experiences and finds validation in current research and standards.

Focus Questions

1. What does experience mean to you?
2. How is technology used in schools?
3. In what ways do you use technology in your daily routines?
4. How do you think NCLB supports and, at the same time, prevents the use of technology for learning in schools?

Dewey died in 1952 and had lived over 92 years through perhaps the most innovative period in global history. When he was born in 1859, many of the conveniences of the modern world such as automobiles, antibiotics, the telephone, and airplanes were yet unknown. Before he passed, he witnessed the first computers and the detonation of the atomic bomb.

Almost to the end, he remained in relatively good health and continued to work prodigiously. His earlier experiences of starting the laboratory school at the University of Chicago and his eventual displacement to Columbia University, where he held dual positions in the philosophy department and Teachers College, provided the ideas for his greatest comments on educational philosophy, including the role of technology.

Despite the vast changes in technology when Dewey wrote some of his most seminal works, including *The Child and the Curriculum* (1902/2001), *How We Think* (1910/2007b), *The School and Society* (1899/2001), *Democracy and Education* (1916/2007a), and *Experience and Education* (1938), he provided elements for understanding the proper role and elusive integration of information technology for teaching and learning. The technology includes computer-based software and hardware.

In the modern world, Dewey advocated a philosophy of pragmatic instrumentalism and examinations of social occupations. By situating technology within these two ideas, we can develop a better sense of using technology to educate the whole student.

Dewey's philosophy of pragmatic instrumentalism regarded knowledge as an instrument for addressing human needs. If one juxtaposes computer technologies in this system of ideas, the technology can be conceptualized as an inquiry tool in a social and cultural context. In other words, when students successfully engage in technological inquiry, they use computer tools to resolve conflicts and develop new ideas such as theories and concepts to engage in further inquiry.

Likewise, it is in this context that education finds relevancy for informing the curriculum and drawing on the teacher's expertise. Dewey recognized that the transmission of knowledge occurred in an environment with many forces exerting influences on the immature mind, including sources such as family, religion, school, and all formal and informal social associations.

Compared to the associations outside of school, schooling was relatively artificial. Therefore, the curriculum, according to Dewey, should begin with young children in an "unscholastic" manner because it looked to the real, outside social world for relevancy. In other words, effective education—especially for beginning learners—depended on connecting previous experiences of the outside world to new experiences, expertly guided by the efforts of the teacher.

Today, when we look at a typical child's daily experiences, we discover a technological world of cell phones, text messaging, digital media such as iPods, video games, and much more. In contrast, when we look inside schools, we see a curriculum and methods closer to the comprehensive schools of the 1920s than the mediated environment of the 2000s. In general, when students enter school, they are required to switch off their cell phones, pack away their iPods, and slip into a world of rigidly aligned desks, teacher-centered instruction, and low-level uses of technology.

THE IMPORTANCE OF FIRSTHAND EXPERIENCES AND SOCIAL OCCUPATIONS

Dewey's epistemology, or his theory of knowledge, explained how individuals constructed meaning in sociocultural contexts, which sharply differed from a traditional approach to knowledge that recognized fixed, universal truths. Because individuals constructed their own knowledge, Dewey's views on subject matter and curricular resources dictated that teachers use firsthand experiences and social occupations to connect to students' lives in meaningful ways.

For Dewey, the most important aspect for the study of subject matter was the selection of curricular resources "which at the outset fall within the scope of ordinary life-experience" (Dewey, 1938, p. 73). Thus, educators provided the problems, which served as the stimulus for thinking, with ever-increasing sophistication and organization approximating that of "the skilled, mature person" (p. 74).

Likewise, the selection of important problems involved making cognitive connections to previous experiences, which "have the promise and potentiality of presenting new problems which by stimulating new ways of observation and judgment will expand the area of further experience" (p. 75). Dewey conceived one rich source of experiences in social occupations, which may hold great promise for understanding the integration of technology in education.

Even around 1900 industrial America, Dewey envisaged work with natural materials such as wood and metal as a method for learning, despite and indeed because of factory production. He believed that bringing children in contact with the natural world while engaging in social practices mirrored life in the community, and therefore, made schooling relevant and interesting.

For younger children, material should be integrated sequentially in the following order: (1) family and local community life; (2) social occupations; and (3) a historical treatment of common, contemporary occupations and the social processes associated with them. In the early twentieth-century world, this often began with the factories and nature surrounding urban centers.

For example, in his elementary laboratory school at the University of Chicago, Dewey and the teachers selected occupations that would stimulate inquiry because they related directly to human needs and evolved in a clear historical progression. One example was the textile industry. Students began with the study of primitive clothing such as animal pelts and skins. Next, they focused on the domestic production of clothing by one or more family members from raw materials to usable garments.

As the Industrial Revolution began, cottage industries within the homes produced some of the finished products for larger consumption, followed by the establishment of factory production. Students at the school participated in the crude manufacture of yarn and clothing while instruction was provided in a historical context (Tanner, 1997). In *The School and Society* (1899/2001), Dewey went as far as creating diagrams of traditional school organizations replete with renderings of ideal school arrangements of classrooms, nature, and the home—no doubt culled from his experiences at the Chicago Laboratory School.

The laboratory school also provided the means for studying children engaged in activities leading to Dewey's elaboration of children's growth stages. In an article titled "Science in Elementary Education" published in the *Elementary School Record*, Dewey (1900) presented a case for engaging children with curriculum activities based on three stages of growth.

The first stage ranged from the age of four to about seven or eight. According to Dewey, children participate unreflectively in activities as part of a social experience and that is what they remember, not the knowledge and steps of the process. He illustrated this step by describing children of this age refining flour from raw wheat. As a group, they crushed the wheat to release the husk and bran, and then milled the remainder into fine flour.

What the students remembered later was the social activity with their classmates, not the actual process of refining flour. What the children were doing was gaining firsthand experiences with a social occupation, which he defined as the "observation of natural phenomena through their connection with some use, either by child or by man" (Dewey, 1900, p. 157). And subsequently, this social engagement provided the elements for inquiry in the first stage and offered an immediate connection to young children's lives.

The second period of growth begins at about the age of eight and is characterized by children's ability to understand processes and make generalizations about the world. As compared to the first stage, children move from their own immediate sphere to making connections with real people geographically and historically. Dewey explained, "The main purpose is to build up an idea of the physical world as a whole, while making connections through their social interests with definite areas in widely separated parts of the world" (p. 160).

At the same time, cultivating student interest in the subject matter was still dependent on a social approach to learning. Dewey described how children at the laboratory school began their historical studies with a sweeping history of the world followed by specific activities to study the Great Lakes, the emergence of British colonies, and other facets within a spiraling curriculum with emphases on experimental activities. This middle stage occurred between the unreflective nature of the first stage and the highly specialized aspects of the last stage.

While the first two stages of growth occur in a typical elementary school setting, the last stage is characteristic of secondary school. In the last stage students continue to grow intellectually through experience. While they are not able to think abstractly in the beginning of this stage, by the end they are capable of utilizing abstract thought for social purposes. As we shall see later, the three stages provide insights into how the teacher can provide effective experiences using technology. However, first we need to recognize the crucial importance of experience in Dewey's epistemology.

EXPERIENCE AND GROWTH

Originally published in 1916, *Democracy and Education* provided an extensive elaboration of Dewey's education philosophy advocating a more democratic approach to teaching and learning. The book encompassed an enormous scope with typical Dewey obfuscations, so much so that later, in 1938, he felt the need to offer an abbreviated account with the publishing of *Experience and Education* (Pring, 2007).

In this spare book, Dewey offered a concise description of a theory of experience and the arrangement of the curriculum, crucial for understanding technology. By analyzing the commensurate parts of experience, we may be able to shed light on why technology has failed to live up to its potential in education, while at the same time recognizing the manner in which it has revolutionized the way we live and work.

According to Dewey, by definition, an individual's encounter with the external environment created experiences. However, Dewey was quick to point out that not all experiences were educative. In fact, he offered a list of categories for experiences that were "mis-educative," because they retarded or thwarted "further experience."

Dewey articulated these types as follows: (1) experiences that produced "callousness" resulting in "insensitivity" leading to a lack of "responsive-ness"; (2) experiences that degenerated into routines, which inhibited richer experiences because the individual was "in a groove or rut"; (3) experiences that were enjoyable but ended with a "slack and careless attitude"; and (4) experiences that were not cumulatively linked together resulting in an internal loss of control "and a person becomes scatterbrained" (Dewey, 1938, pp. 25–26).

As shall become evident later, when technology is used in learning, it is often infused into the curriculum in mis-educative ways, which may illuminate why, overall, technology has not been widely adopted within the schools. Further, Dewey gave us guidance to assess the quality of an experience.

DEWEY'S QUALITATIVE DESCRIPTION OF EXPERIENCE

Dewey talked about the "*quality*" of the experience. He explained that there were two characteristics to an experience, the first being the positive or negative response of the learner and the second being the effect on future experiences. The educator's responsibility was to arrange for experiences that captured the interest and attention of the learner over the long haul and "that live fruitfully and creatively in subsequent experiences" (Dewey, 1938, p. 28). Additionally, Dewey viewed all educative experiences as growth.

The growth—or culmination of experiences—could become a momentous force if they motivated students to learn more. The role of the teacher was to select the experiences based on two criteria: she must consider the moving force of the experience and the social aspects because all experiences involved human interaction. Therefore, Dewey engaged in a type of moral relativism, which stressed change and growth while rejecting fixed, absolute truths.

He believed that teachers had a moral obligation to take into account a student's previous experiences grounded in concrete situations. When that did not occur, as in a traditional educational setting, dualisms resulted such as the separation of mind and body. He emphatically proclaimed,

In a word, we live from birth to death in a world of persons and things which in large measure is what it is because of what has been done and transmitted from previous human activities. When this fact is ignored, experience is treated as if it were something which goes on exclusively inside an individual's body and mind. It ought not to be necessary to say that experience does not occur in a vacuum. (Dewey, 1938, pp. 39–40)

In order to connect to student experiences, history and geography became important curricular considerations as noted with the textiles lesson before, beginning with the upper elementary students. Keeping in mind that Dewey formulated much of his philosophy at the turn of the twentieth century when nature and factories were part of many students' daily existence, knowledge of local conditions facilitated the connections.

Further, he coined the term "interaction" to describe the situation when the "objective" social world encountered the student's internal perspective. In sum, the two aspects of an experience are the *continuity* from perpetual growth as each new experience affected another, and the *interaction* of the individual's cumulative experiences with the social world. Dewey also referred to these as the "longitudinal" and "lateral" characteristics of experiences (p. 44).

The longitudinal, or continuity aspect of the experience, required a consideration of the future throughout the entire learning process. As immature minds matured, earlier experiences prepared for larger and more sophisticated experiences later on. This entire educational process was growth, characterized by "continuity, reconstruction of experience" (p. 47).

In addition, Dewey asserted, even more important than learning the prescribed curriculum was the effect on future endeavors because students would develop the interest in further learning. This was at the heart of Deweyan democracy: Not only should individuals have the freedom to freely associate with others politically and socially in a decentralized manifestation of democracy, but also the freedom to experience growth, leading to one of his most famous remarks, "The only freedom that is of enduring importance is freedom of intelligence, that is to say, freedom of observation and of judgment exercised in behalf of purposes that are intrinsically worth while" (p. 61).

Exercising intelligence involved active firsthand experiences and meaningful reflection, resulting in thinking and self-control. Having students sitting at desks engaging in passive learning for long intervals was considered artificial, especially for young children. Likewise, enforcing silence only exacerbated the artificial conditions relative to the outside world while negating the social aspect to learning. Moreover, Dewey equated physical movement with the development of sound bodies and minds.

Hence, following physical learning activities, he advocated brief periods of deep reflection. The reflection nurtured growth by harnessing the active impulses directing a reconstruction of the experience. The remaking process guided future plans leading to the declaration, "Thinking is thus a postponement of immediate action, while it effects internal control of impulse through a union of observation and memory, this union being the heart of reflection" (p. 64). Consequently, the intelligent movement forward provided purposes.

In *Experience and Education*, Dewey (1938) succinctly explained how learners used intelligence to form purposes. First, the student analyzed the situation and local environment. Second, the learner recalled personal experiences and sought guidance and advice from others about similar past situations. And third, the student evaluated observations of current conditions and synthesized those elements with the recalled knowledge. Without this intelligent framing of purposes, impulses went unchecked.

Dewey worked out this inquiry process several years earlier in *How We Think* (1910/2007b), in a series of problem-solving steps sometimes referred to as the Dewey Sequence. The Dewey Sequence involved two premises, "a state of perplexity, hesitation, doubt" and an active "investigation directed toward bringing to light further facts which serve to corroborate or nullify the suggested belief" (p. 9).

The problem-solving steps were (1) define the problem; (2) analyze the characteristics of the problems; (3) propose possible solutions; (4) select a solution, which Dewey forcefully stated was *"the steadying and guiding factor in the entire process of reflection"* (p. 11); and (5) systematically test the solution. According to Dewey, the educator's role in this process was to provide the experiences that resulted in problems for reflection, specifically through the organization and facilitation of content matter in a manner consistent with how things are accomplished outside of school.

Taking into account information technology's infiltration into nearly all aspects of the modern world—including its use in myriad social occupations for inquiry—why have educators failed to utilize it to create consistent and even learning experiences across diverse student populations?

TECHNOLOGY AND THE NO CHILD LEFT BEHIND ACT

Explicitly acknowledging the importance of educational technology and the current state of inequity, Title II, Part D of the No Child Left Behind Act of 2001 contains provisions to bridge the abyss between affluent and high-poverty school districts by providing state grants to support the use of technology for teaching and learning through the Educational Technology State Grants Program.

According to the rules, the states can allot up to 5 percent of the grant money for the state level, with the remaining amount being equally proportioned to Title I recipients and other high-need districts and partnerships as long as they demonstrate poverty and direct the money toward an underperforming school or demonstrate a severe deficit in technology.

The grants can be used in the following five ways: to (1) provide administrative and instructional development, (2) purchase technology and build or enhance networks, (3) facilitate the development of technology and curriculum, (4) foster parental participation, and (5) leverage data to make informed decisions.

Moreover, the grants require that the districts spend 25 percent of the funds on professional development, except in the cases where districts can prove that they already provide substantial and high-quality development for the use of technology. If the states accept the grant money, they can also use a portion of the funding to develop required accountability measures as part of their technology plans.

The No Child Left Behind Act also contains provisions requiring the Department of Education to evaluate the effectiveness of educational technology on student achievement using an experimental design with control conditions, often referred to as scientifically based research. However, as illustrated by a 2003 study conducted by Mathematica Policy Research, Inc., and SRI International, adhering to these provisions can produce artificial circumstances.

For instance, in collaboration with the Department of Education, the researchers decided that the study should focus on reading and math software products in low-income schools, embrace an experimental design, and base achievement outcomes on student performance on standardized tests. Moreover, the researchers solicited companies for software, then selected from them based on evidence of previous effectiveness.

From a pool of 160 products, only 16 were selected for the study. Further, the product vendors recommended the selection of schools for the study. While the teachers were provided training for their products, they did not select the software. In sum, the software was selected based on the needs of the study, rather than the needs of the teachers and learners (Dynarski et al., 2007).

UNINTENDED EFFECTS OF HIGH-STAKES TESTS ON EDUCATIONAL TECHNOLOGY

High-stakes testing places stresses on the learning community by narrowing the curriculum and reducing opportunities for student use of technology in meaningful ways (Al-Bataineh, Anderson, Toledo, & Wellinski, 2008; Ertmer, 2005; Franklin, 2007; Scott & Mouza, 2007). Students use computers in schools in low-cognitive ways to search for information on the Internet, word processing activities, and reward and free time (Cuban, Kirkpatrick, & Peck, 2001).

High-stakes testing may even retard these low-cognitive uses because teachers may be hesitant to have students use word processors because the state tests are in paper-based form (Russell & Abrams, 2004). This may be particularly true for high-needs and bubble students, meaning those students designated as close to passing the state's test, because of the perceived advantages to practicing for the test using actual testing conditions. Similarly, disadvantaged students are often exposed to computer technologies in drill-and-practice exercises.

Subsequently, an entire software industry has emerged because of testing ("EM exclusive: Riverdeep," 2006). Quite simply, teachers and administrators have failed to adopt technology integration in a way that lived up to its initial expectations of promoting a student-centered classroom. And when technology is used in authentic and higher-cognitive-use ways, evidence suggests that it occurs mostly in classrooms with higher socioeconomic student populations.

TECHNOLOGICAL BARRIERS TO INTEGRATING TECHNOLOGY IN TEACHING AND LEARNING

Since the 1970s, a reform movement to integrate technology into the curriculum has flourished with a mandate to promote authentic learning and student-centered classrooms. Despite the spending of billions of dollars on equipment, software, and training, teachers still teach much the same way without incorporating technology, even when it is readily available (Russell, O'Dwyer, Bebell, & Tao, 2007).

Cuban (2001) conducted a seminal study in the late 1990s to examine how teachers and students used computer technologies in schools in the Silicon Valley area of California. First, he selected six preschool and five kindergarten classrooms based on the availability of the technology, the diverse socioeconomic status of the students, and the willingness of the participants.

Next, he and his assistants studied two technology-rich high schools to determine the extent to which these schools followed national patterns in technology integration. The study team looked at teachers who integrated technology into their curriculum to determine if they used technology to sustain traditional teaching practices.

After examining the preschool and kindergarten classrooms, the researchers concluded, "[T]he teachers we studied adapted computers to sustain, rather than transform, their philosophy that the whole child develops best when both work and play are cultivated and 'developmentally appropriate' tasks and activities are offered" (Cuban, 2001, pp. 65–66). This conclusion produced a sort of paradox because the teachers and parents also expressed a core belief that their children would need computer skills for future jobs, and hence, even young students would benefit from using computers in school.

From the high school observations, the researchers also concluded that despite greater access to computers, most classrooms perpetuated a teacher-centered environment, following "a familiar repertoire of instructional approaches" (p. 95) consisting of lecture, whole-class discussion, homework review, in-class assignments, and the occasional use of videos and the overhead projector. However, a few of the teachers integrated computers in more meaningful ways.

The study featured three teachers who infused technology into their daily teaching: Esperanza Rodrigues, a preschool teacher; Mark Hunter, a kindergarten teacher; and Alison Piro, a high school humanities teacher. What these teachers had in common was their positive attitudes about using technology, similar views of technology as a tool to enhance learning within a larger arsenal of practices, and propensities to place students in groups, resulting in student-centered classrooms.

The preschool and kindergarten teachers used technology in their classrooms in similar ways. Both set up learning centers around their respective rooms and incorporated computer stations. Esperanza Rodrigues teaches in a preschool in a poor San Francisco Bay neighborhood, which primarily consists of a Latino population.

The researchers observed a lesson on geometric shapes, which the teacher initiated with a song, followed by a display of large paper cutouts, and the distribution of individual smaller cutouts, which the students arranged while the teacher pointed to the shapes on a computer monitor. The students responded in English and Spanish. Later, the students utilized the computer learning centers to practice math skills using "Millie's Math House" and other multimedia learning activities.

Similar to the preschool teacher, Mark Hunter used the computer to begin whole-class instruction in his kindergarten classroom. He used the computer to play software featuring the letters N, O, and P on a large monitor. The software incorporated catchy music and animation, which the students sang while emulating the gyrations of the animated figures.

Every day, the students selected from a variety of learning centers, which also included the five computers used for composing a daily message, playing games, and engaging with reading software. Like Ms. Rodrigues, Mr. Hunter also directed the students to whole-group instruction, which often involved student performances and physical games.

Both teachers placed the students in pairs when using the computers, resulting in negotiated meanings. For example, the observer noted that one boy ended his daily message with a comma, which sparked a conversation with the other boys at the computers about whether it was proper to end a sentence in that manner.

The third featured teacher, Alison Piro, taught two sections of an interdisciplinary humanities class at a Silicon Valley high school. She facilitated student computer use in her classroom in multiple ways, including research on the Internet, writing, electronic presentations, and creating and editing videos.

Moreover, she described how she incorporated technology in her classroom in three ways: giving her students access to information and ideas, including primary sources; having her students create multimedia presentations by combining ideas, images, sound, and video; and by motivating her students through active learning. Students typically used computers in her classroom about twice a week as they completed projects.

Likewise, the teacher spent a considerable amount of time determining what types of practices to select for stimulating student learning, including whether integrating technology was the best choice. Ms. Piro, like the preceding teachers, attempted to integrate computer technologies into her daily teaching and learning. However, these three teachers featured in Cuban's study were the exception, not the rule.

Despite the availability and access to computer technologies in the San Francisco Bay area schools, most teachers used computers for e-mail communications and locating online curricular materials, and for sporadic student use with word processing, Internet searches, free-time activity, and drill-and-practice software. Remarkably, in the 10 years since Cuban reported his findings, other studies persistently reaffirmed these low-level technology uses (Ertmer, 2005; Scott & Mouza, 2007).

Research over the years has focused on a variety of reasons, particularly teacher beliefs, teacher demographics, teacher technology and content knowledge, access to technology, technology support, and the availability of curriculum materials. Even when teachers are provided the resources and are more inclined to support the use of technology, self-reports and observations reveal that the pressure to prepare students for high-stakes tests leads them to more traditional, nontechnological teaching methods and resources even when evidence suggests that using technology effectively can result in enhanced test achievement (Ertmer, 2005; Hermans, Tondeur, van Braak, & Valcke, 2008).

TECHNOLOGY AND STUDENT TEST ACHIEVEMENT

As noted earlier, Title II, Part D of the No Child Left Behind Act of 2001 provided states money to distribute to Title I schools through the Educational

Technology State Grants Program. Upon acceptance, the states also agreed to institute accountability measures to examine the effectiveness of the technology integration.

One study looked at Tennessee's efforts to promote the integration of technology in learning through the statewide program, Tennessee EdTech Launch (TnETL), where the funds were used to integrate research-based technology into pedagogy and practice, provide professional development to facilitate the integration, and explore ways that technology could be used to enhance instruction and student performance.

In order to accomplish the technology integration goals, Tennessee's director of technology led an effort to identify proven barriers and then devised a plan to spend the grant money in each of these areas. These efforts yielded six general barriers as follows: (1) access and availability of computer technologies, (2) appropriate teaching and learning resources, (3) teacher beliefs about technology, (4) background statistics of the teachers, (5) teacher knowledge related to technology and content expertise, and (6) the availability of technical and moral support.

The grant purchased significant technological resources for a small number of schools, rather than smaller grants for many; technology experts developed teaching and learning materials; technology coaches worked with individual teachers; coaches and teachers were matched according to demographic characteristics; through the interactions with the coaches and peers, the teachers developed content and technological expertise; and the technology-rich schools were provided technical support, administrator training, and regular meeting opportunities. Consequently, a study was launched to evaluate the effectiveness of the program.

This large-scale study involved 54 schools with two distinct cohorts of students in a mixed-methods design. The research team addressed four questions concerning the following: student achievement, teacher attitudes about and aptitude for using technology in instruction, student engagement levels, and student abilities in using technology. For the achievement measure, student test scores on Tennessee's high-stakes tests in mathematics and language arts were analyzed at the fifth and eight grade levels. The results indicated that the treatment groups performed as well or better, except in one instance with the second cohort on both fifth grade measures.

Further, observations revealed that the treatment classrooms "were significantly more engaged in student-centered learning activities such as experiential, hands-on learning, independent inquiry/research, and cooperative learning" (Lowther, Inan, Strahl, & Ross, 2008, p. 22). Likewise, teacher technology skill levels were higher in the treatment schools and they felt more comfortable aligning technology with the curriculum and standards compared to the control teachers. Positive results also were evident in the use of best practices.

In addition to the evidence of more student-centered classrooms, the researchers also concluded that the treatment teachers integrated computers into the curriculum in more meaningful ways. In fact, the treatment students and teachers tended to concentrate more on academics, and the students exhibited greater interest in the subject matter than the control teachers and students.

Despite the overall positive results, the researchers also pointed out that teachers would probably have benefited significantly from more professional development to promote consistency and to address implementation issues. Moreover, the mixed results on the high-stakes tests may have resulted from the relatively short study duration, students' mixed use of computers for low- and high-level tasks, and teachers' lack of personal choice in selecting tasks.

TECHNOLOGY AND HIGH-NEEDS STUDENTS

In keeping with the No Child Left Behind spirit of assisting high-needs and at-risk populations in urban environments, another study focused on enhancing middle school student science achievement in the Detroit Public Schools, which are almost completely populated by African American students and a small percentage of Latinos and ethnically diverse immigrant children (Geier et al., 2008).

The school system partnered with the University of Michigan and a National Science Foundation–funded organization called the Center for Learning Technologies in Urban Schools (LeTUS) to develop inquiry-based projects for the science curriculum. In addition to creating technology-rich problem-based curriculum, the consortium also provided teacher development activities and a variety of other systemic supports.

The curriculum consisted of a series of units lasting from eight to ten weeks. Technology was embedded into the curriculum to support student inquiry, which was propelled by generative questions. For instance, in one unit, students evaluated the quality of the air in the community compared to historical standards and other metropolitan areas.

They used data probes for collecting and analyzing air samples and multivariate modeling software to explore further questions and generate different types of data representations. In the three years of implementation concluding with the 2000–2001 academic year, 37 teachers from 18 middle schools participated with nearly 5,000 students in two cohorts. Participating students, moreover, scored significantly higher on the Michigan Educational Assessment Program (MEAP) standardized tests in science.

The MEAP measures the science content areas of earth, physical, and life sciences as well as reflection and construction of knowledge in the skill parts. In both cohorts, the students scored significantly higher in all five areas relative to their peers. These finding were bolstered by significant effect sizes. When the findings were further analyzed they revealed that male participation in at least one of the science units helped close a significant achievement gap with girls, which is typical in high-minority, urban districts, thus providing evidence of increased engagement with at-risk learners.

Another large-scale study examined the digital divide, broadly defined as the gap between those with or without access to computer technologies, in Florida schools to determine whether students from different socioeconomic backgrounds had similar opportunities to use and learn with computer technologies. Hohlfeld, Ritzhaupt, Barron, and Kemker (2008) studied data from over 2,000 of the state's K–12 public schools.

The researchers used a theoretical framework based on three levels of the digital divide: first level, access to and support for computer technologies; second level, frequency of use and purposes of the technology; and third level, ways in which the technologies are used to empower individuals in school. Similar to Cuban's (2001) findings, they noted that access to computers in schools has increased over the years. Further, they detected statistically significant differences in the equitable use of technologies between high and low socioeconomic status (SES) schools.

Students from higher-income families enjoyed greater access and use of production software at all levels of schooling, had more content software installed on their middle school computers, had a greater proportion of teachers using technology for curriculum delivery and administrative purposes than their counterparts from low SES backgrounds. Production software implies that students are learning content by making electronic products, which inherently creates a student-centered classroom.

For instance, students could create a concept map infused with words, symbols, and images to illustrate the parts of a novel. On the other hand, the findings also indicated that students in low SES elementary and middle schools were exposed to content delivery systems much more often than the high SES students.

This finding supports other evidence that suggests marginal students, often from minority populations, engage in learning with computers through tutorials and drill-and-practice exercises in a teacher-centered environment. One glimmer of hope emerged from the study: low SES elementary and middle schools tended to have higher levels of technology support, which may indicate a gradual shift to more equitable access and student use of technology in those schools.

A third research endeavor that involved high-stakes tests and at-risk student populations was a pre-NCLB 2000 case study at a Massachusetts high school where the teachers and administrators embarked on remediation strategies to target low-achieving tenth grade student performances on the math section of the Massachusetts Comprehensive Assessment System (Hannafin & Foshay, 2008).

The strategies included aligning the curriculum with the standards; providing professional development focusing on pedagogy, enhancing traditional instruction, and planning standards-based lessons; facilitating organizational and study training for at-risk students; and building a computer-based instruction (CBI) experience, which consisted of a series of modules that the students practiced for mathematical mastery.

The students spent four days a week in the computer lab for about 45 minutes each session. Students could not advance to the next module until they scored a minimum of 80 percent. The researchers reported that passing rates for the low-ability students improved significantly more than the high-ability students. Compared to the statewide results, the tenth grade math scores improved more dramatically as well.

The researchers established a statistically significant correlation between the number of modules completed and the scale scores. Despite this statistical relationship, the study did not purposefully focus on the individual parts of the overall strategy. Therefore, the combined efforts of the strategy or other unforeseen factors may explain the correlation. So, what can Dewey inform us about technology's effectiveness in a high-stakes testing climate based on these studies?

HOW DEWEY CAN INFORM US ABOUT TECHNOLOGY

In spite of a paucity of research, a pattern emerges suggesting that students benefit from using technology in schools, with one outcome being better performance on high-stakes tests. Yet, because of many barriers to integration—including the narrowing of the curriculum and perceived time constraints to cover tested topics—many teachers are loath to integrate technology consistently in the learning process. Dewey provides us with the means to analyze the successful use of technology in schools by placing research in the context of his stages of growth and educative experiences.

A starting point for understanding the integration of computer technologies in learning is the three stages of growth that Dewey (1900) described in the *Elementary School Record*. As mentioned earlier, in the first stage from the ages of about four to eight, children are mainly unreflective, and instead, recall the social experience of engaging with others in work and play. While in the second stage beginning at about the age of eight and lasting to around twelve, students develop historical and geographical awareness of others.

At these early stages, teachers should carefully provide learning opportunities based on first-hand experiences such as the milling of flour described previously. Dewey was deeply affected by Darwin's theory of evolution and believed that learning originated from a survival instinct found in nature. Students learned to develop theories through manual activities with nature, resplendent with possibilities and sometimes lurking with dangerous consequences.

The flour milling project brought students in direct contact with nature (something that becomes increasingly distant with high-stakes testing and a narrowing curriculum). Students were engaged in a team project that emphasized practical, manual, and social skills. At the same time, the process informed students about conditions for human survival and the laws of nature. These types of projects excited students' interests as long as the teacher properly directed the impulses within the framework of the disciplines' bodies of knowledge.

Dewey would not have supported technological experiences as a substitute for firsthand experiences, especially in the elementary grades. However, coming of age during the Great Industrial Revolution, Dewey "knew that *all* human experiences were mediated by technological culture, and he deplored blanket rejections of technological trends" (Waks, 2001, p. 417). Therefore, Dewey would have supported the integration of technology, particularly in the elementary grades, inasmuch as it reflected and supported the social aspects of play and work, and elements of the larger community beyond the school walls.

One reason that Dewey would embrace the integration of technology into the curriculum is the fact that it permeates the spheres of "play and work, similar to those in which children and youth engage outside of school" (Dewey, 1916/2007a, p. 147), meaning as social occupations. Social occupations provided continuity by linking an individual's experiences into a coherent whole. Dewey believed that an effective school was a minicommunity reflective of the larger community.

In spite of the artificial conditions associated with schooling experiences, Dewey believed students should learn in a manner consistent with the larger culture. Dewey insisted that the learning that occurs within a school should intersect with "numerous points of interest between the social interests of the one and of the other" (p. 261). When we look back at Cuban's study focusing on the preschool, kindergarten, and high school classrooms, we see models of effective technology use. For the young children, the teachers used technology to enhance pedagogy using multimedia to teach shapes and letters. Later, the students worked socially in pairs at computer learning centers, actively engaging with multimedia.

The teachers expertly combined physical and computer activities into unified learning experiences. Moreover, certainly by the time they enter preschool, even young children have developed a sense of computers being used in this manner in the real world for work. Likewise, according to the Pew Research Center (2009), preteens and teens use the Internet often to play games, post to social networking sites to communicate with friends, and create and respond to personal blogs. In fact, one estimate claims that 51 million out of 53 million school-age children play video games, representing approximately 93 percent of the K–12 population (Etuk, 2008).

In the last stage of growth beginning at the age of about 12 or 13, students develop the ability for abstract thinking, where symbols and language become representations of a real world and students develop even more sophisticated understandings of social occupations. In nearly all the aforementioned studies, the older students used computer technologies to enhance inquiry.

In Alison Piro's Silicon Valley High School classroom, students responded to inquiry tasks by accessing information and ideas, and consequently synthesizing new meaning by producing electronic products such as multimedia presentations with images, video, and sound. In the other large-scale studies, we find similar uses of production software, characterized by enhanced motivation, social learning, and student-centered classrooms, which demonstrated to be beneficial for high-poverty populations and resulted in increased achievement on high-stakes tests.

In other words, when we examine the educational integration of technology through the lens of Dewey's stages and social occupations, students engage deeply with subject matter in an authentic way and appear to perform better on tests. Furthermore, analyzing the *experience* of technology integration may provide more clarity.

In Dewey's epistemological system, not all experiences are educative; some are mis-educative because they thwart, prevent, or distort further experiences. As mentioned earlier in the chapter, Dewey provided four conditions for mis-educative experiences. We can find many instances where technology in the classroom was used in a way that resulted in these types of experiences.

In the first condition, described as an experience resulting in a lack of sensitivity and reaction on the part of the learner, we can surmise that the eventual outcome of limiting high-poverty students to drill-and-practice type tutorial programs to practice tested skills—while somewhat effective in the short term—will eventually lead to a lack of responsiveness (Hohlfeld et al., 2008). From my own first-year teaching experience as an out-of-field, seventh grade math teacher at a Title I urban school, I was charged with bringing my students to a computer lab once a week to sit quietly in front of a computer and toil with math drills similar to problems on the state's high-stakes test.

In the beginning, the students enjoyed the multimedia. However, within a few weeks they tired of the drudgery and no longer participated enthusiastically, much to the chagrin of the laboratory coordinator. The end result of the lack of student interest led to the second condition where student activities degenerated into tiresome routines.

The third condition produced enjoyable circumstances, but resulted in a lack of focus on the learning. A recent trend has blurred the distinction between education and entertainment, resulting in a new genre of technology called edutainment. An example is simulation software, which imitates real-life circumstances. Often these games incorporate a clear beginning and end, competitive elements, and rewards for success.

Education games tend to be less sophisticated and appealing than commercial games because of the massive development costs, which range from $500,000 to $2.5 million (DeVary, 2008). Children may enjoy playing the games, but critics suggest they are not really engaging in critical-thinking skills and other desirable behaviors because they are either focusing on the play or reward aspects. In fact, some evidence suggests that many students may outwit the gaming technology in pursuit of these mis-educative experiences, and when benefits do occur, it enhances learning primarily for already successful students (Ito, 2006; Okan, 2003).

The final condition happened when the experiences were not arranged in a logical manner, resulting in confusion. When teachers incorporate technology into the curriculum for technology's sake—rather than for a cumulatively linked learning experience focused on the subject matter and learner needs—students become perplexed.

Alison Piro from Silicon Valley High School understood the importance of this principle because she chose experiences based on student needs, not on the availability of the technology. She often selected nontechnological experiences because "[i]t depends . . . on what the teaching and learning goals are" (Cuban, 2001, p. 70). Additionally, when technology is infused into the curriculum in meaningful ways, it can result in educative experiences.

Educative experiences have two characteristics, interaction (lateral) and continuous (longitudinal), and result in positive effects on student learning or growth. The lateral quality of experience exists when the outside social world collides with the student's internal thoughts. Teachers in the studies also selected experiences where students worked in pairs, cooperative learning groups, and other group configurations. Students were able to shape and perfect their peers' experiences.

Free associations with others provided a cumulative effect on growth as more perspectives were considered; others' past experiences were taken into account, especially valuable were those from wider, deeper, and diversely different conditions and situations. In almost all the reported studies, when the students used technology, the classrooms became student centered. In the Tennessee study, the researchers noted a dramatic difference in student engagement with the subject matter between the treatment and control classrooms. Further, educative experiences also embody a continuous or longitudinal aspect.

The continuous aspect creates conditions for a reconstruction of experience and a desire for further learning. In the research studies cited earlier, the younger students participated in work and play with computers where they sang, imitated the movements of the multimedia characters to learn shapes and letters, used word processing software to produce daily messages, and interacted with learning software. In these instances, the computer technologies were used as tools to aid in the reconstruction of experience.

The teachers selected these integrated computer and physical experiences because they provided a moving force for growth. The students consistently participated in the computer centers, which derived meaning and potency from social occupations, those uses that students witnessed in the real world. The teachers carefully prepared lessons building on previous ones, changing the focus of content and skills by replacing software or adding to something already in use.

The researchers in nearly every study reported enthusiasm and motivation for learning because the teacher skillfully integrated technology in the experiences. For example, the high-poverty, mostly minority male population in the Michigan study registered statistically huge achievement gains because of increased engagement with the curriculum. The engagement came in the form of inquiry learning.

Inquiry learning embodies many concepts when it is placed in the social milieu of experiences. One instance occurs when learners recall past experiences; another occurs when individuals seek counsel from those with different and varied experiences. However, according to Dewey, the most important type of inquiry was gained through the scientific method.

The aforementioned Dewey Sequence is an example of scientific inquiry, or as Pring (2007) eloquently stated, "the systematic suggestion of actions in order to bring about predictable results, and the testing of those suggestions (or hypotheses) against experience" (p. 151). Educational technology is a tool and symbol of social occupations, which can ignite, nurture, and sustain inquiry. Further, when teachers *authentically* infuse technology into the curriculum to promote the construction of knowledge, disciplined inquiry, and the communication of results through discussion, products, or performances, student achievement on tests increases.

AUTHENTIC INTELLECTUAL WORK

As recalled from chapter 1, the term *authentic intellectual work* (AIW) emerged from a massive undertaking in which a group of researchers examined over 2,000 assignments from more than 400 elementary classrooms in 19 high-needs schools in the Chicago Public Schools district (Newmann, Bryk, & Nagaoka, 2001; Smith, Lee, & Newmann, 2001).

They designated high-quality assignments as those that demanded intellectual rigor through the construction of knowledge, disciplined inquiry, and elaborated communication, which had value beyond school. Disciplined inquiry meant that students engaged in real-world, adult-style tasks where students gained a prior knowledge base, developed in-depth understanding, and then communicated their findings in an extensive way.

The researchers correlated the results of the analysis on the performance of over 5,000 students on standardized test measures for reading, writing, and mathematics. The assignments allowed the researchers to determine the type of instruction used in the classrooms from various forms of didactic and interactive methods. Didactic is teacher-led instruction, which usually involves a traditional approach to teaching and learning with students reproducing information in answers to questions or on tests and may require them to transfer the knowledge to new situations.

Mastery is determined by absolute answers to these short assessments. Interactive, on the other hand, usually involves students asking questions, formulating new ways to test for answers, often with other students, then providing justifications for their answers through more extensive means of communication. Even after controlling for prior achievement, gender, and socioeconomic status, the researchers discovered that students who engaged in interactive and authentic intellectual work scored higher on standardized tests than those with traditional types of assignments.

The types of assignments that teachers used were primarily a function of the teacher's personality and belief system. Moreover, low-achieving students benefited more than their high-achieving peers when they were exposed to rigorous, AIW mathematics assignments. The opposite was true for reading, where high-achieving students showed more significant gains than the lower-achieving students. A companion study also affirmed that students exposed to interactive pedagogy also scored higher on standardized tests. In multiple ways, the success of AIW validates Dewey's teachings.

THE INTERNATIONAL SOCIETY FOR
TECHNOLOGY IN EDUCATION STANDARDS

The International Society for Technology in Education's (ISTE) National Educational Technology Standards (NETS) and Performance Indicators for students and teachers were originally conceived in the late 1990s and were recently updated in 2007 and 2008 respectively. There are six student standards combined with four performance indicators for each. Likewise, for teachers, there are five standards with four performance indicators. The general theme is for students to use technology to form learning communities both while in school and during nonschool times.

The student standards promote the appropriate and meaningful use of technology in nearly all facets of life. The six standards are as follows: (1) creativity and innovation; (2) communication and collaboration; (3) research and information fluency; (4) critical thinking, problem solving, and decision making; (5) digital citizenship; and (6) technology operations and concepts (International Society for Technology in Education, 2007). There are heavy emphases on inquiry, social collaboration, and democratic practices, containing many elements of Dewey's educative experiences (see textbox 5.1).

Textbox 5.1.   The 2007 ISTE National Educational Technology Standards (NETS-S) and Performance Indicators for Students.

1. Creativity and Innovation
Students demonstrate creative thinking, construct knowledge, and develop innovative products and processes using technology. Students:

a. apply existing knowledge to generate new ideas, products, or processes.
b. create original works as a means of personal or group expression.
c. use models and simulations to explore complex systems and issues.
d. identify trends and forecast possibilities.

2. Communication and Collaboration
Students use digital media and environments to communicate and work collaboratively, including at a distance, to support individual learning and contribute to the learning of others. Students:

a. interact, collaborate, and publish with peers, experts, or others employing a variety of digital environments and media.
b. communicate information and ideas effectively to multiple audiences using a variety of media and formats.
c. develop cultural understanding and global awareness by engaging with learners of other cultures.
d. contribute to project teams to produce original works or solve problems.

3. Research and Information Fluency
Students apply digital tools to gather, evaluate, and use information. Students:

a. plan strategies to guide inquiry.
b. locate, organize, analyze, evaluate, synthesize, and ethically use information from a variety of sources and media.
c. evaluate and select information sources and digital tools based on the appropriateness to specific tasks.
d. process data and report results.

4. Critical Thinking, Problem Solving, and Decision Making
Students use critical[-]thinking skills to plan and conduct research, manage projects, solve problems, and make informed decisions using appropriate digital tools and resources. Students:

a. identify and define authentic problems and significant questions for investigation.
b. plan and manage activities to develop a solution or complete a project.
c. collect and analyze data to identify solutions and/or make informed decisions.
d. use multiple processes and diverse perspectives to explore alternative solutions.

5. Digital Citizenship
Students understand human, cultural, and societal issues related to technology and practice legal and ethical behavior. Students:

a. advocate and practice safe, legal, and responsible use of information and technology.
b. exhibit a positive attitude toward using technology that supports collaboration, learning, and productivity.
c. demonstrate personal responsibility for lifelong learning.
d. exhibit leadership for digital citizenship.

6. Technology Operations and Concepts
Students demonstrate a sound understanding of technology concepts, systems, and operations. Students:

a. understand and use technology systems.
b. select and use applications effectively and productively.
c. troubleshoot systems and applications.
d. transfer current knowledge to learning of new technologies.

Source: "The ISTE National Educational Technology Standards (NETS-S) and Performance Indicators for Students." Retrieved April 29, 2009, from www.iste.org/Content/NavigationMenu/NETS/ForStudents/2007Standards/NETS_for_Students_2007_Standards.pdf. Copyright 2007 by the International Society for Technology in Education. Reprinted with permission.

The five teacher standards provide measures for facilitating and modeling student technology use while advocating professional growth. The five standards are (1) facilitate and inspire student learning and creativity, (2) design and develop digital-age learning experiences and assessments, (3) model digital-age work and learning, (4) promote and model digital citizenship and responsibility, and (5) engage in professional growth and leadership (International Society for Technology in Education, 2008). Furthermore, the teacher standards promote student learning in communities of practice similar to Dewey's philosophical pragmatism and AIW (see textbox 5.2).

Textbox 5.2.   The 2008 ISTE National Educational Technology Standards (NETS-T) and Performance Indicators for Teachers.

1. Facilitate and Inspire Student Learning and Creativity
Teachers use their knowledge of subject matter, teaching and learning, and technology to facilitate experiences that advance student learning, creativity, and innovation in both face-to-face and virtual environments. Teachers:

a. promote, support, and model creative and innovative thinking and inventiveness.
b. engage students in exploring real-world issues and solving authentic problems using digital tools and resources.
c. promote student reflection using collaborative tools to reveal and clarify students' conceptual understanding and thinking, planning, and creative processes.
d. model collaborative knowledge construction by engaging in learning with students, colleagues, and others in face-to-face and virtual environments.

2. Design and Develop Digital-Age Learning Experiences and Assessments
Teachers design, develop, and evaluate authentic learning experiences and assessments incorporating contemporary tools and resources to maximize content learning in context and to develop the knowledge, skills, and attitudes identified in the NETS-S. Teachers:

a. design or adapt relevant learning experiences that incorporate digital tools and resources to promote student learning and creativity.
b. develop technology-enriched learning environments that enable all students to pursue their individual curiosities and become active participants in setting their own educational goals, managing their own learning, and assessing their own progress.
c. customize and personalize learning activities to address students' diverse learning styles, working strategies, and abilities using digital tools and resources.

d. provide students with multiple and varied formative and summative assessments aligned with content and technology standards and use resulting data to inform learning and teaching.

3. Model Digital-Age Work and Learning

Teachers exhibit knowledge, skills, and work processes representative of an innovative professional in a global and digital society. Teachers:

a. demonstrate fluency in technology systems and the transfer of current knowledge to new technologies and situations.
b. collaborate with students, peers, parents, and community members using digital tools and resources to support student success and innovation.
c. communicate relevant information and ideas effectively to students, parents, and peers using a variety of digital-age media and formats.
d. model and facilitate effective use of current and emerging digital tools to locate, analyze, evaluate, and use information resources to support research and learning.

4. Promote and Model Digital Citizenship and Responsibility

Teachers understand local and global societal issues and responsibilities in an evolving digital culture and exhibit legal and ethical behavior in their professional practices. Teachers:

a. advocate, model, and teach safe, legal, and ethical use of digital information and technology, including respect for copyright, intellectual property, and the appropriate documentation of sources.
b. address the diverse needs of all learners by using learner-centered strategies and providing equitable access to appropriate digital tools and resources.
c. promote and model digital etiquette and responsible social interactions related to the use of technology and information.
d. develop and model cultural understanding and global awareness by engaging with colleagues and students of other cultures using digital-age communication and collaboration tools.

5. Engage in Professional Growth and Leadership

Teachers continuously improve their professional practice, model lifelong learning, and exhibit leadership in their school and professional community by promoting and demonstrating the effective use of digital tools and resources. Teachers:

a. participate in local and global learning communities to explore creative applications of technology to improve student learning.
b. exhibit leadership by demonstrating a vision of technology infusion, participating in shared decision making and community building, and developing the leadership and technology skills of others.

(continues)

c. evaluate and reflect on current research and professional practice on a regular basis to make effective use of existing and emerging digital tools and resources in support of student learning.
d. contribute to the effectiveness, vitality, and self-renewal of the teaching profession and of their school and community.

Source: "The ISTE National Educational Technology Standards (NETS-T) and Performance Indicators for Teachers." Retrieved April 29, 2009, from www.iste.org/Content/NavigationMenu/NETS/ForTeachers/2008Standards/NETS_T_Standards_Final.pdf. Copyright 2008 by the International Society for Technology in Education. Reprinted with permission.

DEWEY, AIW, AND EDUCATIONAL TECHNOLOGY BEST PRACTICES

When we examine the ISTE student and teacher standards, AIW, and Dewey's theory of experience and education, we discover the major elements of Dewey embedded throughout current indicators and best practices (as shown in table 5.1). In AIW, the process of constructing knowledge comes from the core beliefs of Dewey's epistemology.

Disciplined inquiry follows from Dewey's writings about problems serving as the stimulus to thought and inquiry. Disciplined inquiry, together with elaborated communication, relates to the concept of social occupations. Therefore, in comparison, AIW follows the Deweyan dictates of educating the whole child. Moreover, by placing the affordances of computer technologies into the AIW paradigm, we can begin to understand the power of technology.

When an individual constructs knowledge, she or he is individually making meaning in a sociocultural context. Rather than focusing on the subject or lesson being taught, the emphasis is on the learner's thinking about thinking. Unlike traditional conceptualizations of learning, constructivists believe that knowledge independent from the learner does not exist.

To place this in historical contexts, while Plato suggested that true knowledge could be remembered from dimly viewed perfect ideas (remember the shadows on the cave walls), Enlightenment philosophers created ways of thinking that established whole canons and taxonomies of knowledge, much of which led to the scientific revolution and great discoveries of the modern world. Dewey (and later others such as Piaget and Vygotsky) turned this world upside down by claiming that it was prior experiences interacting with new ideas in the meaning-making process that mattered.

Newmann, Bryk, and Nagaoka defined disciplined inquiry as the accumulation of a prior knowledge base, the active development of deep understanding,

Table 5.1. Comparison chart of Dewey's experiences, authentic intellectual work (AIW), and the ISTE National Educational Technology Standards (NETS) and Performance Indicators for Teachers and Students

Steps	Dewey (DE, EE, HWT, SS)	AIW	Teacher and Student ISTE NETS
1	Teacher selects curricular resources taking into account: • Previous student experiences • Natural materials • Social occupations	Teacher selects assignments and interactive methods similar to work that skilled adults engage in	Teacher standards 1, 2, 3, 4, and 5
2	The selection of resources creates student interest by directing student impulses, tendencies, and instincts, which are: • Sociocultural engagement • Inquiry • Active learning with creating and making Communication and expression	Construction of knowledge • Use words and concepts to solve real problems • Elaborated communication	Student standards 1, 2, 3, 4, 5, and 6 • Communication and collaboration • Inquiry • Products and processes
3	Properly directed student interest results in educative experiences and has two qualities: • Lateral 　◦ Outside social world interacts with internal thoughts • Longitudinal 　◦ Desire to go on learning 　◦ Promotes reconstruction of experience	Disciplined inquiry Motivate and sustain students in the hard work that learning requires	Student standards 1, 2, 3, 4, 5, and 6 • Interact, collaborate, and publish with others • Positive attitude

Table 5.1. *(continued)*

Steps	Dewey (DE, EE, HWT, SS)	AIW	Teacher and Student ISTE NETS
4	Reconstruction of experience • Student impulses are checked by the intelligent framing of purposes through: 　○ Examining the situation and local conditions, defining and analyzing the problem 　○ Recalling personal experiences and learning from others 　○ Reflecting (and synthesizing new elements with recalled ones), and then proposing possible solutions 　○ Selecting a solution 　○ Testing the solution	Disciplined inquiry Elaborated communication • Build on prior knowledge • Deep understanding when one looks for, imagines, proposes, and tests relationships among key concepts in order to clarify a specific problem or issue	Student standards 1, 2, 3, 4, 5, and 6 • Locate, organize, evaluate, synthesize, and ethically use information • Identify and define authentic problems • Collect and analyze data to identify solutions • Report results
5	The process continues indefinitely in a unified fashion providing all the criteria are met resulting in democracy	All students benefit Enhanced test scores	Standard 5 • Digital citizenship

Note: DE = *Democracy and Education*; EE = *Experience and Education*; HWT = *How We Think*; SS = *School and Society*.

and the socioculturally situated conduct of learning and presenting of the results. They posited, "Students must acquire the knowledge base of facts, vocabularies, concepts, theories, algorithms, and other conventions necessary for their inquiry" (Newmann et al., 2001, p. 15). Dewey would have insisted that this process begin with the younger students being exposed to firsthand experiences. In most schools, this step is usually part of teaching basic skills using direct instruction techniques.

The researchers also recognized that AIW involved developing deep understanding of issues by studying particular problems. This application of knowledge to inquiry produces a much more powerful form of learning, much like Dewey articulated in great detail with problems serving as the stimulus to thinking, followed by a postponement of action to control impulses through the reflection process. What does this process look like?

The study authors claim "Such understanding develops as one looks for, imagines, proposes, and tests relationships among key concepts in order to clarify a specific problem or issue" (Newmann et al., 2001, p. 15). Moreover, technology in the real world is an important tool in the inquiry process offering ways to access information, organize content, analyze, and act with solutions often in the form of digital presentations.

As examined throughout this chapter, recent research supports the use of technology in a Deweyan or authentic intellectual way, especially because of the positive impact on learning and test achievement. In one additional example, a laptop initiative examined the effects of two teachers' laptop integration on their students' learning experiences at a high-poverty, minority elementary school (Mouza, 2008).

Two similar, traditional (i.e., no laptops) classrooms at the school served as the control groups based on the same student profiles and similar teacher characteristics. The students under study were given refurbished laptops, but were not able to connect to the Internet or printers because of a lack of infrastructure. However, a couple of desktop computers in the room provided those capabilities. The laptop students used computers to play games, explore various websites, listen to music, and use productivity software such as word processing, concept mapping, and presentation software.

The qualitative data collected came from student focus groups, teacher interviews, student surveys, and classroom observations. The researcher reported four main findings related to the laptop integration: (1) enhanced student motivation and perseverance in completing assignments, (2) increased social interactions among students and with the teacher, (3) increased confidence in students' learning abilities, and (4) significant achievement gains in mathematics and writing within the laptop group. Using the laptops created a student-centered classroom with many instances of students interacting together to learn the various technologies and academic content.

The productivity software facilitated student's organizational skills for writing. The concept mapping and word processing software aided student spelling and grammar, improved communication skills, allowed students to focus more fully on content rather than the mechanics of writing, which ultimately allowed the students to produce longer and more complex writing samples.

Further, the use of spreadsheets in mathematics allowed students to enhance their graphing skills while manipulating data sets. Results indicated that students were able to use the spreadsheets to compare data sets, which facilitated students' inquiry into further questions about the data. When comparisons were made between the third and fourth grade treatment classrooms, data indicated that "third graders exhibited higher creative tendencies than fourth graders and more positive attitudes toward curricula and school context" (Mouza, 2008, p. 467). The researcher surmised that this may be due to the effects of a more complex curriculum and the pressures associated with high-stakes testing. The fourth graders and their teacher reported frustration with the amount of time used for test preparation, which may have led to a lessening of intrinsic motivation.

The last AIW element, elaborated communication, turns to the adult world for validation, akin to Dewey's notion of social occupations in work and play. Twenty-first-century workplaces demand that employees communicate socially and present the results of their work, which often use tools that are "verbal, symbolic, and visual" and may involve elaborated discourses among many other things (Newmann et al., 2001, p. 15). Furthermore, modern social occupations infuse technology in myriad ways through perpetual innovation cycles.

CONCLUSION

Dewey has often been criticized erroneously for his child-centered approach to learning (Darling, 1994; Pring, 2007). Contrary to some reports, he did not espouse a position that curriculum follow the interests of the child. Instead, the development of interest was a consequence of educative experiences. Nor did he reject the past and traditional forms of knowledge. Rather, he recognized the expertise of the teacher in facilitating the continuity of experiences for growth and by fostering the desire for further growth.

Dewey respected the canons of knowledge, which grew exponentially during the Enlightenment period, and understood the importance of learning about the past through the curriculum. It was in the teacher's best judgment to begin with firsthand experiences and employ other methods and ways reflective of the way people work and play in the pursuit of social occupations.

Clearly, in the twenty-first century, most social occupations involve some form of computer technologies.

Social occupations can also inform experiences in ways other than providing authenticity. Hickman (2001), building on Dewey's ideas, distinguished between technology and the technical, which he labeled a form of naturalized technology. He asserted that cognition resulting from the use of tools or artifacts external to the individual is an application of *technology* on experiences. When, through repeated applications or continued use, the process became habituated in routine, then desired results become part of a *technical* experience.

Whenever a new problem arose that the old technical routine could not address, a new technology response became a necessity. He concluded, "Technology is what we use to tune up the way we experience the world, and the way we experience the world is increasingly technical" (p. 23). Moreover, the collective effect of everyone's experiences in this technical world has often been cited as a source for school reform.

Interestingly, nearly all recent pronouncements for education reform—particularly with those advocating the use of technology—begin with the premise of preparing students for jobs and skills of the twenty-first century. Following that clarion call has probably led to mis-educative experiences because Dewey tells us that the focus should be on the subject matter, where technology evident in the mediated world is integrated by the skilled teacher as a way to learn that subject matter.

Discussion Questions

1. What is pragmatic instrumentalism?
2. Why did Dewey advocate that teachers provide firsthand experiences?
3. What does the term *social occupation* mean? How does the term fit into Dewey's epistemology, or theory of knowledge?
4. Describe Dewey's growth stages. How does each stage relate to learning with technology?
5. What are the conditions for mis-educative experiences? Describe one that you have experienced.
6. What are the characteristics of experience? How do experiences relate to growth?
7. Compare and contrast the Dewey Sequence to the scientific method.
8. Elaborate on the effects of NCLB on students using technology to learn in schools.
9. In what ways should teachers incorporate technology into learning for young children and adolescents?
10. Explain how recent technology studies validate Dewey's philosophy.

Further Reflection

1. What technologies are available for learning in your school? In what ways do students use these technologies to support firsthand experiences?
2. Describe how technologies in your school resulted in educative and mis-educative experiences.

Chapter Six

Advocating for the Disenfranchised Exceptional Child in an Era of High-Stakes Education

Just as Aristotle rationalized slavery by showing how natural it was for those superior by nature to constitute the ends for others who were only tools, so we, while marveling perhaps at the callousness of the Greek philosopher, rationalize the inequities of our social order by appealing to innate and unalterable psychological strata in the population.

—Dewey (1976c, p. 289)

The historical isolation of the handicapped from the flow of events resulted in precisely this devolutionary situation, wherein the actual handicap became a minor and subsidiary problem in comparison to being cut off from the avenues and possibilities of future experience.

—McDermott (1992, p. 238)

The old time general, academic education is beginning to be vitalized by the introduction of manual, industrial and social activities; it is beginning to recognize its responsibility to train all youth for useful citizenship, including a calling in which each may render useful service to society and make an honest and decent living.

—Dewey (1922, p. 366)

In the early twentieth century the state educational systems in the United States experienced profound changes in reaction to social, scientific, and economic conditions. With the invention of intelligence tests and emphases on economic efficiencies, norms were established based on cultural constructs, which were later used to divide special student populations. Dewey adamantly opposed the use of intelligence tests and anything else that placed people in socially constructed categories because philosophically every individual had the potential to grow and affect the experiences of others.

After the establishment of institutions such as reformatories and asylums to house those deemed mentally deficient, compulsory school attendance laws were eventually enforced. A hodgepodge of state laws across the nation denied access to millions of exceptional students until the 1970s, when a sympathetic Congress and more socially conscious citizenry advocated for national legislation. Since that time, schools and communities have moved toward embracing inclusive education for all beginning with President Ford's signing of the Education for All Handicapped Children Act of 1975. Congress made significant changes in 1997 with the law's reauthorization as the Individuals with Disabilities Education Act (IDEA). The No Child Left Behind Act of 2001, which provided more resources and mandates for passing the tests, again spurred a reauthorization of IDEA in 2004. Despite the resources and emphases placed on exceptional students, the rationale for high-stakes testing and the use of large-scale studies to guide pedagogy and student practice contradicts many of the current best practices producing unintended results.

Focus Questions

1. Who are the exceptional children?
2. What are the pros and cons for exceptional children being required to take the high-stakes exams under NCLB?
3. Why do you think Dewey would be against using intelligence tests to sort students into categories?

———◦◦◦———

Dewey situated his philosophy of American pragmatism in historical, geographical, and sociocultural contexts. In turn-of-the-century America, schools sluggishly adapted to the changing economic and social conditions brought on by the dizzying pace of industrialization. As ideologies and businesses embraced scientific management such as Taylorism, which advocated a focus on empirical methods for decreasing waste and enhancing efficiency, some educators voiced support for intelligence tests to channel students into courses and career paths.

The first usable intelligence test was invented by Alfred Binet around the same time that Taylor had published his seminal work, *The Principles of Scientific Management* (1911). Working for the French government, Binet developed a test consisting of various tasks such as putting items in order and naming objects, for example, in order to establish baselines of intelligence corresponding with a person's chronological age. The purpose of the test was to identify students who required extra assistance to succeed academically. However, Binet and others, including Dewey, cautioned vigorously against the misuse of intelligence tests for larger purposes.

Reacting to the inaugural address by the president of Colgate University, George B. Cutten, Dewey, in the *New Republic* in the fall of 1922, passionately derided the use of mental tests for maintaining a privileged aristocracy. Cutten spoke of the American government as a constitutional monarchy headed by an authoritarian president. Drawing on Lincoln's wartime governing, Cutten posited that the greatest American rulers were autocratic. As reported in a front-page article in the *New York Times* on November 26, 1922, Cutten also alleged,

> There used to be a saying that the hope of democracy lay in education, but that was founded on the hope that everybody could be educated. We have found out the falsity of this. The mental tests recently made on one and three-quarters million men in the United States Army showed us not only that they were not equal mentally, but revealed even larger proportions in the extreme classes than we had supposed possible. With only 13½ per cent. of the population able to get through college well, 15 per cent. able to get through at all, and 25 per cent. unable to comprehend the significance of the ballot, democracy is out of the question. (Bent, 1922, p. 111)

These comments so incensed Dewey that he responded shortly thereafter with two articles in the *New Republic* published a week from each other in December 1922. In these articles, Dewey argued that citizens in the contemporary industrialized world focused too much on efficiencies and numbers, which led to a natural inclination for placing individuals into groups and subgroups. Furthermore, the transfer of this business paradigm to individuals, he continued, resulted in the preservation of traditional authoritarian, antidemocratic power.

Dewey viewed Cutten's remarks as a repudiation of the Darwinian principle, diversity of life, and as a threat to individuality and democracy. He emphatically declared, "Our new feudalism of the industrial life which ranks from the great financier through the captain of industry down to the unskilled laborer, revives and re-enforces the feudal disposition to ignore individual capacity displayed in free or individualized pursuits" (Dewey, 1976b, p. 296).

In one fell swoop, Dewey cut to the heart of the matter: normality was a sociocultural construct that placed individuals in artificial groupings, thus denying these individuals the opportunity to make unique contributions and, at the same time, preserving political and economic power for the privileged few. In Dewey's system of ideas, any individual—"barring complete imbecility"—had the ability to realize her or his potential (Dewey, 1976c, p. 294), and by doing so, she or he practiced democracy ideally and morally, not just in a narrowly defined political arena.

In small and sometimes large ways, individual actualization changed the established order of things by making every individual a change agent, which over time, improved conditions for all. Every human being was an aristocrat according to Dewey.

Today, despite the good intentions of NCLB to address the needs of exceptional children, the legislation's emphasis on interventions originating from large-scale scientifically based research and testing formats infusing content based on a constructivist accumulation of knowledge is in direct conflict with the spectral nature of most exceptional populations. Many of the effective best practices originate with small qualitative studies and the teaching of discrete skills and knowledge belying the spectral nature of exceptional children.

EXCEPTIONAL CHILDREN

The Council for Exceptional Children, or CEC, is the largest professional organization in the world advocating for the causes of disabled, gifted, and/or talented students (www.cec.sped.org). The CEC defines 13 broad areas of exceptionality: (1) autism/Asperger's syndrome, (2) attention deficit hyperactivity disorder, (3) behavior disorders/emotional disturbance, (4) blindness/visual impairments, (5) communicative disorders, (6) developmental disabilities, (7) gifts and talents, (8) learning disabilities, (9) mental retardation, (10) other health impaired, (11) physical disabilities, (12) traumatic brain injury, and (13) twice exceptional.

In the first area, individuals with autism have difficulties communicating and interacting with others. Within the first three years of life, specific behaviors emerge, which are spectral in nature, meaning they affect individuals in different ways and to varying degrees. A recent report from the Centers for Disease Control and Prevention estimates that the rates of autism are rising afflicting about 1 in every 150 U.S. children, and even more alarmingly, 1 in every 94 boys, or over 1 percent of the male child population.

Currently, there are about 1.5 citizens living with some form of autism. In a child's early years, parents and professionals can identify autism by the following characteristics: difficulties with the development of spoken languages, repetition of spoken phrases or physical movements, difficulty making eye contact, little or no effort to form peer relationships, a fascination with individual parts of objects, and little impromptu play or make-believe behaviors. One example of a type of autism is Asperger's syndrome, which is loosely defined by the person's willingness to interact socially, but it usually results in social awkwardness.

The second exceptionality area is attention deficit hyperactivity disorder, also known as ADHD. ADHD is a neurological malady affecting about 3 to 5 percent of the school-age population who may have challenges with concentrating, controlling impulses, and in some cases, hyperactivity. Often children with ADHD experience difficulties in all spheres of their lives including the community, home, and especially in school, where their behaviors may be interpreted as discipline related.

In the third exceptionality category, the name "behavior disorders" is the currently preferred designation over "emotional disturbances" because of negative connotations associated with the latter, and is characterized by severe excesses or deficits of fixed behavioral patterns over time. These behaviors include difficulty with learning that cannot be explained by other disabilities or health issues, trouble with peer and teacher relationships, socially inappropriate feelings and behaviors, general unhappiness or clinical depression, and a propensity to exhibit physical symptoms or irrational fears related to personal or school issues.

In the fourth area, visual impairments and blindness, about 1 in 1,000 students experiences some degree of impairment, and of these individuals, about 10 percent are blind. While most of these students are able to use vision for some tasks, a vision evaluation can help determine the level of accommodations and services needed for complete participation.

The fifth classification is communication disorders, a condition where students have difficulty trading information with others. The difficulties comprise writing, reading, hearing, and/or speaking. Hearing disabilities include hearing loss and deafness, while hearing difficulties include problems with speech and/or language.

Speech also includes challenges with articulating words intelligibly and clearly, voice, and stuttering. Communication disorders can result from many causes, including neurological deficits or other exceptional area conditions such as autism and traumatic brain injuries. Further, students may have difficulty understanding tasks and communicating ideas in the classroom.

In the sixth category, developmental disabilities can encompass many of the previous categories and are defined according to the Developmental Disabilities Assistance and Bill of Rights Act of 2000. A developmental disability is a serious, chronic condition that afflicts individuals at birth or in childhood and disrupts normal functioning in one or more aspects of life.

According to the Institute on Community Integration at the University of Minnesota, a developmental disability is a chronic condition that

- is attributable to a mental or physical impairment or a combination of mental and physical impairments;
- is manifested before the person attains age 22;

- results in substantial functional limitations in three or more of the following areas of major life activity:
  - self-care
  - receptive and expressive language
  - learning
  - mobility
  - self-direction
  - capacity for independent living, and
  - economic self-sufficiency;
- reflects the person's need for a combination and sequence of special, interdisciplinary, or generic care, treatment, or other services which are of lifelong or extended duration and are individually planned and coordinated;
- except that such term when applied to infants and young children means individuals from birth to age five, inclusive, who have substantial developmental delay or specific congenital or acquired conditions with a high probability of resulting in developmental disabilities if services are not provided. (Institute on Community Integration, 2009, About section, para. 1)

The wide definition of developmental disability can include specific handicaps such as autism, mental retardation, neurological injuries, and Down syndrome.

In the seventh category, gifted and talented children are endowed with certain abilities that allow them to interact at high levels in an academic context and/or in other environments. While not everyone agrees on a specific definition or even uniform standards for defining talents and giftedness, some general characteristics emerge, which can help educators to identify this type of exceptional student.

A gifted or talented child may exhibit keen reasoning powers and problem-solving abilities, show marked intellectual curiosity, develop an array of interests with some depth, use words and language in sophisticated ways, become an avid reader, learn effortlessly, grasp mathematical concepts with ease, engage in high levels of creative expression, show intense concentration, set high standards for self-achievement, exhibit enthusiasm for intellectual challenges, examine issues/problems from multiple perspectives, be receptive to new ideas, exhibit social grace and maturity, and engage in a complex form of humor.

While no individual is fully endowed with all of these gifts and talents, about 10 to 15 percent of students fall within a general gifted range. Those who perform exceptionally well are often referred to as geniuses.

The eighth area of child exceptionality is individuals with learning disabilities. Like gifted or talented students, these children may have above-average intelligence, but some also have typical levels. What defines this category is the difficulty these students face with academic achievement because of deficits with recall, metacognition, and social abilities.

Specific areas where learning disabled students encounter difficulties include reading, writing, mathematics, recall, metacognition, and social interactions. Reading disabled students may face difficulties with comprehension, word recognition, word decoding, or challenges with maintaining their places while scanning text. A common type of reading disability is dyslexia, a condition where in early childhood, a student experiences difficulty in learning spoken language, and later, decoding and comprehending texts.

A ninth category is mental retardation, which by definition manifests before the age of 18. Further, retardation is also characterized by degrees of intellectual functioning and an individual's adaptability. A score of 70 or lower on an IQ test is usually the benchmark for a clinical diagnosis of mental retardation.

Those scoring about 70 to 55/50 are considered mildly retarded, 55/50 to 40/35 moderately, 40/35 to 25/20 severely, and those below 25/20 profoundly affected. The causes of mental retardation can vary from hereditary conditions to reckless behavior during pregnancy such as fetal alcohol syndrome. Students with mental retardation generally experience difficulty with learning because of cognitive deficits and may also have neurological and physical disorders.

In the tenth area of exceptionality, a child may be considered health impaired because of some acute or chronic health problem. These children may be sapped of strength or face challenges with alertness. They may also experience a heightened awareness to the environment because of underlying conditions. Examples include students with heart conditions, diabetes, Tourette syndrome, and cancer.

The eleventh category focuses on physical disabilities. A student may have difficulties performing academically because of abnormalities related to disease, congenital anomalies, and other causes. An example of a disease includes poliomyelitis, a congenital condition such as the absence of a limb, and other factors could include neuromuscular disorders such as muscular dystrophy. The severity of the condition determines the challenges faced by the students.

Traumatic brain injury (TBI) frames the twelfth exceptionality area and results from either a blunt blow to the head or the consequences of a child being shaken violently. The damage can cause the child to endure physical challenges such as seeing, talking, and hearing as well as more specific cognitive problems such as memory recall, problem solving, abstract thinking, and comprehension. The child may also suffer physical impairments from the trauma.

In the last and thirteenth category, twice exceptional, a student may be gifted and also suffer a debilitating condition. In these cases, a student may score well on standardized measures but fail to live up to her or his potential academically in the classroom. Often these children are difficult to identify because they intelligently mask their disabilities. For instance, a student with a learning disability may use a sophisticated spoken vocabulary but be unable to express herself or himself clearly in written form. These students may develop coping mechanisms to compensate for a disability.

An exceptional child often experiences more than one type of deficit; therefore, she or he can also claim membership in more than one of the CEC areas. Heredity and environmental influences produce variability across individuals throughout society creating a rich range of potential behaviors.

Dewey tells us that individuals matter and diversity enriches inquiry for all (see chapter 2 for a detailed analysis). Furthermore, he also objects to the creation of rigid categories, which separate individual humans rather than bringing them together in dialogue and genuine mutual respect. Today, mainstream educational thought embraces inclusion, but that was not always the case when we take an historical view of special education.

HISTORY OF SPECIAL EDUCATION
IN THE UNITED STATES

A special education for exceptional children emerged from the common school and compulsory attendance in the nineteenth century. By democratizing education for all, school officials were left with the conundrum of what to do with those students who could not easily pass through the graded curriculum, meaning special and delinquent populations. In traditional society predating the Industrial Revolution, enlightened ideals and the apprenticeship system provided special education services outside the home by binding out a young girl or boy to a master over a specified period of time.

However, as apprenticeship succumbed to the modern world, the common schools became the primary education agent. Before mandated attendance could be promulgated effectively, special places to handle these populations had to be established in the form of institutions and reformatories. The pattern of separating these populations continued into the 1970s until the passage of the Education for All Handicapped Children Act of 1975 (Richardson & Parker, 1993; Winzer, 1993).

Clearly, throughout Western history, individuals with deviations from the norm suffered great hardships. While the ancient Greeks engaged in the infanticide of deformed children, the Romans codified disabilities in great detail to dictate property rights and define citizenship responsibilities. Roman subjects deemed mentally deficient were placed under the care of guardians.

Other Roman laws specified citizenship rights for deaf individuals, distinguishing between those who could speak (and exercise those rights) and those who could not (and were not able, according to the law). Later in the sixth century, after Rome was overrun by the barbarians, Emperor Justinian uniformly codified the scattered and sometimes contradictory edicts and laws "that encompassed mental defectives (*mente capti, fatul*), the deaf, the dumb, and those subject to incurable malady" (*cura debilium*; Winzer, 1993, p. 19).

Because many of these Roman ideals were adopted by the various Germanic invaders, it was the emergence of the apprenticeship system in the Middle Ages that initially offered a pseudoinclusive educational system outside the home. Apprenticeship developed as the production and reproduction of goods and services moved from the home to the greater society.

The family of a young man or woman would typically agree to a term of servitude of about four to seven years. For the upper-class families of the merchant, artisan, and professional classes, the apprenticeship was often exercised through guilds with the primary focus being on the acquisition of vocational skills. For the lower classes, apprenticeship was a way to contract out surplus labor with the expectation that sons and daughters would acquire some training along the way.

However, there were no guarantees for the poorer families because some masters would often attempt to exploit as much hard labor as possible at the expense of education. Further, the system was far from uniform in all places and primarily served the sons over the daughters. Within this economic and social arrangement, individuals with ranges of behaviors including mental and physical defects received education and vocational training outside the home, sowing the seeds for an inclusive education for the modern world (Richardson & Parker, 1993).

With the waning of the apprenticeship system and the rise of manufacturing, the states began to take on many of the educational functions outside the home. Likewise, Richardson and Parker (1993) assert, "The decline of apprenticeship undermined the capacity of local communities to rely on family members to care for the indigent and infirm members . . . [and] states imposed labor requirements on the indigent and dependent, turning poorhouses into workhouses" (p. 362).

Similar to how new industries focused on averages and efficiencies, states began to conduct censuses to determine the numbers of poor and defective individuals in order to set up institutions for these special populations. The establishment of reformatories and asylums paved the way for compulsory public school attendance laws and, at the same time, signaled a willingness on the part of the state to provide services to special populations, albeit with uneven uniformity and mixed intentions.

With the blossoming of Enlightenment thought, Great Britain and Europe began to recognize the need and value of educating disabled populations in the eighteenth century, and the United States and Canada followed thereafter in the nineteenth century. The typical progression for providing these services began with deaf students, followed by the blind, and later, mentally retarded individuals.

In the United States, the first school for disabled students was the Connecticut Asylum for the Education and Instruction of Deaf and Dumb Persons, which opened in 1817 in Hartford. Later, in 1832, the Massachusetts Asylum for the Blind welcomed its first students after a census concluded that there were 400 youths in Massachusetts and another 1,500 in New England who would benefit. While mental asylums had been around since the eighteenth century in the United States, insanity was thought to come from immoral behavior, and the centers only featured adult patients who were often victims of humiliating circumstances, including the institutional practice of charging the general public small admissions to see the lunatics.

However, by 1848, the founder of the Massachusetts Asylum for the Blind convinced the state legislature to open an experimental school for feeble-minded youth within the asylum explicitly to prove that mentally retarded students can be educated to be productive members of society. The experiment proved successful, and the Massachusetts legislature later authorized the first permanent institution in 1850. Moreover, until mental retardation gained recognition as a distinct disorder, severe emotional disabilities were often lumped together with retardation (Winzer, 1993).

At the same time that mental retardation and severe emotional disabilities were emerging as distinct disorders, surging populations produced bustling urban centers, which, in turn, visibly elevated the sheer numbers and profiles of gangs and delinquents. Through much of the first half of the nineteenth century, juvenile delinquents were often detained and incarcerated similarly to the adult populations of criminals and ruffians.

However, beginning in about the middle of the century, a more benevolent attitude emerged with an emphasis on training and rehabilitation. Child reformers recognized that schools were unable to cope with truant and delinquent behavior, so many sought to establish special schools that in the beginning of the nineteenth century resembled prisons more than institutions for learning and reform. The reformers' answer was to establish industrial schools, which combined elements of public school, home life, and the manufacturing culture.

Industrial schools were less punitive than the reformatories and stressed the values of hard work, Christianity, and Victorian mores. Further, they were meant to be preventative in nature unlike the reformatories, which were often used as prisons for adults and youths alike. While boys were overwhelmingly the focus of such efforts, some reformers sought to protect girls from degenerating into prostitution and promiscuity (Winzer, 1993).

Likewise as Richardson and Parker (1993) conclude, "The backward child was many things: slow in mind and often defective in body, poor in family background, and lazy but defiant in school. But above all these things, the backward child was 'bad' and male" (p. 365).

In general, most states established asylums first, and then later, built reformatories for delinquent boys. By creating these institutions, the way was cleared for the firm establishment of the common school.

Unlike the apprenticeship system, which was hierarchical in nature, the emerging system of private and semipublic asylums, reformatories, and vocational training institutions offered several modes of differentiated instruction controlled at the local level, meaning separate and distinct forms took shape around the United States. Many of the institutions avoided becoming incarceration facilities, and instead the trustees and administrators often contended that their purpose was part of the common schooling experience (Richardson & Parker, 1993).

Perhaps even more interesting, as boys were often separated from family members and the schools themselves began to take on more of a vocational character with an emphasis on job skills, the schools often developed broader pedagogies than the common schools to educate the whole student. Evidence of this broad pedagogy included the concomitant teaching of literacy with manual skills and practical arts.

And secondly, these schools began the practice of segregating slow and troublesome students, tailoring instruction and conditions to meet their needs. This arrangement was later copied in the common schools of the 1920s for dealing with truant and troublesome students (Richardson & Parker, 1993).

With the establishment of special schools for all types of children and the rise of the child-study movement of the late nineteenth century, services for exceptional children were becoming more commonplace in the United States and Europe. Moreover, the turn of the nineteenth century witnessed an emphasis on science and special education with new methods and ways of classifying exceptional children.

Beginning in the latter half of the 1800s, special tests were developed to measure blindness and deafness. In the early years of the twentieth century, Binet created the intelligence test. Likewise, new terms such as *moron, feeblemindedness,* and *mental retardation* became part of the American vernacular. Science and morality shaped the perceptions of exceptional children throughout the time period and, by the new century, public support for disabled student education was waning (Winzer, 1993).

With the dawn of the twentieth century, many people began to believe that children were exceptional because of genetic reasons, and thus were not able to benefit from education. In an effort to control deviant behavior, mentally retarded and severely deviant children were warehoused—often in abominable circumstances—in state-run institutions.

In response to the belief that feeblemindedness was something that should be controlled, medicine provided one solution with forced sterilization practices while states sponsored institutionalization and marriage restrictions. However, by 1940, attitudes again shifted and most states abandoned these harsh measures for controlling the mentally disabled population and a discernible shift was made from isolation to segregation (Winzer, 1993).

While the roots of segregation were planted in the 1880s, urban school districts by the 1910s were under immense pressure to accept and educate a wider range of children including the immigrants who were flooding into many cities. In order to promote harmony and discipline within the schools, administrators began to segregate populations within the schools, creating special classes for exceptional children.

As compulsory attendance laws were initially directed at the nonexceptional population, by the twentieth century they were directed at all students and were also enforced much more vigorously and consistently. At the same time, institutions for the deaf and blind became regarded as educational institutions rather than merely charitable asylums. In fact, the word *asylum* was dropped from many of their names, reflecting this new reality. These new emphases on education meant that special curricula were needed to serve the segregated populations (Winzer, 1993).

Throughout the twentieth century, schools moved from accepting mildly disabled children to embracing a much more cognitively diverse clientele. At the same time, better testing and diagnostics led to finer categories as well as the redesignation of some conditions. Likewise, the profession evolved with better instructional techniques, challenges from the legal system, and the embracement of new learning theories and philosophies.

However, throughout most of the century, the profession and mainstream citizens adopted a deficit model of disabilities with terms such as *handicapped*. In other words, rather than focusing on what an individual could do well, they emphasized how the exceptional child was qualitatively weaker on some measure compared to a "normal" student.

Winzer (1993) declared, "The early twentieth century also witnessed a more careful distinction between children with mental retardation and children who appeared to possess normal intellectual ability but still failed to achieve adequately" (p. 339). In response to all the new diagnoses and categories, the term *learning disabilities* came into use in 1963. It was also during this decade that schools began to accept and educate severely emotionally disturbed children.

Earlier in the twentieth century, Lewis Terman conducted a series of experiments involving gifted students. These tests marked an important turning point for the education of the gifted and talented because, before this perceived scientific validation, they were considered precocious. Using intelligence tests and teacher recommendations, Terman believed that intelligence differed from talent and creativity mainly through an individual's ability to learn and manipulate concepts.

Compared to other special education classes, gifted classes were meagerly funded and much less prevalent. In 1952, Kansas became the first and only state to include gifted students in the exceptional population. The concern had been for many years that gifted students would become bored in schools, and, in some cases, disrupt the classroom because of a lack of intellectual challenge.

The 1950s also began a period of enhanced funding and national emphases on exceptional children that flowed into the 1960s. By the 1970s, a more humane consensus emerged that exceptional children should be moved into normal living and working conditions as much as possible. The mainstreaming movement became codified in the Education for All Handicapped Children Act of 1975.

Before 1975, schools were able to legally turn away exceptional students, but with President Ford's signing of the Education for All Handicapped Children Act, or PL 94-142, schools became legally obligated to provide an appropriate education for all children. For many special education students, the new law meant individualized instruction in the least restrictive environment, collaborative involvement among school personnel and families, unbiased testing and evaluation, and due process rights and responsibilities.

Previous congressional investigations had concluded that perhaps 1 million exceptional children had been turned away from public schools, languishing either at home or in the care of nonprofit organizations and charities. Millions of others were attending public schools undiagnosed as exceptional. Or when they were recognized as exceptional, they were unable to receive the appropriate services. A socially conscious Congress of the 1970s brought parent and professional groups together to forge a solution resulting in the landmark legislation (Itkonen, 2007; Jimenez, Graf, & Rose, 2007).

Following the president's signature on November 29, 1975, PL 94-142 remained mainly the same for nearly 20 years with only some minor tinkering with language. However, other ideological forces—specifically, the standards and outcomes movement—germinated in the 1980s and became manifested across education programs in the 1990s as part of Goals 2000 in 1994 (see chapter 1).

With the reauthorization of the Elementary Education Act of 1994, states would receive Title I funds only after implementing performance standards and assessments. From that legislation forward, the focus of special education also shifted from issues of access to questions about results and quality. Further refinements were made just a few years later when schools and other stakeholders became concerned with the cost and effectiveness of the supplemental services and programs.

Taking into consideration two decades of research, Congress determined that exceptional students benefited from greater accessibility to general education. In the 1997 reauthorization, the law was renamed the Individuals with Disabilities Education Act (IDEA), which required that most special education students participate in the state examinations, and general education teachers attend individual education plan (IEP) meetings (Hardman & Dawson, 2008; Itkonen, 2007; Jimenez et al., 2007).

In 2004, IDEA was reauthorized with even more of an emphasis on mainstreaming special education students into general education classrooms. Schools were required to place students in the least restrictive environments possible, mainly education classrooms with removal for special services. The law also made clear that the IEP should be used to determine appropriate services rather than what was convenient for the schools. According to Jimenez, Graf, and Rose (2007),

> As a result of the law's increasing emphasis for more inclusive experiences for students with disabilities, more students receive special education services within general education settings than ever before . . . [including] not only students with high incidence, mild to moderate disabilities (e.g., learning disabilities, speech and language disorders) but also students with more severe cognitive impairments. (p. 43)

In addition to greater inclusion, Congress also required that disabled students take the high-stakes examinations.

NO CHILD LEFT BEHIND AND EXCEPTIONAL CHILDREN

One of the main reasons that Congress altered IDEA in 2004 was because of the requirements of the No Child Left Behind Act of 2001. The focus on quality meant that political forces joined together to apply the same performance and accountability measures to disabled students as those in general education programs. One of the reporting requirements of NCLB states that schools must disaggregate assessment data by disabilities.

Moreover, schools are also required to provide "reasonable" accommodations during test-taking times. Likewise, in the original bill, states were required to set adequate yearly progress goals for the special populations and ensure that at least 95 percent of the group members were tested. Currently, the legislation also provides funding for professional development at the early childhood level to train teachers and other school employees to implement effective practices for children with disabilities and special needs. In general, special needs children are given high priority status because of the law.

One area where students with disabilities (and other special needs children) benefit from NCLB is the Reading Is Fundamental (RIF) program. The federal government formed a partnership with the private program to provide books to low-income areas, particularly targeting schools where there are concentrations of special needs children such as students with disabilities.

According to current guidelines, the federal government pays for 75 percent of the costs with the remaining 25 percent coming from private sources. However, in extreme circumstances, the federal government will pay up to 100 percent of the costs if the organization can demonstrate that it would not be able to participate in the community without the extra funding.

The program serves the birth to twelfth grade student population. Another area where students with disabilities rank higher in priority is with grants related to star schools, where districts may set up virtual schools to target certain populations and subject matters. In fact, students with disabilities are given priority in nearly all grant and funding areas including those for Alaskan, Hawaiian, and Native Americans.

In addition to students with disabilities, NCLB also contains provisions to promote achievement with gifted and talented students. With an emphasis on scientifically based research—which favors large-scale quantitative designs—the law provides funds for the development of curriculum and materials for this subgroup.

The legislation also stipulates the creation of the National Research Center for the Education of Gifted and Talented Children and Youth, a national consortium of higher education institutions and other educational agencies dedicated to the advancement of resources and methods for this population. Schools and districts may also use this source of funding for technology to disseminate curriculum to students who would normally not have access to such resources (U.S. Department of Education, 2002b).

Recently, the U.S. Department of Education introduced new regulations under the auspices of increasing flexibility for schools and districts by addressing the needs of children with severe cognitive disabilities. Essentially, the new regulations allow school districts and states to apply alternative standards and levels of proficiency to this slim number of students, no more than 1 percent of district's population.

However, if district administrators can prove that more than 1 percent of the students are severely impaired, and the district has developed effective assessment programs for disabled children, then they may seek a higher limit. Moreover, the 1 percent rule does not necessarily apply to individual schools; rather it is an average across the district and state. Further, the new regulations maintain that most students with disabilities will be measured against normal, grade-level standards (U.S. Department of Education, 2008).

EXCEPTIONAL CHILDREN BEST PRACTICES FOR SOCIAL DEVELOPMENT

Dewey tells us that diversity is desirable for the development of intelligence, and as Skrtic (2005) also expresses, "[I]t is an asset, an enduring source of uncertainty, and thus the driving force behind innovation, growth of knowledge, and progress, which in organizational terms makes educational equity a precondition for educational excellence" (p. 150). Likewise, Dewey also recognizes the importance of socially useful skills. While many exceptional children suffer from social dysfunction as a direct result of disabilities such as autism, others may experience social isolation because of interpersonal and emotional problems.

Special needs children often must deal with frustrations related to their learning difficulties, which may disrupt their ability to form positive and healthy social relationships in schools. They also tend to suffer from higher levels of depression, which correlates with suicidal tendencies. One of the greatest challenges in conducting research for special education is the variability of the population. Despite the 13 groups identified by the Council for Exceptional Children, within each group there exists a wide range of behaviors and abilities, and therefore, a wide range of best practices.

NCLB dictates that practitioners should employ interventions based on scientifically based research (SBR), although what exactly constitutes this body is in some dispute. In addition, much of the useful research and resultant interventions come from qualitative studies because of the spectral nature of most disabilities, not experimental studies with large sample sizes and randomly assigned control groups (Odom et al., 2005).

Autism and Asperger's Syndrome

Because the defining characteristic of autism and Asperger's syndrome is social dysfunction, best practices often focus on strategies to improve social relations. Earlier strategies focused on adult-style, behavioral types of therapy that isolated particular behaviors for extinguishing, increasing, or acquiring purposes. Today, the field has embraced a naturalistic approach with a focus on peer interactions because some evidence suggests that the adult interactions do not generalize across other areas (Volker & Lopata, 2008).

For preschoolers, interventions that emphasize positive adult to child relationships show great effectiveness. Interventions can include play and other forms of communication. Moreover, therapies for children with some verbal ability may include targeting key behaviors, which in turn will affect others indirectly through the use of pivotal response techniques such as offering choices and reinforcements; another is the use of visual cues during playtime to initiate social interactions. Further, current research trends favor peer interactions (Rogers, 2000).

In the past few decades, a growing corpus of evidence supports the promotion of peer interventions with autistic preschool children. Using peer-mediated techniques, adults train typical children to initiate contacts through normal play and resources. The process unfolds with adults offering the typical students reinforcements for their initiating behaviors, and, over time, the reinforcements are reduced, and then eliminated.

Many variations of this durable and powerful technique, which have been studied over time, have been used successfully at home with siblings. Similar to peer mediation, peer tutoring involves the training of typical children to deliver short bursts of incidental teaching of about five minutes. It also involves adult reinforcement that is eventually faded. While other strategies not mentioned here have also been shown to increase social exchanges, research suggests that peer-mediated interventions are most effective (Rogers, 2000).

Like the preschool children, school-age children—including adolescents—also benefit from the same interventions and also several others. For example, adults have successfully created games based on autistic obsessions, which has led to greater social interactions among autistic students and their peers. Other approaches include the use of visual cues in work schedules, objects for sharing, self-management strategies such as maintaining eye contact, friendship circles, and social skills groups. Many of the strategies evoke mechanisms that are faded over time.

In an exhaustive review of scientifically based research, Simpson (2005) concluded that despite the current status of autism spectrum research being in its infancy, certain skill-based and cognitive strategies were either backed by strong empirical evidence or held great promise for later validation. The stronger evidence indicated that applied behavior analysis, discrete trial teaching, and pivotal response training were often effective, and concomitantly many of the play strategies had the potential for future scientific validation.

Attention Deficit Hyperactivity Disorder

Also known as ADHD among other names, attention deficit hyperactivity disorder manifests in combinations of two elements: the inability of the student to maintain attention and hyperactive impulsiveness. In diagnosing ADHD, a variety of evaluations can be employed focusing on three areas: emotional, educational, and medical. Diagnosis is an essential component because a child may have ADHD and it may not interfere with the learning process, hence she or he would not be eligible for additional services. In the emotional evaluation, a variety of ADHD-specific rating scales exist to quantify the severity of the condition.

For educational assessment, teachers and school personnel may use periodic reviews of academic progress as well as direct observations for telltale signs of ADHD, such as when a child is constantly fidgeting while sitting down. While a medical evaluation may not be required, in 2000, the American Academy of Pediatricians recommended the use of DSM-IV (*Diagnostic and Statistical Manual of Mental Disorders*, 4th ed.) guidelines as well as the testing for coexisting conditions such as depression and emotional disorders.

DSM-IV guidelines consist of two checklists of behaviors: one is based on inattention while the other is hyperactivity. The child must have engaged in six of the behaviors for at least six months on one or both of the checklists in a way that is incongruent with the child's developmental level. In this manner, medical experts can determine possible combinations of inattention and hyperactivity for possible treatment options (U.S. Department of Education, 2003).

The main treatment options available for children who are diagnosed with ADHD include behavioral, pharmacological, and multimodal approaches. Behavioral treatment—as the name suggests—implies that changes are made to the child's physical and social surroundings. In the classroom, teachers mainly use direct instructional methods with reinforcements such as token economies and "timeouts." A paucity of research, moreover, indicates limited effectiveness.

A pharmacological approach to treating ADHD remains controversial and may include a variety of stimulants such as Ritalin or antidepressants or other medications for those students who do not respond well to one type of medication. Further, research suggests that a multimodal approach may work best to lessen the symptoms associated with ADHD.

This approach includes a combination of drugs and behavioral strategies administered and applied consistently at home and school. In consultation with the IEP team, teacher best practices may include (1) designing lessons so the ADHD student is working on the most challenging concepts in the beginning of the school day, (2) chunking directions into smaller pieces of information, (3) offering a variety of pacing and types of activities throughout the day, and (4) instituting accommodations specific to the needs of the child (U.S. Department of Education, 2003).

Behavior Disorders and Emotional Disturbance

Students who exhibit emotional and behavioral disorders (EBD) act out persistently across different settings without regard to social and cultural norms. A central emphasis of many interventions is self-control and the promotion of positive social skills. According to the research, the most effective type of intervention involves direct instruction, modeling, and guiding.

One cognitive behavioral strategy is ZIPPER, which is an acronym for Zip your mouth. Identify the problem. Pause. Put yourself in charge. Explore choices. Reset (Patterson, Jolivette, & Crosby, 2006). Likewise, a comprehensive approach also can include a variety of best practices to manage disruptions such as making clear the expectations and consequences, establishing a cooling off area, engaging students in role playing, and providing a highly structured classroom.

Blindness and Visual Impairments

According to the American Foundation for the Blind (AFB), blind or low vision students may experience difficulties in learning concepts because visual perception is an organizing tool for learning about the world. When a student is diagnosed as blind or visually impaired according to her or his respective state guidelines, the child has the right to use the services of a certified teacher for the visibly impaired (TVI).

Further, all teachers should provide as many opportunities as possible for allowing students to experience the world in other ways. One method may be to enhance visual ability through optical devices such as magnifiers. Another may be facilitating access to information through large-print texts or Braille. And certainly, assistive technologies can be used to create audio of longer texts or provide many of the same accommodations as magnifiers and large-print items. A combination of strategies may be necessary to provide equal access to the core and expanded curricula.

In addition to the formal, academic core curriculum, visually impaired students face many challenges related to regular functioning in society. Most people learn life skills by observing what others do, which may not happen or happen partially depending on the degree of visual acuity. Therefore, many of these students also engage in an expanded curriculum that may assist them in living independently.

For instance, learning how to orient themselves and travel would be necessary skills for active independent living. Related to mobility, visually impaired individuals would also need to know how to engage in physical activities and recreation. Other areas would include learning how to manage personal finances, prepare meals, maintain proper hygiene, and gain the education and training for lifelong careers.

In order to allow equal opportunities for visually impaired students, teachers should provide accommodations whenever possible. Testing may include combinations of Braille and assistive technologies among other resources. Students may also provide answers via a variety of ways such as orally. Teachers may place visually impaired students in small groups when completing in-class assignments and projects. Students may receive scheduling accommodations such as extra time to complete an assignment. And finally, students should have access to tactile objects and assistive technologies when needed.

Communicative Disorders

The prevalence of communicative disorders is defined by an individual's inability to comprehend and/or speak. The conditions can result from disease or trauma or a person may be born with some sort of developmental disability making it difficult for her or him to communicate. Like other exceptional child interventions, the focus of current communicative disorder strategies is on natural social settings.

These strategies encompass voice, gestures, and graphic representations of communication either individually or in some type of combination. While traditional strategies mainly emphasized direct instruction, in the past decade a consensus has emerged where the expert chooses "the least intrusive strategy that makes it possible for the learner to produce a correct communicative utterance with minimal struggle" (Reichle, 1997, p. 121).

Natural setting strategies include a technique called response facilitation. One of the most studied types of response facilitations is milieu language instruction. In this approach, the learner gestures or points to a desired object, and then the interventionist verbally asks what the learner wants.

The facilitation escalates with modeling if the learner does not respond to the verbal request. If the learner responds correctly, then the learner receives a verbal affirmation and the requested item. This type of strategy is most effective with students who have the ability to imitate and exhibit limited verbal skills.

Another technique involves effective patterns of interaction. There is a positive correlation between the learner's improvement in communication and the quality of the interactions with the people surrounding the learner. For instance, the more parents interact with their children in meaningful ways, the better the child with communicative disorders will improve.

While the first two strategies are indirect in nature, direct instruction has proved effective, particularly with children experiencing severe communicative disorders. These children usually have little opportunity to learn in the early years through literacy and play activities, which may explain the need for more direct avenues. In daily routines, interventionists may try to situate artificial interventions within natural settings, giving them the ability to eventually fade the artificial approaches (Reichle, 1997).

Developmental Disabilities

Students with developmental disabilities have chronic conditions caused by physical and/or mental impairments such as autism, hearing loss, cerebral palsy, and visual impairment. Because the range of conditions is so wide and varied, general guidelines for the classroom may include strategies such as the use of visual cues, posting a daily schedule, verbal prompts, varying of the pacing, and a variety of groupings and strategies to increase social interactions.

Gifts and Talents

Because the federal government does not mandate services for gifted and talented children, the services available vary from state to state. Further, most experts have moved away from relying on one measure to determine if a child is gifted and/or talented. Instead, they may look at general and specific intelligence measures together with environmental and chance factors such as a child's cultural background and diligence (Johnsen, 2009).

In order to accommodate the needs of these children, teachers should provide differentiated instruction that allows the students to delve deeper into certain content areas as well as allow for acceleration of learning. One way to do this is to provide modeling on expert behavior in a particular domain. In this way students can act like experts such as by being exposed to primary and secondary sources or the manipulation of raw data. Carefully crafted questioning techniques such as Socratic methods can also help lead the students to new understandings (Scot, Callahan, & Urquhart, 2009).

Learning Disabilities

According to the National Research Center on Learning Disabilities (www .nrcld.org/), the current focus on learning disabilities is early intervention based on accurate diagnoses followed by the appropriate levels of services. Services may be thought of as consisting of levels of tiers. In the first tier, a student may thrive in the general education classroom. For others, it may involve more intense interventions such as additional reading instruction and some other areas where the student may be struggling. The key to best practices is early identification and intervention strategies, using data to guide decisions, and appropriate tiers of intensity.

Mental Retardation

Students with mental retardation, developmental delays, or mild intellectual disabilities benefit from efforts at self-determination, allowing individuals to formulate personal goals that promote autonomy and strengthen interpersonal relationships through a variety of appropriate interventions and services. In general, teachers should use simple sentences and uncomplicated instructions, mitigate distractions, teach specific skills, employ alternative pedagogical and assessment forms, enforce consistent behavioral rules, and promote effective social skills through modeling and practice.

Other Health Impaired

Children who experience other health-impaired disabilities have limited strength and vitality due to chronic or acute conditions such as asthma and cancer. Accommodations may include extra time, reduced assignments, safe zones, frequent breaks, and alternative assignments and assessments. Possible strategies include emphases on hands-on learning, visual cues, partner work, and teaching all students about various health impairments.

Physical Disabilities

Perhaps the greatest issue facing children with physical disabilities is positive self-image. Teachers can offer activities and strategies that build on these special children's strengths. At the same time, teachers must also cultivate an inclusive environment that is safe and accepting, meaning intolerance to rude remarks and any type of comments that trivialize or demean disabilities.

Further, teachers and students should not pity the physically disabled children. Accommodations should be made based on the type and severity of the disability. Likewise, some students may suffer from life-threatening illnesses. Teachers must acquire the specific skills to deal with emergency situations, such as when a diabetic student experiences surges or dips in glucose levels.

Traumatic Brain Injury

School-age children are at greatest risk for experiencing traumatic brain injuries, resulting in varying degrees of cognitive impairments. These impairments may include communicative disorders, difficulty with memory and learning, sophisticated information processing, and perception. Because of the wide variability of disorders, best practices usually include combinations of approaches such as task analysis to align the difficulty with the students' abilities, inclusion, self-management techniques, and direct instruction such as the teaching of reading and math skills (Arroyos-Jurado & Savage, 2008).

According to New York State guidelines, IEP teams should determine high-priority areas such as what is most important for normal functioning and what is easily accomplishable to give the learner a sense of progress. New skills and concepts may need to be broken down into discrete components, and students may need to be taught compensatory strategies such as using highlighting or underlining to focus attention in specific areas to improve concentration. Further, the student may require environmental modifications such as the use of a buddy to direct the student to the correct classrooms.

Also, teachers should make curricular modifications as well as teaching modifications to suit the needs of the learner. For example, a student with TBI may have difficulty with some lower-level skills while being able to master higher-order ones, which means that the traditionally hierarchical curriculum would have to be modified. Additionally, there are many other modifications that could be instituted to address orientation (e.g., the use of cues), attention/concentration (e.g., slow-paced instruction), visual/perception (e.g., arrows), organization (e.g., key word lists), memory (e.g., summarization techniques), problem solving (e.g., modeling), and initiation (e.g., visual cues) (New York State Department of Education, 2002).

Twice Exceptional

Gifted or talented children with special needs face unique challenges such as encountering tasks that are either too easy or too difficult. Furthermore, twice exceptional children may exhibit outstanding abilities in some areas, and, at the same time, appear lazy with a discrepancy between what is expected and actual achievement.

Teachers may also notice that these types of students may have difficulty getting along with other children or show characteristics of low self-esteem. These children often benefit when a team of educators support the child through assistive technologies, tutors, mentors, flexible groupings, and, in some cases, counseling services. Teachers can build on a student's strengths to achieve in other areas as well.

UNINTENDED EFFECTS OF NCLB
ON EXCEPTIONAL CHILDREN

While most educators and the public in general welcome the attention NCLB has showered on special populations, the legislation has also produced some unintended effects. As discussed earlier in the chapter, NCLB places emphases on research interventions based on large-sample, quantitative research studies.

Yet, the spectral nature of exceptional child interventions supports in-depth qualitative studies with small numbers of research participants. In addition to fulfilling the mandates of scientifically based research, other effects include some problems with mainstreaming and selecting appropriate high-stakes tests.

The past few decades have witnessed a dramatic shift in mainstreaming exceptional children into regular classrooms and placing them in natural social environments. One of the goals of this strategy is to increase social competence, meaning individuals control their own needs and wants with as much independence as is possible. Some research indicates that some exceptional students, such as those suffering from autism, may become more socially isolated as their social skill deficits become more pronounced in general education classrooms.

These students may feel isolated and withdrawn as a consequence of being rejected by their peers. Moreover, the isolation may lead to other cognitive developmental difficulties. Therefore, providing effective intervention strategies and services in the mainstream classroom becomes even more important (Stichter, Randolph, Gage, & Schmidt, 2007).

Another consequence of NCLB concerns the question "What is appropriate testing?" Many of the high-stakes tests require students to draw on vast amounts of knowledge gleaned from a constructivist approach to learning. Yet, effective strategies with disabled students often involve the teaching of single and discrete skills in small chunks because of cognitive overload. Furthermore, because of the wide range of abilities and behaviors associated with exceptional children, it becomes difficult to pinpoint a specific type of high-stakes test based on IEP recommendations.

Depending on the state in which the child attends school, she or he may be required to participate in grade-level assessments, below-grade-level tests, or a unique assessment designed by the IEP team. Additionally, if the IEP team determines that the child is unable to perform satisfactorily on any type of test, then she or he may be able to opt out of assessment completely. Other options may include the use of assistive technologies and/or other testing accommodations such as additional time. Layton and Lock (2007) suggest that a better approach in some circumstances may be the use of authentic assessment because it fulfills the intention of NCLB and IDEA by focusing on the individual student and produces results that can guide daily practices.

Specifically, they suggest 20 authentic assessments as follows:

1. Collect daily work samples to show the student's actual progress.
2. Ensure that the IEP reflects the student's instructional level.
3. Create curriculum-based assessments (CBA) to link student performance to the curriculum.
4. Establish a baseline using CBA.
5. Rely on curriculum-based measurements for determining the effectiveness of instruction.
6. Use a portfolio to provide a direct bond between instruction and the general education classroom curriculum.
7. Maintain classroom portfolios to create a detailed and complex picture of the student's mastery over time.
8. Perform direct observations to record behavior.
9. Employ direct observations to document the inclusion of research-based strategies.
10. Draw on environmental assessments to analyze the instructional cycle.
11. Examine environmental assessments to identify staff training needs.
12. Generate questionnaires to gather different perspectives.
13. Interview all stakeholders in the student's academic life.
14. Explore the results of checklists based on state-mandated goals.
15. Survey the success and use of modifications and accommodations in a variety of environments.
16. Capture student achievement over time through rating scales.
17. Develop communication notebooks to inform parents.
18. Journal to corroborate student progress on IEP goals and objectives.
19. Document the correct choice for the level of state-mandated assessment.
20. Base assessment decisions on NCLB and IDEA mandates. (pp. 170–172)

Of course, best practices always involve the use of frequent formative assessments in the classroom.

CONCLUSION

As long as an individual had the ability to interact with others in some manner, Dewey believed that individual had the capacity to grow and become a change agent. Dewey's position undergirds one of the conflicting theories of disabilities, something Danforth (2008) called "the social model of disability" (p. 46). Much like Dewey espoused when he rejected the use of intelligence tests to sort intellectual ability nearly a century ago, today the social model of disability recognizes that we have created various categories of disabilities based on sociocultural contexts.

In other words, abnormalities and deficiencies only occur within cultural frames of reference. In contrast to this recognition, the other theoretical perspective, labeled "the medical model" (p. 46), relies on psychological and medical opinions to view any abnormalities as deficits or individual defects.

The problem with the latter theory, which pervades education and is encapsulated in NCLB with a reliance on testing and scientifically based research interventions, is that it leads to labeling special students as needing fixing based on some notion of pure science and measurement. In the past, this has meant separating special populations from the mainstream, which still occurs to some extent today.

On the other hand, the social disability model values and respects all children. As Danforth (2008) states,

> Disability is understood not to be a bodily or mental anomaly or a deficit in functioning. It consists of the variety of social interpretations of human difference that construct disability by assigning to it particular linguistic, interpersonal, and political meanings, often limiting the access, status, and participation of disabled persons. This social retheorizing of disability does not deny the presence of individual bodily or mental differences across the population. But it effectively shifts theoretical and practical attention away from diagnostic and remediation goals . . . and toward ways of organizing schools and classrooms as democratic communities, interactive spaces where a diverse range of individualities are respected and valued. (p. 46)

In effect, this is the heart and soul of Deweyan democracy with a caveat: not only must schools engage in democratic practices that embrace and value the contributions from all its members, but the members must also share the common goals and experience contentment with the process.

Discussion Questions

1. How did the advancement of science and psychology affect education?
2. What arguments did Dewey use to refute George Cutten's remarks?
3. List the 13 groups of exceptional students. Compare and contrast each group. What did you discover?
4. Of the 13 groups identified by the Council for Exceptional Children (CEC), which one or ones seem most unlike the others? Why?

5. How does the history of special education in the United States relate to compulsory education for all?
6. In the overview of best practices, how do the interventions reflect Deweyan philosophy about individuals? Why?
7. In the overview of best practices, which interventions seem contrary to Deweyan philosophy? Why?
8. What are the unintended effects of NCLB? How can those effects be mitigated?
9. What is authentic assessment? Why might authentic assessment be more valuable in the classroom?
10. What are the differences between the social and medical models of disability?

Further Reflection

1. How can NCLB be modified to further aid and build respect for exceptional children?
2. Can Deweyan democracy ever be achieved with NCLB? Why?
3. As an educator, reflect on ways that NCLB has improved opportunities for exceptional students. In what ways can it be improved?

Chapter Seven

Realizing Our Ethical Responsibilities as Educators

Just as physical life cannot exist without the support of the physical environment, so moral life cannot go on without support of a moral environment.

—Dewey (1934/2005, p. 359)

To teach is to take an ethical stance in the world. It is we teachers who must stand with the child. . . . Teaching is a relationship founded on such ethics, and the satisfactions of teaching are achieved in the difficult achievement of that ethical stance.

—Block (2008, p. 417)

A narrow and moralistic view of morals is responsible for the failure to recognize that all the aims and values which are desirable in education are themselves moral.

—Dewey (1916/2007a, p. 262)

This chapter underscores the importance of realizing and actualizing the ethical dimensions of our work as educators. Drawing from some of Dewey's works, among other prominent philosophers and educators, this chapter presents an argument for educators to examine carefully their motives, aspirations, and hopes for teaching the whole child. In an era of heightened accountability and onerous adherence to rigid and narrow pedagogical and curricular practices, attention to ethical imperatives for addressing the educational and emotional needs of the whole child is axiomatic. The theoretical frame, supporting mindful attention to nurturing the development of the whole child, draws from concepts and issues of social justice, cultural diversity, constructivism, differentiated instruction, and an ethic of caring. In the end, educators must vigilantly remain on the forefront by asserting their ethical obligations for promoting best interests of children.

Focus Questions

1. What are your first recollections about considering teaching as your career? Why have you decided to teach? Why does teaching matter?
2. What ethical issues do you confront in your work as an educator?
3. Can you think of an instance when your personal values or ethics came into conflict with school or district policy? Explain how you resolved the dilemma.
4. Do you feel empowered or powerless to effect change in your school environment? Explain.
5. As you read this chapter, what lesson(s) might you learn about how best to advocate for the best interests in children, educationally and emotionally?

———

I want to share a story about John Dewey. No, I never had the honor of meeting him; I, Jeffrey, was two when he passed away. But, for me and my generation of educators-in-training at Teachers College, Columbia University, Dewey was both feared (really held in awe) and admired. He was "feared" certainly because of the immensity of who he was and the prodigious writing and thought he produced. In my day, we often boasted of having "read Dewey."

Even today, I presume, saying you are reading or studying Dewey might imply that you must be very smart or, at least, courageous. Dewey's writing has been described as brilliant, insightful, cutting edge; he himself characterized as iconoclastic and prophetic. Yet, he has been criticized for his "thick" writing style, deliberate, long-winded, and abstract. Perhaps, that's why many of us would "fear" reading Dewey.

My story hasn't begun. I once had the honor and pleasure to study (take a course) with Lawrence Cremin, a student of John Dewey and famed educational historian at Teachers College. Cremin, also "feared" by us, would have his teaching assistant (TA) handle course logistics, including session introductions, course requirements, and so on. Then, Professor Cremin would walk in, usually five or ten minutes after the official start of class, to begin his lecture on the history of education. By the way, many of his ideas he would later publish were field-tested in our class.

Now, I want to caution the reader. I am uncertain that what I am about to relate represents accurately Cremin's everyday teaching style as I can't honestly recall and I did only take one course with him. Parenthetically, though, it was one of the most important courses I took because my final paper in that course led to my dissertation work on the history of supervision in the United States, which in turn led to my first published book (Glanz, 1991).

Nonetheless, my recollections here are subjective and represent only my perceptions and memories, as flawed as they might be. So, Professor Cremin would lecture in a most captivating, enthralling manner, pacing back and forth in front of the room (actually, he was standing on an elevated stage, which added to his mystique). He might occasionally field a question, but I don't recall many brave students in that course asking anything. I certainly did not!

At any rate, to make a long story a bit shorter, one day an assignment was given to select a prominent educator of the past and to briefly describe his or her contributions and relevance to education in the present (which was 1974 or 1975). I foolishly chose Dewey. I submitted my five-page paper. Whenever we submitted work we would never hand it to Professor Cremin, but only to his TA. By the way, that TA was Ellen Condliffe Lagemann, who is now a prominent scholar and former dean at the Harvard Graduate School of Education. She in fact earned her Ph.D. in history and education at Teachers College.

I have never met her since or spoken with her, but my memories of her were that she was warm and approachable. I am sure many would say the same about Lawrence Cremin, but he was, after all, "our professor," whom we all held in esteem. Such awe of him probably precluded any personal contact with him; I am certain others had approached him to find him engaging, interested, and kind, as one colleague of mine later reported.

Okay, so Ms. Lagemann, as I called her, would take our papers and answer any questions we might have about the assignment. She would also return our graded papers. The rumor was that she, not Professor Cremin, had graded our papers. We heard he would occasionally read certain papers that his TA thought were worthy or, as in my case as you'll soon hear, problematic. In these cases, the professor would speak to us privately, usually after class in front of the auditorium.

Well, one evening after class as I was about to leave, I heard Professor Cremin call out, "Mr. Glanz, please see me." Stunned, frightened, my knees quivering (I exaggerate not), I slowly and hesitatingly approached my professor, who had descended from the podium to engage me privately to the side. "Mr. Glanz," he started, "Have you ever read Dewey?" "What?" I thought to myself. Continuing my thoughts, "Well, the paper after all was on Dewey, . . . uh, sure I've read Dewey." Silence. He reiterated the question.

I think I nodded affirmatively and muttered something about Dewey. He said, calmly yet assertively, and I now paraphrase because I wasn't in clear mind to recall his precise words, "Many students are fearful of Dewey, so they read people who write about Dewey, . . . so you are not unusual. . . . My suggestion, Mr. Glanz, is to read John Dewey in the original . . . you'll find him quite refreshing." He then handed back my paper, on which these words were written: "Please read Dewey and resubmit." His comments to me were communicated in a forthright, encouraging manner.

I later realized, without really intending to, that I had not read Dewey, but, in fact, based my five-pager on the writings of others who discussed Dewey. I consciously acknowledged at that moment my fear of Dewey, probably having read him a bit in the past, but giving up. So, I took Professor Cremin's advice and reread Dewey, patiently this time. In many ways, I discovered, Dewey was more comprehensible than many of the folks who wrote about him! I resubmitted the paper, successfully.

Since then, I have read, and reread, Dewey, still not always with perfect comprehension, but his ideas are embedded in my own. My own personal educational philosophy is influenced by Dewey. I often will say or write something that I think is my own idea, without citing Dewey, realizing that it's based on a Deweyan concept. I present this story here for several reasons: One, to encourage readers to read not only us, but to "read Dewey in the original" (start with his "My Pedagogic Creed," then *Experience and Education*); and two, to say that the ideas I express in this chapter are not always attributed to Dewey, but I acknowledge they are Dewey-influenced, and so if I don't quote him at every turn, do realize I write, or at least try to, with a Deweyan intent.

One more caveat: I don't agree with everything Dewey said or believed. His political philosophy, for instance, probably influenced by his time, is, I think, misguided. Moreover, if Dewey were able to read this chapter, he might not agree with everything I have to say about his view of ethics and education.

In fact, my ideas here are extrapolated from Dewey to ideas or topics he might not have even discussed. But, in earnest, I have tried to write this chapter keeping true to some of Dewey's fundamental principles on the subject, at least as I understand them. First, education and teaching, by extension, are moral activities. To paraphrase Huebner (1996), teaching is moral work; it is never amoral, but can be sometimes immoral. Second, educators must actualize their moral and ethical influence that nurtures the whole child. Third, and fundamentally, teachers play a vital role in society and their influence on children is immeasurable; teaching matters.

WHY TEACHING MATTERS

Education is much more than transmitting some set of prescribed cultural, societal, or institutional values or ideas. Education is an ongoing, spirited engagement of self-understanding and discovery. Etymologically, the word *education* comes from its Latin root "educare," meaning to draw out or to lead. That is, in fact, our goal as educators—to draw out that unique latent potential within each student. As Smith (cited in Slattery, 1995, p. 73) poignantly explains, "[E]ducation cannot simply tell us what we are, but what we hope to become."

When we teach our students, regardless of the subject, we serve as a catalyst for them to reach their potential. A fundamental human quest is the search for meaning. The process of education becomes a lifelong journey of self-exploration, discovery, and empowerment. Teachers play a vital role in helping students attain deep understanding. As Rachel Kessler (2000) concludes in her *The Soul of Education,*

> Perhaps most important, as teachers, we can honor our students' search for what *they* believe gives meaning and integrity to their lives, and how they can connect to what is most precious for them. In the search itself, in loving the questions, in the deep yearning they let themselves feel, young people can discover what is essential in their own lives and in life itself, and what allows them to bring their own gifts to the world. (p. 171)

As educators, we affirm the possibilities for human growth and understanding. Education embodies growth and possibility, while teachers translate these ideals into action by inspiring young minds, developing capacities to wonder and become, and facilitating an environment conducive for exploring the depths of one's being. The capacity for heightened consciousness, the emphasis on human value and responsibility, and the quest of becoming are quintessential goals. Teaching thus becomes not only meaningful and important, but also exciting.

Extraordinary times call for extraordinary teachers. We need teachers who can challenge others to excellence; teachers who love what they do. We need teachers who help students achieve their potential; teachers who help students understand why and how to treat others with respect, dignity, and compassion.

Haim Ginott (1993) made the point that education is more than teaching knowledge and skills in dramatic fashion when he related a message sent by a principal to his teachers on the first day of school:

Dear Teacher:
   I am a survivor of a concentration camp. My eyes saw what no man should witness:
   Gas chambers built by *learned* engineers.
   Children poisoned by *educated* physicians.

Infants killed by trained nurses.

Women and babies shot and burned by *high school* and *college* graduates.

So, I am suspicious of education.

My request is: Help your students become human. Your efforts must never produce learned monsters, skilled psychopaths, educated Eichmanns.

Reading, writing, arithmetic are important only if they serve to make our children more humane. (p. 317)

The challenges of teaching are certainly awesome. Overcrowded classrooms, lack of student interest, absenteeism, lack of preparedness, high incidence of misbehavior, lack of parental support—compounded by social problems such as drugs, unstable family life, teenage pregnancy, poverty, child abuse, violence, and crime give pause to think. But think again. If not for these challenges, the rewards of teaching would not be so great. Our work matters. We make a difference.

Margaret Mead once said, "Never doubt that a small group of thoughtful, committed citizens can change the world, for indeed it is the only thing that ever has." It is up to each of us to change our world, touch a life, and to make a difference. We are involved in what Gary Zukav (2000) calls "sacred tasks." In his words, "Your sacred task is part of the agreement that your soul made with the Universe before you were born. When you are doing it, you are happy and fulfilled. You know that you are in a special and wonderful place. . . . When you are not doing your sacred task, you are miserable" (p. 241).

People have different sacred tasks. For some, starting a business might serve as a path for fulfillment; for others, it might be raising a family, or cooking. For us, it is teaching. Sharing, guiding, assisting, communicating, praising, encouraging . . . touching another's soul. Moving students to realization and understanding. Recognize your sacred task. Never forget why you are a teacher.

Each of us entered teaching to make a difference in the lives of our students. We see the uniqueness of each child and try our utmost to light that spark of potential that lies dormant within. We realize that our task also is not just to help our students do well in school, but, more important, to succeed in life. We encourage our children by teaching them to be caring, moral, and productive members of society.

In the end, our destination is to create a vision of possibilities for our students, a journey of self-discovery. We are reminded of Robert Browning's observation that "a man's reach should exceed his grasp or what's a heaven for?" Browning gives us a moral message and serves as a moral compass. As we work against tough odds, we persevere. In doing so, we inspire our students to achieve excellence. We play a vital role. We shape lives. We touch the future. Christa McAuliffe was right. The Boris Pasternak poem from *Dr. Zhivago* comes to mind:

> You in others—this is what you are.
> Your soul, your immortality, your life in others.
> And now what?
> You have always been in others and you remain in others.
> This will be you—the spirit that enters the future
> And becomes a part of it.

Our legacy is the future, our students. And that's why teaching matters. But, the manner in which we shape that future is critical.

OUR ETHICAL RESPONSIBILITIES TOWARD EDUCATING THE WHOLE CHILD

Ethics deals with actions that are commonly seen as right or wrong. Ignoring a student's emotional well-being by focusing exclusively on building content knowledge can lead to disastrous consequences. In such a situation, the ends justify the means. If embarrassing a student will encourage him to study harder next time to pass a spelling test, for instance, then such practice might seem justified.

When my oldest son, Daniel (J. Glanz's son), was in first grade he came home crying one day. After I finally calmed him down, he explained that the teacher had placed him outside the classroom in the hallway as the class was celebrating his birthday. Yes, you read this right. That day was his birthday, and so my wife had delivered cupcakes to be distributed after lunch to celebrate his birthday. My wife left. Apparently, here is what transpired. Before the birthday celebration was to commence, the teacher returned graded spelling tests. After seeing that Daniel had failed, yes once again, she placed him outside the classroom; then she distributed the cupcakes to his classmates.

When I personally called her to task for such egregious behavior, or at least I thought it was egregious, she explained her decision, calmly, as follows: "Daniel is a bright boy who just doesn't try hard enough. I am certain, Mr. Glanz, that Daniel will do very well on future spelling tests." I exaggerate not; this is a true story. Maybe not the norm in all schools, but instances of denigrating students' emotional well-being are all too frequent in schools. Daniel, by the way, just turned 30, and to this day recalls nothing about first grade but this incident, and not positively as you might understand. And, he is still a horrible speller!

An ethical educator strives to do the right things as well as do things right. Morality deals with a system of values that undergirds ethical behavior. A moral and ethically responsible educator will demonstrate a caring attitude and approach to all students. Teaching matters, as we demonstrated in the previous section, because educators understand that their responsibility is to nurture a child's welfare, educationally, socially, and emotionally.

Ethics also deals with implementing a diverse and culturally responsive curriculum. Teaching the whole child takes into consideration that each child is culturally unique and that we as educators, who espouse a sense of ethics, work arduously to ensure that culturally responsive teaching and a curriculum that is culturally sensitive are set in place. Not unrelated, ethics too addresses issues of equity that promote a sense of social justice.

What does promoting social justice have to do with our ethical responsibility of teaching the whole child? Attending to the needs of the whole child requires that we ensure that barriers to learning are removed for all students so that all students have an equal opportunity to reach their potential. Under this rubric, providing accommodations and modifications as necessary are viewed as ethical imperatives.

Teaching practices too are scrutinized under the ethical lens that attempts to teach the whole child. Constructivist practices and differentiated instruction are affirmed as valued and necessary in order to practically address each child's needs, holistically.

Undergirding a sense of justice, an appreciation for cultural diversity, an eye toward constructivist practice, a commitment to teach every child through differentiated instruction, and a vision of caring form an undifferentiated unity or, more pointedly, an ethical responsibility as educators to teach the whole child. The ensuing subsections in this chapter attempt to describe each of these ethical constructs in more detail.

THE CONCEPT OF SOCIAL JUSTICE IN SCHOOLS

The concept of social justice has received wide attention in the literature (see, e.g., Bogotch, 2000; Bowers, 2001; Brown, 2004; Connell, 1993; Furman & Shields, 2005; and Rapp, 2002). The subject of promoting social justice in schools is vast so our attention to it in this section will remain introductory. Calls for social justice abound because many critics over the years have pointed to significant social, political, economic, and educational inequities in schools (see, e.g., Apple, 1986; Giroux, 1991; Ogbu, 1978; Spring, 1994).

Schooling, for these critics, perpetuates and reinforces social, racial, and gender stratifications. Inequities in allocations of school finances (Kozol,

1991), socially stratified arrangements through which subject matter is delivered known as tracking practices in schools (Oakes, 1985), biased content of the curriculum (Anyon, 1981), patriarchal relations through authority patterns and staffing (Strober & Tyack, 1980), differential distribution of knowledge by gender within classrooms (Sadker & Sadker, 1994), and the influence of teacher expectations (Rosenthal & Jacobson, 1968) are examples of inequities decried by these critics.

What are teacher expectations? How might they function to stifle individual autonomy and perpetuate stereotypical relationships? and What impact might they have on students? are important questions (Good & Brophy, 2007). Coined by Robert Merton and first researched by Rosenthal and Jacobson (cited by Tauber, 1997), the "self-fulfilling prophecy" is a phenomenon that has relevance in education.

Aware of the limitations of this concept, researchers have documented its effects in and outside the classroom (see, e.g., Ogbu, 2003; Seyfried, 1998). Expectations are sometimes communicated directly, more often indirectly or unconsciously. Assumptions are sometimes made based on a student's family background, religious or cultural environment, or past academic performance. A teacher who tells Charles he might as well not study for the exam since he's failed prior exams may affect the student in marked emotional and academic ways.

Social justice advocates point out that educators should remain vigilant and aware of the force of expectations so that students are not treated differentially due to some unfounded or grossly misinterpreted characteristic. Educators who seek to promote social justice in the classroom might posit the following question: "How might I, as the classroom teacher, promote the ideals of equality, justice, and opportunity in my classroom by communicating positive expectations to students?" (see Yonezawa & Jones, 2006, wherein they report findings of a study in which students, who oppose tracking, call for teachers to teach for equity and to have positive attitudes toward all students).

Tauber (1997), proffering advice to teachers about remaining conscious of the power of their expectations, asks:

> Do you assign tasks on some gender basis? Does it just seem natural to assign heavier and dirtier tasks (i.e., carry this, move that) to the "stronger sex" and the more domestic activities (i.e., wash this, clean that, serve this) to the "weaker sex"? When leaders are selected, whether for a classroom or a playground activity, are males more often chosen than females? When creative activities (i.e., decorating for an upcoming holiday) are undertaken, are females more likely than males to be called upon?
>
> When you conduct demonstrations, are males more often asked to assist you and females more often asked to be "recording secretaries"? Do you let female

students get away with inappropriate behavior that you would discipline male students for? If you are female, do you catch yourself identifying more with the female students than with the male students? And the list goes on and on. (pp. 47–48)

Although Tauber discusses gender issues, the inferences are nonetheless pertinent, if not obvious. If a teacher lowers expectations for a student simply because of an academic or intellectual label placed on her (see, e.g., Rist, 1970), or because of some cultural consideration, then social justice activists would point to an injustice. What is our moral commitment to avoiding negative or low expectations so that we ensure justice in our schools for all students?

The call for social justice talks to the heart of concepts of respect, equality, and equity. For Dewey (1976a), justice "sums up morality," and "it is not a virtue, but it is virtue" (p. 371). John Dewey (1916/2007a) articulated a commitment to these ideals in his monumental *Democracy and Education*. He also addressed them even more fully in his "The Ethics of Democracy" and "Individuality, Equality, and Superiority" (Dewey, 1967; 1976b).

He said, in an another essay titled "Creative Democracy—The Task Before Us," that the "democratic faith in human equality is belief that every human being, independent of the quantity or range of his personal endowment, has the right to equal opportunity with every other person for development of whatever gifts he has" (Dewey, 1981, pp. 227–228). More succinctly and directly, Dewey (1976b) said, "[E]quality is moral, a matter of social justice secured, not of physical or psychological endowment" (p. 299). Dewey (1976a) explained:

> Justice, as equity, fairness, impartiality, honesty, carries the recognition of the whole over into the question of right distribution and apportionment among its parts. The equitable judge or administrator is the one who makes no unjustifiable distinctions among those dealt with. . . . [T]he idea of social justice due to the growth of love, or philanthropy, . . . [is] a working social motive. (pp. 372–373)

In the ensuing years other progressive and neoprogressive educators made similar pleas. Recently, attention has been drawn to the ethical and moral responsibilities of school leaders to pursue and uphold such concepts (Theoharis, 2007).

John Rawls (1971), moral philosopher and academician, in his groundbreaking work in political philosophy, *A Theory of Justice*, and in consonance with Deweyan philosophy, provides the conceptual grounding for educational leaders and others committed to respect, equality, and equity. He posits a Kantian interpretation that conceives justice idealistically as fundamentally grounded in human respect. On a more pragmatic level, he sees justice as an accommodation between competing political and philosophical positions in which individuals with differing opinions learn to cooperate without coercion.

For Rawls, moral persons are ones who are willing and able to appreciate both the idealistic and pragmatic views of justice. Rawls believes that development of a sense of justice is a high-order human characteristic or personality state that includes developing multiple relationships with diverse groups of people and learning to respect and treat each justly. For Rawls, such action is moral affirmation. Education, in general, and schools in particular, play a critical role in fostering such respect and cooperation (Strike, 1991).

The social justice literature differentiates between issues of equality and equity. Individuals concerned with fostering social justice ensure that each individual or group receives what is needed (Strike & Soltis, 1992). An ethic of justice is affirmed when equality and equity are employed. The authors cite Aristotle who held "that justice consists of treating equals equally and unequals unequally." Using this premise, "if high-school grades are the basis of admission into a university, then two people with the same grades should receive the same treatment, either both should be admitted or both should be rejected" (p. 46); thus justice is affirmed on the basis of equality.

Equity on the other hand, in the Aristotelian sense, means if a student needs an accommodation to assist learning, I treat him fairly by providing that instructional prompt, for instance; in other words, he gets what he needs. No one else would complain of unfairness for not receiving that particular prompt. So, when people differ in relation to some characteristic or condition, they receive different treatment based on their particular needs. Thus, in the ethics of justice, both are affirmed.

More fundamentally, Rawls (1971) bases his theory of justice on a notion of fairness as well. In a school setting, one fourth grader might need remedial assistance in reading, for instance, while another enrichment. Equity, not equality (i.e., getting the same thing), is achieved given the fact both students' needs are accurately and unbiasedly assessed. Both individuals are treated evenhandedly in pursuit of a good life, liberty, and happiness.

On an individual level, social justice advocates ensure that all individuals are treated equally, that is, given what each needs without preferential treatment or differences in resources expenditures. Expectations here are held in check and dispensed fairly without bias. Equality doesn't really address group differences though. Let's say one group of students is African American, and the other is Caucasian. If African American students are placed uniformly in remedial classes without attention to their academic ability and needs, and Caucasian students automatically placed in upper tracks, inequity and thus injustice prevail.

An inequitable situation is one in which a group has not historically been treated fairly or justly, or given equal treatment. Members of the group are often viewed as inferior, or at the very least considered less, and consequently oppressed or disadvantaged. Equity goes beyond racial, ethnic, and gender inequalities to also include social class, disability, and exceptionalities (Shapiro & Stefkovich, 2005).

PROMOTING CULTURAL DIVERSITY

The arena of cultural diversity and multicultural education is vast. In order to provide theoretical grounding for the positions taken in this chapter, I have decided to focus on one aspect of the topic, this is, the relevance of culturally relevant teaching. Multicultural education, though, serves as the moral underpinning for this discussion. According to Boyer and Baptiste (1996), multicultural education transforms "education so that its reality for students includes equity for all, a true spirit of democracy, freedom from prejudice and stereotypes of discrimination, and appreciation for cultural diversity" (p. 2).

Multicultural education consists of five dimensions (Banks, 1997): content integration (the degree to which, for example, teachers use examples from a variety of cultures), equity pedagogy (teaching, for example, that facilitates achievement for all students), empowering school culture and structure (practices, for example, that avoid labeling), prejudice reduction (activities, for example, that promote positive interactions with those different from oneself), and knowledge construction (examining, for example, who determines what gets taught).

Appreciating and capitalizing upon cultural diversity to enhance learning is very much an extension of the work of those educators committed to multicultural education. Support for deep learning based on sound psychological learning theory was reported by Lambert and McCombs (2000) in a comprehensive review of latest research on learning theory amplified upon a fundamental psychological principle relating to the learning process and the learner.

They explain that social and cultural diversity are important factors in enhancing the learning experience. Learning, they explain, is "facilitated by social interactions and communication with others in a flexible, diverse (in age, culture, family background, etc.) and adaptive instructional setting" (p. 509). Learning is enhanced by interacting with diverse abilities, cultures, values, and interests.

Learning environments should allow for the appreciation of and interaction with diverse learning styles. The principle states that "[l]earning settings that allow for and respect diversity encourage flexible thinking as well as social competence and moral development" (p. 509). Multicultural communities, according to Strike (2007), are characterized "by a sense that we are all in this together while also respecting differences and individual rights" (p. 146).

Educators who teach from a culturally relevant frame understand that all students can learn, albeit at different paces and in different ways. Although not the first to articulate a culturally relevant stance in regard to teaching, Ladson-Billings (1994) compares culturally relevant teaching with what she terms assimilationist teaching. An assimilationist believes that ethnic groups should conform to the norms, values, expectations, and behaviors of the dominant social and cultural group. Culturally relevant teachers, by contrast, believe that all students can learn, albeit differently. Assimilationist teachers believe that failure is inevitable for some students.

Culturally responsive teachers (Jordan Irvine & Armento, 2003) are responsive to their students by incorporating elements of the students' cultures in their teaching. They make special efforts to get to know their students well. They might ask their students to share stories about their family and cultural heritage. Students are encouraged to express themselves openly about their culture.

Students obtain a tremendous sense of pride and a feeling of being appreciated. A teacher, for instance, might assign her students a homework assignment to write a story about their family. Culturally responsive pedagogy is integrated into the curriculum and lessons on almost a daily basis, not just around holidays or special commemorations.

According to Lindsey, Roberts, and Campbell Jones (2005), culturally relevant educators affirm justice and opportunity for all students in their school and work to create an ethical learning environment that supports and encourages all students to succeed, academically and socially. Although not couched in similar semantics, Dewey's writing affirms such a commitment.

CONSTRUCTIVISM AS PEDAGOGY

How do people learn best? John Dewey (1899/2001) said that people learn best "by doing." Hands-on instructional tasks encourage students to become actively involved in learning. Active learning increases students' interest in the material, makes the material covered more meaningful, allows students to refine their understanding of the material, and provides opportunities to relate the material to broad contexts.

Constructivism also supports the social dimensions of learning: people learn best when actively working with others as partners, for example, cooperative learning (see Johnson, Johnson, & Johnson-Holubec, 1994). Thus, constructivist pedagogy is aligned with the moral commitment to provide all students with developmentally appropriate instruction (Nalder, 2007; Udvari-Solner & Kluth, 2007).

Constructivism is aligned with progressive thinking (Twomey Fosnot, 2005). Constructivism is not a theory about teaching and learning per se; rather, it is a theory about the nature of knowledge itself. Knowledge is seen as temporary, developmental, socially constructed, culturally mediated, and nonobjective. Learning, then, becomes a self-regulated process wherein the individual resolves cognitive conflicts while engaged in concrete experiences, intellectual discourse, and critical reflection (Foote, Vermette, & Battaglia, 2001; Rodgers, 2002).

The principles of constructivist paradigms support the view of educators as informed decision makers. Accordingly, learning is a socially mediated process in which learners construct knowledge in developmentally appropriate ways, and real learning requires that learners use new knowledge and apply what they have learned (Vygotsky, 1934/1986; Bransford, Brown, & Cocking, 1999). These beliefs emphasize "minds-on" learning.

This endorses the belief that all learners must be intellectually engaged in the learning process by building on their previous knowledge and experiences, and applying their new learning in meaningful contexts. To become a constructivist (mediator of learning) the teacher preparation candidate must be guided by the development of the child, motivation, and learning. Thus, central to expert instruction is a deep understanding of child development and a broad knowledge of the principles of pedagogy that serve as the blueprint for design of instruction that leads to student learning.

Many of us, including Dewey, of course, would applaud such efforts because students are actively involved in meaningful and relevant learning activities. However, as O. L. Davis Jr. (1998) has reminded us, hands-on "activities that do not explicitly require that pupils *think* about their experience" can simply mean "minds-off" (p. 120). Davis explains further:

> Raw experiences comprise the grist for thinking. They are necessary, but not sufficient, instructional foci. For the most part, hands-on activities must include *minds-on* aspects. That is, pupils must think about their experience. They must, as Dewey noted, reflect about what they have done. Consciously, they must construct personal meanings from their active experience. . . . Indeed, for hands-on activities to qualify as educationally appropriate tasks, teachers must work with pupils before, during, and after these engagements so that pupils maintain a minds-on awareness of their unfolding experiences. (p. 120)

Working from a constructivist pedagogic frame is challenging (Windschitl, 2002) but rewarding because when students actively engage in the learning process all their sense and emotions are involved and nurtured. Thus, such pedagogy is ethical, for Dewey, because it addresses the educational and the healthy development of the learner. Learning is not fragmented, nor isolated from the wholesome development of the learner.

A RATIONALE FOR DIFFERENTIATING INSTRUCTION

Calls for differentiating instruction have gained strength in education literature over the past decade. Conceptually and theoretically grounded in the work of progressive education (Dewey, 1899/2001), child development (Erikson, 1995), social and intellectual development (Vygotsky, 1934/1986; Piaget, 1936), learning styles (Dunn, 1995), and multicultural education (Banks, 2004), differentiated instruction has been most recently articulated and promulgated through the work of Carol Tomlinson (2001, 2003).

Teaching for a diverse student population is certainly challenging. Then again, teaching well is itself a challenging enterprise requiring knowledge expertise, talents in communication, pedagogical savvy, appreciation of varied student learning styles, and so on (Parkay & Stanford, 2006). The problem of reaching all students academically, however, has become more critical as schools have become more ethnically and linguistically diverse.

Teaching, historically, has been plagued by a one-size-fits-all mentality. As Tomlinson (2005) simply yet accurately posits, "[W]e teach as we were taught" (p. 183). Classrooms have always been heterogeneous. Yet, when students, to teachers, appear alike ethnically, linguistically, or culturally educators have made the erroneous assumption that all students learn the same way, hence teaching becomes unifaceted.

Recently, George (2005) has articulated a rationale for differentiating instruction. He argues that a heterogeneous classroom is critically important for several reasons. Since students in the future will likely live and work in diverse environments, classrooms should model such diversity. He explains, "[T]he heterogeneous classroom can provide a real-life laboratory for the development of important interpersonal and social knowledge, skills, and attitudes essential to success in adult life, while simultaneously providing opportunity for varied types and degrees of academic achievement" (p. 186).

Besides goal consistency, George asserts that heterogeneous grouping will aid in accurate placement of students without erroneous labeling. "When students learn together in diverse classrooms, without the need to classify students according to their ability, there is also much less risk of labeling or stigmatizing high or low achievers" (p. 187). Furthermore, George states that such grouping accentuates the awareness of individual differences. If a teacher perceives his class as uniform, she is more likely to teach in a uniform manner.

Teachers, he continues, are more sensitive to individual learning needs of students in mixed-ability classrooms. "In an effective heterogeneous class-room (one where curriculum and instruction are properly differentiated), stu-dents and teachers, I think, are more likely to view their differences as assets that strengthen the whole school" (p. 187).

Moreover, he argues that effort and persistence are enhanced in a differ-entiated classroom. The classroom is also more equitable in that "there is a much greater chance for equitable distribution of teaching talent and other school resources" (pp. 187–188). "Heterogeneous classrooms help ensure that all students are exposed to a complex, enriched curriculum, and to spir-ited instruction" (p. 188). In Deweyan tradition, such efforts are essential to connect learning and personal growth.

BUILDING AN ETHIC OF CARING

Dewey stressed that social morality was based on a fundamental premise of caring that he called an "[A]ttitude of willingness to reexamine and if neces-sary revise current convictions, and even if that course entails the effort to change by concerted effort existing institutions, and to direct existing tenden-cies to new ends" (Dewey & Tufts, 1909, p. 777). The work of Nel Noddings (1984, 1986, 1992), characteristic of and influenced by Dewey's work, cen-ters on the ethic of caring.

An "ethic of caring" affirms a belief that educators and children alike are to be caring, moral, and productive members of society (Jordan Irvine, 2001). As Noddings (1992), extending Dewey's views, posits, "The traditional or-ganization of schooling is intellectually and morally inadequate for contem-porary society" (p. 173). Although appropriate at some point in educational history, the traditional model of bureaucratic school organization in which organizational needs supersede individual interests is no longer appropriate.

Dewey (see Mayhew & Edwards, 1965) knew this well when he said the problem of education was the "harmonizing of individual traits with social ends and values" (p. 465). Nurturing an "ethic of caring," principals, as do teachers, realize their ultimate motive is to inspire a sense of caring, sensitiv-ity, appreciation, and respect for human dignity of all people despite travails that pervade our society and world.

Organizations are not autonomous independent entities but are rather made to conform to and meet the needs of people. Noddings (1992) makes the point related to the purpose of education: "We should educate all our children not only for competence but also for caring. Our aim should be to encourage the growth of competent, caring, loving, and lovable people" (p. xiv).

Feminist organizational theory (Blackmore, 1993; Regan, 1990) informs this ethic of caring by avoiding traditional conceptions of teaching and leading. Feminist theory questions the legitimacy of the hierarchical, patriarchal, bureaucratic school organization. Challenging traditional leadership models, feminist theory encourages community building, interpersonal relationships, nurturing, and collaboration as of primary interest (Ferguson, 1984).

Supportive of this feminist view of school organization, Henry (1996) explains how feminist theory opposes bureaucracy:

> The feminist approach that I have developed in this study places people before mechanical rules or bureaucratic responses. Feminism stems from a concern not just with humankind, but with all living things and their interdependence in the universe, with a view to redefining male-female and other relations away from a notion of dominance and subordination and toward the ideal of equality and interconnectedness. . . . All human beings are seen as enriched by a feminist way of seeing and relating to the world. Instead of autonomy, separation, distance, and a mechanistic view of the world, feminism values nurturing, empathy, and a caring perspective. (pp. 19, 20)

Noddings (1992) has led a feminist critique challenging traditional conceptions of education by advocating an ethic of caring "to enable schools to become caring communities that nurture all children, regardless of their race, class, or gender" (Marshall, Patterson, Rogers, & Steele, 1996, p. 276). Unlike traditional humanistic models of administration, "caring" is inclusionary, nonmanipulative, and empowering.

Whereas the main objective of bureaucracy is standardization, caring inspires individual responsibility. Caring "is a situation- and person-specific way of performing in the world that requires being fully and sensitively attuned to the needs of the cared for by the person caring. Caring cannot be transformed into policies mandated from above, but caring can give form and coherence to our schools" (Marshall et al., 1996, pp. 278–279).

Although defining "caring" has been difficult (Beck, 1994), scholars who have explored this topic in depth note that caring always involves, to some degree, three activities: (1) receiving the other's perspective, (2) responding appropriately to the awareness that comes from this reception, and (3) remaining committed to others and to the relationship.

What do caring educators do? According to Marshall et al. (1996), they "frequently develop relationships that are the grounds for motivating, cajoling, and inspiring others to excellence. Generally thoughtful and sensitive, they see nuances in people's efforts at good performance and acknowledge them; they recognize the diverse and individual qualities in people and devise individual standards of expectation, incentives, and rewards" (p. 282). With students, teachers would remain sensitive to their social, emotional, and academic needs.

Caring educators would make certain that students respect each other, and that the values and traditions of each individual, regardless of religious affiliation or cultural background, are affirmed. Caring educators would remain sensitive to the needs and feelings of all students.

The relationship between an ethic of justice and an ethic of caring is instructive (see Katz, Noddings, & Strike, 1999). An educational commitment to seeking justice in terms of promoting equality, equity, and respect in the classroom for all students is fundamentally premised on an ethic of caring. Caring about the worth and needs of the individual student, not necessarily the needs of the school as an organization, is of utmost concern to educators who work from an ethic of caring and justice.

Parenthetically, one difference between the two ethics should be pointed out as well. Justice generally strives for a sense of impartiality: that is, right is right, wrong is wrong. An ethic of caring, in contrast, avoids impartiality. Moral reasoning is passionate and involved. Gilligan (1993) and Noddings (2003), in Deweyan tradition, argue that moral detachment is not feasible. Caring rests philosophical laurels on compassion in which equity is placed at the core, not equality.

CONCLUSION

Dewey (1938), in his *Experience and Education*, posits three fundamental aspects of curriculum: the development of intelligence, the development of socially useful skills, and the healthy growth of the individual. Addressing the needs of the whole child, he feels, is not only a curricular imperative, but an instructional and ethical one as well.

The moral vision needed goes beyond the ordinary, mundane, or established ways of conceiving teaching and learning (Brown & Duguid, 1991). From a Deweyan (1916/2007a) perspective, this vision "entails a constant expansion of horizons and a consequent formulation of new purposes and new responses" (p. 206). We need new responses to deal with a plethora of challenges we face in education. This new vision cannot be framed in isolation of a community of concerned individuals seeking to improve education and curriculum, more specifically.

What is our moral commitment to such ideals in regard to promoting the best education of the whole child? The moral imperative, we discussed in this chapter, involves much work as we strive to enhance an ethic of caring, justice, and constructivist work within a differentiated instructional environment. To accomplish this imperative requires moral recommitment to affirming the value of taking responsibility for teaching the whole child. Beyond and fundamental to this imperative is Dewey's enduring belief that education is moral activity, and "ethics is understood as the art of helping people live more richer, more responsive, and more sensitized engaged lives" (Fesmire, 2003, p. 92).

Discussion Questions

1. Describe how a school you are familiar with addresses or doesn't adequately address the "teaching of the whole child." If the school is inadequate in doing so, describe what changes you might advance to create a more holistic curriculum, for instance. Be as descriptive and specific as possible.
2. How do you, in your interactions with students, foster a sense of justice and display an "ethic of caring"?
3. How has Dewey's work and influence, as described in this chapter, helped you better understand your own personal ethical responsibilities?
4. How do concepts and issues of social justice, cultural diversity, constructivism, differentiated instruction, and an ethic of caring promote a moral climate in a school or classroom?
5. Discuss your experiences with trying to differentiate instruction. Highlight successes and challenges.
6. React to the criticisms of those who claim that schools should, indeed, not have to address the "whole child" in the sense that a school should be solely accountable for instilling knowledge, and preparing future competent workers and good citizens in a democracy.
7. To what extent does your school address issues related to cultural diversity? Explain with specific strategies employed.
8. How has constructivism influenced your practice?
9. Some people say we overemphasize constructivist practice because some children are not yet ready to work independently and need directive or frontal teaching. How would you respond to such a statement?
10. What else strikes you about the ideas highlighted in this chapter?

Further Reflection

1. Interview a colleague to ask how concepts and issues of social justice, cultural diversity, constructivism, differentiated instruction, and an ethic

of caring influence her practice. Record her responses and then discuss how her responses connect in some way to the ideas you read about in this chapter.

2. Observe three colleagues and compare and contrast their culturally responsive styles of teaching. What conclusions can you make about the ethics of cultural diversity?

3. What did Dewey refer to when he said, "A narrow and moralistic view of morals is responsible for the failure to recognize that all the aims and values which are desirable in education are themselves moral"? How does this quotation reference the material addressed in this chapter?

Part Two

VOICES FROM THE FIELD

Chapter Eight

The Relevance of Dewey's Work

I hope that somewhere in the book you will address the fact that we quote Dewey endlessly but neglect to implement his lessons, especially those pertaining to his research.

—John I. Goodlad (Personal correspondence with the authors, 2009)

The purpose of this part of the book is to share with readers the views of selected scholars in the field who generously responded to our request to assess the impact of Dewey's work on the field today. We posed some specific questions. We pose these very same questions in Focus Questions below. Not everyone we solicited responded to our request. We culled names from the list of members of the John Dewey Society, from scholars we personally know who we thought would have interesting insights to offer, and from some scholars who have published on various aspects of Dewey's work. We feel that sharing their thoughtful insights with our readers will concretize our work here and serve to highlight some of the major themes we have tried to address in this volume. We also highlight two specific implications from this research, namely, the nature of school reform (NCLB) and the dire need to attend to poverty in our country. A perusal of the views proffered in this section will underscore the import and relevance of Dewey's thought but, at the same time, the lack of seriousness we take in terms of relating Dewey's ideas to policy making. Sarason's (1996) timeless adage finds much relevance here: "The more things change the more they tend to stay the same" (p. 233).

Focus Questions

Here is what we wrote each scholar soliciting his or her participation. We ask that you respond as well, and please feel free to e-mail us your responses for possible inclusion in another edition of this book.

> We are currently writing a book about educating the whole child in the era of high-stakes testing in the context of John Dewey's educational philosophy. We invite your *brief* participation. As a leading educational scholar, your insights and observations are invaluable for assessing and guiding current education policy. In formulating your response, you may want to consider *one or more* of the following questions:
>
> 1. Is John Dewey relevant today? Explain why or why not.
> 2. What might Dewey advise us today in terms of teaching to the whole child?
> 3. In what ways does John Dewey inform current successes and challenges in education?
> 4. What does the future hold for high-stakes testing?
> 5. Are there any particular aspects of No Child Left Behind that are more helpful or egregious for educating the whole student?

In writing this chapter, we consciously made the decision to include whole excerpts from the data we collected via our e-mail survey of scholars in the field. We thought that providing these whole quotations would make for a more interesting read than for us, as editors, to selectively decide which quotations best fit with the arguments we want to make in this section of the book.

So, we have included direct quotations that best represent, in our view, the particular theme or question under discussion. Some respondents said similar things so we selected those quotations that we felt "said it best." We received nearly two dozen responses to our survey but only included what we felt was most representative.

This chapter includes the quotations based on three themes that emerged from our survey. In chapter 9 we highlight the case of New York City school reform as one example of how NCLB impacts school reform. And in chapter 10, we highlight what we consider perhaps the greatest challenge of our democracy today, that is, our inability to eradicate poverty. Each chapter in part two examines its subject in light of Deweyan democratic ideals.

THEME 1: DEWEY'S RELEVANCE TODAY

Many respondents commented that they were happy to find a volume devoted to the application of John Dewey's work in the field of education. Harriet

K. Cuffaro, a leader in the field of early childhood progressive education, stated that she was "delighted to learn that there will be a book that will bring Dewey back to our discussions on education. Thus far, at best, he's been a whisper rather than a voice."

This comment prompted us to momentarily consider renaming this section of our book "Whispers from the Field." Professor Cuffaro more pointedly posited, "If he knew what was happening in American education today, [John Dewey] would be spinning in his grave." Nevertheless, several respondents to our survey indicated quite emphatically that Dewey had much to say about a variety of issues still relevant today.

David C. Berliner, noted educational psychologist and past president of the American Educational Research Association (AERA), provided two striking examples:

Of course Dewey is relevant today. A simple example comes from a recent newspaper article about California's tiny Ross School District, in Marin country. The community held an auction to fund increases in teacher salaries in order to attract the best teachers in the state. A glass of lemonade, with a pass to play golf, went for $1,100. The 240 families in support of this one public school raised $1.3 million over and above the budget the state provided. A Dewey quote is certainly still relevant: "What the best and wisest parent wants for his own child, that must the community want for all its children. Any other ideal for our schools is narrow and unlovely; acted upon, it destroys our democracy."

A second example of Dewey's relevance today is also easy to find. Dewey was concerned about the influential role most people wanted teachers to play in our society, and whether that can ever happen if the scientist or politician were to dictate the behavior of teachers. He said: "Can the teacher ever receive 'obligatory prescriptions'? Can he [sic] receive from another a statement of the means by which he is to reach his ends, and not become hopelessly servile in his attitude?" Dewey's caution of a century ago was certainly *not* heeded in recent years where we saw federal and state governments forcing certain kinds of so-called "evidence-based" teaching practices upon teachers with demands that they comply, regardless of their professional opinions and experience. Government agencies required teachers to use the controversial program known as Reading First, demanded that English Language Learners be educated through Structured English Immersion, and required high-stakes testing to improve learning. Dewey would have seen problems in dictating to teachers even were the science behind these recommendations more solid than it actually is. Dewey simply didn't believe that it was possible to make a system of instruction-through-fiat work. He understood that the interchanges between teachers and students are particularities, determined by socio-cultural history, personal relationships, and immediate context. Thus these interchanges are harder to formulate in ways that science can illuminate except at a very general level. Dewey's thinking turned out to be much closer to Vygotsky's than it was to his contemporary, Thorndike. As these two examples illustrate, Dewey is as relevant today as ever: a democratic and very wise voice amidst the cacophony of voices all trying to shape our educational system.

Joseph S. Renzulli, distinguished professor of educational psychology at the University of Connecticut and founder of Renzulli Learning Systems, stated:

> Candidate Obama said, "If we really want our children to become the great inventors and problem-solvers of tomorrow, our schools shouldn't stifle innovation, they should let it thrive" (Obama, 2008).
>
> Kids can't be innovative or real world problem solvers if everything is pre-programmed to address predetermined standards and standardized tests. This statement by our new president, coupled with growing dissatisfaction of both educators and the general public, may signal a turning point from the disastrous policies of the last administration and may just open the door to a new national resolve that will make Dewey's work relevant in guiding policy and practice.
>
> Our nation and the world are facing unprecedented challenges and it is only by preparing the kinds of creative problem solvers and persons with moral integrity that we can begin to address these problems. John Dewey's pedagogy coupled with remarkable advances in interactive technology can easily transform the work of teachers in the direction that Dewey provided. This technology is readily available and it goes beyond the worksheets-on-line and digital encyclopedias that were the electronic equivalent of Gutenberg's printing press.
>
> New technologies now allow instruction to be based on individual student profiles that document academic strengths, interests, and learning styles and that then match the most appropriate resources to each student's profile. Research has shown that this approach not only improves achievement, but it also makes learning the engaging and enjoyable process it ought to be. But we must start by first addressing the foundation for the very existence of schools—the pedagogy that guides the act of learning.

Noted Deweyian scholar Tom Fallace was a bit more tempered in his view of Dewey's relevance. He explains:

> My answer to whether Dewey is still relevant today is yes and no. I have studied the actual curriculum of the University of Chicago laboratory school very closely, and thus, have come away with both a sense of Dewey's originality and genius, but also how many of Dewey's ideas would be of little use today. Dewey insisted that the traditional curriculum unnaturally severed "form" from "content"—that is, the processes and outcomes of knowledge were severed from the contexts that engendered them. "The defect of the present school," Dewey explained in a 1895 letter to a teacher, "is that it isolates . . . and devotes itself to techniques or symbols (discipline) without reference either to the necessity either of an end or concrete tools. . . . It thus defeats itself, giving a mechanical habit which cannot be applied to new materials or new purposes." Without ap-

preciating the specific contexts from which the problems of the past emerged (form) and its solution (content), students would not be able to intrinsically appreciate learning, nor be able to transfer it to other emerging issues or problems. Regarding standardized testing, Dewey would obviously be opposed to the way most tests present content as ready-made and abstract, facts and processes to be memorized and regurgitated, but in no way linked to the problems that historically engendered them. Dewey's curriculum successfully overcame this by situating all learning in the context of real world "occupations" such as cooking, gardening, and construction. The underlying scheme for the Dewey school curriculum was to "repeat the race experience" in a sequential way that united the form and content of the present world by presenting it in the context from which it originally (that is, historically) emerged. This was a brilliant solution to an enduring problem of how to organize content. However, the shortcoming of such an approach was that students did not learn the abstract symbols of the modern world (that is, the three Rs) until the race had actually done so. In practice this meant that they did not learn how to read and write until the race had done so (i.e., the third year). As one Dewey school teacher explained, the life of the Phoenicians provided the most effective link between primitive and civilized man. At this time, students were introduced to symbolic systems of writing, reading, and arithmetic, not as distinct abstractions of the adult world, but rather "from the child's point of view, [as] an attempt to solve the problem of how he, a merchant trader from the Phoenician tribe, could tell the value of his merchandise as compared with that of other merchants, and how he could record promises to give him or receive from him merchandise." Through this pedagogical approach, the teacher asserted, students "were studying the progress of people towards the conveniences which we now have." This example demonstrates both the genius and shortcomings of Dewey's approach. Dewey's "reliving the race experience" was a brilliant way to unite knowledge with action, theory with practice, form with content, and students' interests with the material of the curriculum. However, I think even the most progressive of educators would be uncomfortable with waiting until 2nd or 3rd grade to introduce students to letters, words, and numbers, despite their abstract nature. In this sense, Dewey is no longer relevant.

Affirming Dewey's relevance, David P. Moxley of the University of Oklahoma, Norman, said:

Writing during a time of dramatic changes in transportation and communication, massive immigration to the US, and concerns about the breakdown of traditional structures of family, neighborhood, and religion, Dewey called for a reconstruction of philosophy, and by implication, of the way we think about education and society. One could well argue that the changes Dewey saw in all of these areas were greater in his time than the corresponding changes today. Thus, even though the schools and society of Dewey's time looked different, his general concern and the solutions he proposed are still vital today.

Scot Danforth of the School of Teaching and Learning at the Ohio State University put it this way:

> Yes. It would be self-indulgent of Dewey scholars to say that the words of their favorite American philosopher had some sort of timeless quality. Dewey himself was very aware of how his ideas were situated within a given historical context, tussling with the problems of the day. That said, Dewey remains highly relevant today because he avoided a series of conceptual and practical dead-ends that continue to lure and trap educational policy-makers, researchers, and practitioners in the twenty-first century. I'll mention two of these.
>
> First, while Richard Rorty's claim that his own neo-pragmatism was a faithful and logical continuation of the work of Dewey was always questionable, what Rorty helped us to see was Dewey's active choosing of practical solutions over epistemological commitments. Educational research—most specifically, as funded by federal agencies—has often based its authority on claims of epistemological supremacy. Frequently, research methods founded on objectivist principles have been touted as superior to more qualitative and practitioner-based genres based on subjectivist or interpretivist epistemologies. Dewey's pragmatic stance eschewed the notion that the quality of research necessarily flows forth from a so-called "best" epistemology. His approach to knowledge was more balanced, open, humble, and inquisitive. If only the federal agencies that fund educational research today would consult Dewey's writings . . . the consultation would be free, and the "cash value" (to borrow James's phrase) would be high.
>
> Second, Dewey believed strongly that teachers had to be deeply involved in educational decision-making, a message that today is forgotten or ignored by so many educational reformers. I think Dewey's position was pragmatic—how can anything good happen in schools without the meaningful participation of the most essential actors? He viewed teachers as thoughtful and devoted professionals long before such phrases became common. I believe, too, that Dewey's understanding of democracy as a daily practice required that all parties involved in the outcomes of decisions have a seat at the table and an active voice in those decisions. In today's context, this would mean that educational reform efforts would need the participation of parents/families and professionals at the local level.

Highlighting Dewey's relevance in light of NCLB, David Powell at Gettysburg College stated:

> My sense is that Dewey is as relevant today as he has ever been, especially in light of the changes brought on by NCLB and the "standards and accountability" movement of the past twenty years. To me, Dewey's most enduring contributions to our culture's educational discourse are his commitments to democracy and child-centered instruction and I see both of those ideas being undermined by the most prominent policy choices being made today. I'm especially concerned

by the rise of for-profit schools and the idea that education can be privatized and commoditized, and I think Dewey would share these concerns. Selling education with the objective of securing a profit seems to me to fly in the face of everything Dewey stood for—not only because it reveals an impoverished view of what education is for and how students "receive" it, but also because it threatens to disrupt any effort to establish a pragmatic/democratic foundation for schooling in a free society. There can be nothing "child centered" about a third party seeking profit from the knowledge generated by a child.

In a similar but slightly more nuanced fashion, Alan W. Garrett at Eastern New Mexico University stated:

John Dewey's work retains its vitality to this day and is especially relevant in the current era of No Child Left Behind, during which high-stakes testing has come to be viewed by many politicians, much of the public, and, unfortunately, an increasing number of educators as the primary, if not sole, reason for maintaining public schools. As an educational scholar and university professor, I study, read, write, and teach about these problems and ponder alternatives to provide more robust educational experiences for all students. As the father of a school-aged daughter, I witness too often attempts to debase the curriculum and degrade the school experience in quests for higher test scores. As a member of a local school board, I oppose continually those who seek to reduce schooling to little more than test preparation. In "My Pedagogic Creed," Dewey correctly observed, "[A]ll reforms which rest simply upon enactment of law, or the threatening of certain penalties, or upon changes in mechanical and outward arrangements, are transitory and futile" (Dewey, 1897/1964, p. 437). Unfortunately, the centrality of high-stakes testing to No Child Left Behind will reduce the quality of the educations of students attending school while that misguided law remains in effect.

Chapter XI of John and Evelyn Dewey's *Schools of To-Morrow* offers an honest critique of the world in which students and educators have been placed and suggests a frightening possible unintended consequence of today's misplaced emphasis on testing. The Deweys (1915) warned against employing "artificial aims" such as "rewards and high marks" (p. 297). Today, including test scores among such artificial aims is both appropriate and necessary. The possible effect on test scores rather than questions of right and wrong or good and bad constitutes the criterion for making far too many educational decisions. In the absence of such "artificial inducements," the Deweys argued, "the child learns to work from the love of the work itself, not for a reward or because he is afraid of punishment" (p. 298). How many of today's students will avoid becoming curious, lifelong learners when they leave school and face no more tests? After all, the message so many of them have been bombarded with for so long is, "You must learn this, because it will be on the test, and you want to do well on the test." The test, rather than the joy, excitement, and satisfaction of learning, has become the reason for attending school. More ominously, the Deweys went on to suggest, "The conventional type of education which trains children to docility and obedience, to the careful performance of imposed tasks because they are imposed, regardless of where they lead, is suited to an autocratic society" (p. 303). A potential and unfortunate consequence of the structure, uniformity, and shortsighted focus that of necessity arises from No Child Left Behind [is] a generation of passive, poorly informed, and incurious students woefully unprepared to assume their rightful roles as active, contributing citizens in a democratic society.

Finally, famed historian Diane Ravitch acknowledges that many today disregard Dewey's admonitions, but on an optimistic note asserts that Dewey will once again rise in recognition:

> He wrote thousands of pages about the role of education in a democracy; about the purposes of public education in promoting democracy; and about the ways in which schools should meet the needs of the child and educate the whole child. Some of his disciples carried his advice to unwise extremes, ignoring the need for a sound curriculum and the importance of studying the academic disciplines. But in his analysis of the most important aspects of education, Dewey was on target. Education is about the making of a democratic society and the development of individuals who will make their own contributions to that society.
>
> Now, in the twenty-first century, we see an emphasis on testing and accountability that has narrowed the curriculum in many schools to only the basic skills because they are the only school subjects that "count." With the growth of charter schools and other efforts to promote private control of public institutions, we see a growing disdain for the democratic purposes of public education.
>
> In these trends, there is little regard for the lessons taught by John Dewey. At some point, there will be a public reaction against the current approach, and Dewey will again be relevant. At that time, we can again debate the different strands in his thought. But that will not happen until the now-dominant enthusiasm for measuring learning via multiple-choice tests, closing schools, firing teachers, and imposing business methods on the schools has passed.

THEME 2: DEWEY AND HIGH-STAKES ACCOUNTABILITY

Despite opposition to high-stakes accountability among university scholars and practitioners, policy makers are still pushing forward with this aspect of the NCLB agenda. Bipartisan support for high-stakes accountability ignores Dewey's admonitions.

Audrey Amrein-Beardsley at Arizona State University shared her view with us:

By Dewey's definition of pragmatism, when one is constructing truth, one must understand the consequences and effects of that which is being examined to come to a logical and holistic formation of what is real. Unfortunately, too many have become accustomed to believing mathematics, because it is a hard science, reveals truth, without understanding that numbers too are constructed and situated within events. Test scores, in this example those derived from high-stakes tests as part of NCLB, are being used to reduce every student, classroom, school, district and state down to one number, or multiple numbers which are averaged into one. And these "objective" numbers are being used to expose what is real and what is true about America's public schools. But people are too often blind to the heroic sets of assumptions they accept when they read the newspaper and rank a school's worth by its test scores or buy a home based on the percentage of neighborhood students who have passed the state's high-stakes test.

What policymakers and America's voters need to understand is that their perceptions are constructed, particularly as furtive events work to skew their conceptions and subconsciously preferred reductionistic understandings about what these tests reveal. They forget that when states, districts, schools, teachers and students take high-stakes tests there are a plethora of unintended consequences and effects that skew the hard numbers spit out of testing machines. What they do not understand is that these test scores are often artificially inflated—that is through things like teaching to the test; narrowing of the curriculum; minimizing hands-on, project-based and experiential education (all promoted by Dewey); via multiple, different iterations of cheating; by exempting, expelling or asking low scoring students to stay home from school on testing days to prevent them from contributing their scores to composite statistics; by encouraging low scoring students to drop out or enroll in alternative degree programs so they will not drag composite statistics down, and the like.

This is hardly progressive, trumped by simple-minded folks who, given their sociologically unconscious view of how high-stakes tests work in practice, back even more high-stakes despite more than 30 years of empirical evidence confirming that they do not work in the ways intended, and if anything work to obliterate the discovery of truth about that which students know.

Jon Bradley from McGill University more pointedly explained:

Testing (high-stakes or otherwise) is most probably here to stay. Conservative educational leaders, such as William Bennett and Chester Finn, ardently advocate a "package" of standardized testing, common curricula, and teacher control. To a certain extent, this really is a non-question in that there has always been testing (even going back to individual colleges having entrance exams) and Latin and Greek being a requirement for medical school. Therefore, while the array and depth of testing may ebb and flow, testing (however defined) will always be part of the overall school system.

The more important issue that sets Dewey and many contemporary conservatives apart is the role, function, and status of the classroom practitioner. Modeling the view expressed a hundred years or so ago by Thorndike (and enforced by generations of rigid curriculum makers) that the classroom teacher (especially so at the elementary levels) is really nothing more than the low-level conduit through which a higher approved and designed curriculum has been imposed, many classrooms have become places of tedium and repetition rather than centers of creative activity.

Dewey always fought against rote memorization for the sake of memorization and consistently stated that mere knowledge for the simple sake of information is rather useless unless internalized and adapted by the individual. However, to the neoconservatives in contemporary America, classroom teachers are not decision makers; rather, they are simply technical implementers. In fact, Chester Finn (in his volume *Troublemaker*, 2008) praises short term teacher preparation programs and strongly advocates against any kind of teacher professionalism.

Dewey, strongly on the other hand, felt that classroom teachers were key components within the educational sphere. He advocated most vigorously at times for teacher unions, associations, and professional status. Long before it was fashionable, he thought that elementary teachers should be academic specialists in their own right.

Dewey's insistence on a scientific language for education was, in part, anchored in his view that education, in general, and teachers, in particular, would never achieve any kind of elevated social status (and therefore power and influence) unless and until a precise and coherent educational lexicon was assumed by all. For much of his writing life, Dewey strove to find such a precise language and this has often led to confusion as he changed and altered terms and words over time as his own thinking progressed.

If one philosophically views education as being a local/provincial matter, then federally imposed standards tied to monetary payouts seems a bit disingenuous.

I do not think that Dewey would look favorably on such legislation. With only one form of success (that of test results), Dewey might well wish that other (and equally valid) measures may have been employed. While such academic testing may accurately test an aspect of academic development, it does little to tease out the creative or musical and other talented traits that exist within any given society.

Later in his life (in his seventies), Dewey took up the role of "the arts." At a time when many men his age could well have rested on past accomplishments, he wrote about how the creative aspects of the individual need to be nurtured and developed. In some ways, this latter career investigation nicely couples with his elementary program years before at Chicago in which he encouraged all kinds of outside activities.

Additionally, Dewey's mid 1930's *Art as Experience* and Louise Rosenblatt's Reader-Response Theory have dramatically altered how the arts are viewed and dealt with in school curriculums. I think that both Dewey and Rosenblatt would ponder how NCLB and its inculcated high-stakes testing can do justice to the arts side of any individual.

The emphasis on end of term/year testing, in and of itself, takes away from educating the whole child. One cannot educate the whole child if, at the end of the day, only a specific element of that child is going to be tested. And, further, based upon that test measure, future educational and funding decisions will be made. Therefore, there is really no room for the whole child within the NCLB plan.

David P. Moxley commented on the escalating effects of high-stakes accountability:

A depressing future scenario for high-stakes testing is that it expands into higher education, and every aspect of the curriculum, all the while becoming more mechanized, reflecting a false scientism. This can happen because of a confluence of corporate interests, simplistic understandings of learning, and unwillingness to trust children, teachers, and ultimately ourselves.

The stated goal of NCLB to ensure equal educational opportunity for all is essential for a democratic society; it's a goal that Dewey would be the first to embrace. There are many examples of, say, NCLB causing schools to offer courses to students who previously had limited opportunity to learn the material in those courses. But on the whole, NCLB manifests a deep misunderstanding of what education could be. It produces failure by setting up unattainable, although ironically, trivial goals. That diverts attention from the very real needs of children and society today. In the final analysis, it promotes an illusory image of education and denies the connection of learning and life.

Dave Powell at Gettysburg College explained concisely:

A related issue, to me, is the rise of standardized testing, which quite clearly contradicts the idea that we have a responsibility to educate the whole child. Standardized tests suggest that we can educate only the part that takes tests, or that the only things worth knowing are things that are testable. If we don't see human experience as more complicated and wonderful than that then we have no business "educating" students in the first place.

Scot Danforth highlights the politicized nature of high-stakes accountability:

I personally view high stakes testing as way to create concrete political symbols out of the learning activities of public school students so that various corporations, organizations, and high profile leaders can struggle, posture, and attempt to influence the public schools. Without test scores, it is very difficult for actors on the national political stage to grasp anything concrete about classroom life. These symbols—test scores—give political operators levers to pull and push, resulting in a feeding frenzy of political maneuvering. But the test scores offer very little of use for the classroom teachers. A cynic would say that since high stakes testing provides little to classroom practice but much fodder for the games of power, these tests are here to stay. I think Dewey would try to decrease their use as political sources of leverage, and as the centerpiece of public dialogue about schooling. He would try to convince us to broaden our discussion of public education to numerous ends and means, to multiple worthwhile goals for young people and many forms of instruction and support within schools.

Geoffrey W. Zoeller Jr., superintendent of schools at the Westwood Regional School District and therefore grounded in the reality of the world of practice, explains:

Ever concerned about test scores, policy makers and administrators who are responsible for making decisions about the school curriculum are often under pressure to implement "new" instructional programs, with the hope that these will provide quick fixes to improve the quality and efficiency of the educational process at a reduced cost. Schools purchase "packages" that are programmatically designed in the Skinnerian model to align and fit objective by objective with a district's academic curricula. In effect, the instructional repertoire is "teacher-proofed," being entirely geared to established-convergent basic education subject matter. It has been noted that "measurement-driven instruction invariably leads to cramming; narrows the curriculum; concentrates attention on those skills most amenable to testing (and today that means skills amenable to the multiple-choice format); constrains the creativity and spontaneity of the teachers and students; and finally demeans the professional judgment of the teachers" (Madaus, 1988, p. 75). This is exactly the consequence of gearing curriculum to the narrow outcomes of high-stakes testing.

In light of the increased emphasis placed on high-stakes testing under the federal No Child Left Behind Act (NCLB), advocates have continued to make claims about the advantages of established-convergent and discipline-centered programmed materials and software designed to address the knowledge and skills students will need to demonstrate on high-stakes national/state testing. As has been warned against, however, "when you buy into an external certification test, you accept ipso facto the straightjacket of constraints on your syllabus and instruction" (Madaus, 1988, p. 101). Is that what we want for our students? A diluted curriculum geared to skill, drill, and kill testing? Perhaps the true import of Dewey today is as an ongoing "call to arms" for those who are willing to see the significant implications to a free society posed by the long-term dilution of the curriculum provided to our country's children.

THEME 3: DEWEY AND TEACHING THE WHOLE CHILD

Dewey's comments on teaching the whole child are often misconstrued. Our participants of this study explain what Dewey meant.

Greg Seals explains, most fundamentally, what Dewey meant by "teaching the whole child":

For Dewey "teaching the whole child" means, in what may be the simplest, most straightforward, commonsense signification of the phrase, "paying close attention to the educative effects of the personal experiences of the learner." Late in his career Dewey stated this connection between education and experience as a hybrid universal or natural law exemplified in the equation he asserts between education and two universal features of personal experience, continuity and interaction: "Continuity and interaction in their active union with each other provide the *measure* of the educative significance and value of an experience" [emphasis added; *Experience and Education* (New York: Collier Books, 1963), 44–45]. Dewey defines continuity and interaction, respectively, as the temporal span of past, present, and future in which any experience occurs and the transaction that occurs between inner and outer states in any experience.

Identification of this general connection between education and experience assures Dewey's relevance to issues of teaching the whole child. Appropriately, he describes the connection as a permanent frame of reference. Dewey's equation between experience and education provides theoretical directive to practitioners, such as teachers, who have a natural interest in constructing lessons with great educative significance. This is what it means to call the view a framework. The permanence of the framework finds its source in the logical status Dewey gives his view. A hybrid universal presumes the necessity of what it claims. Thus, Dewey's presumption that certain features of experience provide the measure of educational significance remains valid until it can be demonstrated that continuity and interaction are not relevant, universal features of experience or that education can be achieved independently of experience.

Jon Bradley comments on Dewey's work in his laboratory schools:

A careful review of the school program that he (and others) instituted at his laboratory school at the University of Chicago (turn of the twentieth century) would clearly demonstrate a concern for the whole child. Any kind of even cursory glance through the yearbooks, photographs, teacher commentaries, and student memories clearly show that the school encompassed the whole child. In fact, the merging of the educational notions of Dewey and Colonel Parker were to commence, in my opinion, the North American view that one must educate the whole child.

It is perhaps a tad unfortunate that Dewey was never really able to institute a demonstration secondary school, that he and Parker never really "hit it off," and that his wife's administrative duties presented a conflict of interest; but it is abundantly clear from his almost ten years of involvement with the primary school (and his further writings on education and the curriculum and society) that he considered the child an "organic organism," a unique and complete individual that learned and acted as a whole and best learned and internalized new material via a "wholistic" approach.

While never embracing Lord Russell or A. S. Neill's "freedom" notions, Dewey was nonetheless opposed to the sharp demarcation of subjects. There was, in a natural way, groups of subjects that complement each other and these, in turn, complemented the organic child as a creative individual. Further, the very things that Dewey felt were necessary to expand the so-called traditional curriculum (gardening, home economics, woodworking, community service, etc.) have been stripped from our own contemporary curricula in a focused race for academic "high standards." Let's keep in mind that some schools are even doing away with recess and shortening lunch periods so as to be able to devote more time to those all-important academic pursuits.

David P. Moxley at the University of Oklahoma, Norman, concisely highlights Dewey's position:

Dewey recognized early on that the breakdown of connections between mind and body, theory and practice, or society and school, were barriers to addressing the challenges of education. He saw further that the separation of subjects, such as mathematics, science, history, and language did not reflect the interconnected world we lived in, he called for connecting learning and life. This meant building upon the child's own experiences, and continually bringing academics back to the problems of everyday life. He might say that we shouldn't teach subjects, but instead the whole child, and foster his or her development as a healthy, inquisitive, and moral being.

Scot Danforth draws upon Dewey's pragmatism:

One very pragmatic piece of advice that Dewey would probably give is to take critical notice any time that the child is sliced into pieces that are then held in isolation. For example, if researchers or policy-makers write about the child's mind (or brain) as isolated from the rest of the child's body, Dewey would advise us to notice how that artificial distinction is used, to what ends, employing what means. Or if educators described child development as discontinuous, as universally segmented rather than a continuous natural process of change and growth, Dewey would ask what this developmental assumption means in practical utilization. The point is not that Dewey embraced some sort of radical ideological holism against all divisions of matter, time, and place. The point is that Dewey was keenly aware that the act of breaking the wholeness of the child and child's experience into additive units involves a degree of theoretical artifice. It is a strategic maneuver that should be examined not in light of whether the child is properly split up or broken down but in relation to the practical, pedagogical results. If we hold that the mind is separate from the body, what useful actions does this allow educators to take? Also, how does this limit pedagogical creativity and effectiveness? Dewey's holism was steered through everyday pedagogy by his pragmatism.

CONCLUSION

Dave Powell of Gettysburg College sums up best this first chapter of part two:

> In short, I think Dewey's work challenges us to turn back the rising tide of privatization and redouble our efforts to focus our educational policy on the needs of children and our collective needs as citizens in a democracy. We would do well to read Dewey more carefully and reconsider his commitments in light of what's happened in the past several decades and I think any effort to overhaul NCLB should begin with the principals involved dusting off a copy of *Democracy and Education*.

Discussion Questions

1. What are the major themes coming from the experts? Which theme is most important to you? Why?
2. List the reasons why the experts believe that John Dewey is relevant today. Do you agree with the list? Why or why not?
3. Why is there bipartisan support for NCLB despite the opinions of our experts?
4. In what ways did our experts interpret Dewey's notion of teaching to the whole child?
5. After reading the experts' responses, how would you define Deweyan democracy?

Further Reflection

1. Which contributors most reflect your opinion of NCLB? Why?
2. Interview an administrator or official from your local school district or school about the effects of NCLB. Does she or he agree with any of the educational experts from this chapter?

Chapter Nine

School Reform in New York City: The Impact of NCLB

The New York City Department of Education directs the largest school system in the United States. In the past decade, top officials, led by Chancellor Joel Klein, have instituted major reforms to bring a seemingly unwieldy conflagration of schools under central control. These reforms happened because of, and in some ways in spite of, NCLB with a movement toward standardizing the curriculum and building in accountability with high-stakes testing. Many of the structural and curricular changes were initiated by noneducators. For example, much of the curriculum was written by representatives of textbook companies. The homogenization of the curriculum and the teaching profession in general in New York City highlights many of the issues and challenges facing school districts around the nation as they grapple with the reality of applying business concepts to a public enterprise in a one-size-fits-all fashion. Moreover, it sheds light on how the legislation has affected the haves and have-nots in a richly diverse society. However, if history is any guide, democracy will most likely prevail in the end.

Focus Questions

1. How does NCLB fit within the historical context of school reform?
2. How would Dewey react to the passage of NCLB?
3. What is the future of NCLB?

In this second chapter of part two, chapter 9, we would like to focus on a major subtext of the "voices" presented in chapter 8, namely, NCLB as a reform movement. Three questions guided our thinking here:

1. How does NCLB fit within the historical context of school reform?
2. How does NCLB, within this historical context, affect Deweyan democracy?
3. Can we conjecture the future of high-stakes testing and the accountability movement based on an analysis of the preceding two questions?

In order to concretize our discussion we would like to select NCLB as a major reform that has received noteworthy attention nationally as a basis from which to direct our response to the aforementioned questions. Keeping Mirel's (1993) observation in mind that the "decline and fall of America's urban public school systems is the greatest educational tragedy of this century" (p. 408), we examine briefly reforms that have occurred in the New York City schools as an example of how NCLB has deeply affected reform movements, at least in big cities.

Although the particulars may vary, the New York City case is indicative of the impact of NCLB on school reform. Over eight years ago, massive reforms were introduced in New York City to restructure and reorganize the school system with a more centralized governance base. Reform efforts in New York City must be viewed within the context of national currents to standardize curriculum and calls for greater accountability via high-stakes testing.

Greater emphasis than ever before has been placed on raising student achievement scores on standardized tests in mathematics and reading, primarily. Much emphasis was initially placed on staff development in New York City in order to provide instructional support for teachers, especially in these aforementioned content areas. Curiously, such efforts have been sidelined; more on this later.

The current strain of urban politics, centralized governance, and bureaucratic mandates in New York City has gained national attention. Educators from many quarters are concerned with the presumed threat to academic freedom that has emerged from educational reform efforts established by administrative fiat by noneducators, many of whom have achieved prominence in business, politics, and other fields unrelated to education (New York City Department of Education, 2003).

Some critics have posited that the national stress many are experiencing seems to parallel threats to academic freedom, professional integrity, and sound educational practice—threats many feel must be challenged to protect democratic traditions. As John Dewey posited: "Since freedom of mind and freedom of expression are the root of all freedom, to deny freedom in education is a crime against democracy" (Dewey, 1936, cited in Nelson, 2003a, p. 66).

Textbook publishers who have supplied their books to schools have written some curriculum. Publishers, according to the New York City United Federation of Teachers (UFT), not only wrote curricula but also contributed to the standardized city tests to go with them. Other prepackaged curricula in literacy and mathematics have also been mandated for most of the city's public schools.

Prescribed, standardized curricula have not proven successful and are a detriment to good pedagogy (Slattery, 1995). Many fear that the de-skilling of teaching, the overemphasis on high-stakes testing, and efforts by noneducators to control curricula and pedagogy will further erode public confidence and support of education (Amrein & Berliner, 2003; McFayden, 2005).

Amrein and Berliner's (2002b) comprehensive study of high-stakes testing in 18 states finds relevance here. These 18 states were examined to determine the extent to which high-stakes testing programs benefited student learning. Data analyses revealed that high-stakes testing efforts were not increasing student learning.

Amrein and Berliner reported, "While a state's high-stakes test may show increased scores, there is little support in these data that such increases are anything but the result of test preparation and/or the exclusion of students from the testing process" (p. 1). The authors also discovered "numerous reports of unintended consequences associated with high-stakes testing policies (increased drop-out rates, teachers' and schools' cheating on exams, [and] teachers' defection from the profession" (p. 1).

The authors acknowledge some benefits of high-stakes testing that include

- Students and teachers need high-stakes tests to know what is important to learn and to teach.
- Teachers need to be held accountable through high-stakes tests to motivate them to teach better, particularly to push the laziest ones to work harder.
- Students work harder and learn more when they have to take high-stakes tests.
- Students will be motivated to do their best and score well on high-stakes tests.
- Scoring well on the test will lead to feelings of success, while doing poorly on such tests will lead to increased effort to learn.

Supporters of high-stakes testing also assume that the tests

- Are good measures of the curricula that are taught to students in our schools.
- Provide a kind of "level playing field," an equal opportunity for all students to demonstrate their knowledge.
- Are good measures of an individual's performance, little affected by differences in students' motivation, emotionality, language, and social status.

Finally, the supporters believe that

- Teachers use test results to help provide better instruction for individual students.
- Administrators use the test results to improve student learning and design better professional development for teachers.
- Parents understand high-stakes tests and how to interpret their children's scores.

Questioning the validity of these benefits by reviewing the literature, however, Amrein and Berliner (2002a) conclude "all of these statements are likely to be false a good deal of the time. And in fact, some research studies show exactly the opposite of the effects anticipated by supporters of high-stakes testing."

The authors then review current high-stakes testing practices in 22 states and indicate that schools have been censured for not meeting state cutoff standards, and administrators are held accountable, many of whom have been replaced. "In low performing schools," they say, "low scores also bring about embarrassment and public ridicule."

As a result of their extensive study they conclude:

> What shall we make of all this? At the present time, there is no compelling evidence from a set of states with high-stakes testing policies that those policies result in transfer to the broader domains of knowledge and skill for which high-stakes test scores *must* be indicators. Because of this, the high-stakes tests being used today do not, as a general rule, appear valid as indicators of genuine learning, of the types of learning that approach the American ideal of what an educated person knows and can do. . . .
>
> Both the uncertainty associated with high-stakes testing data, and the questionable validity of high-stakes tests as indicators of the domains they are intended to reflect, suggest that this is a failed policy initiative. High-stakes testing policies are not now and may never be policies that will accomplish what they intend. Could the hundreds of millions of dollars and the billions of person hours spent in these programs be used more wisely? Furthermore, if failure in attaining the goals for which the policy was created results in disproportionate negative affects on the life chances of America's poor and minority students, as it appears to do, then a high-stakes testing policy is more than a benign error in political judgment. It is an error in policy that results in structural and institutional mechanisms that discriminate against all of America's poor and many of America's minority students. It is now time to debate high-stakes testing policies more thoroughly and seek to change them if they do not do what was intended and have some unintended negative consequences, as well (2002a).

Later, Reese, Gordon, and Price (2004) surveyed 900 Texas teachers on their perceptions of high-stakes testing. Respondents were asked, in part, about the effects of a rigorous and consistent testing program on the school and its curriculum. Results indicated that increased efforts used to prepare students for high-stakes testing resulted in lower levels of student motivation, high levels of teacher and student anxiety, a dumbing down of the curriculum, and overuse of test-sophistication preparation materials in order to teach for the test, especially in low-performing schools.

The authors conclude that the "practice of teaching to the test through 'drill and kill' strategies is distressing in light of research that indicates authentic instruction, including 'higher order thinking,'" (p. 491) is so critical. The study, in sum, reflected great teacher dissatisfaction with high-stakes testing.

Our purpose here is not to conduct an in-depth analysis of the pros or cons of high-stakes testing. Rather, our purpose is to describe how such testing, reliance on overly rigid standards-driven reforms, and resultant accountability measures have impacted educational reform in New York City with particular attention to democratic thought and practice.

BACKGROUND AND THEORETICAL FRAMEWORK: HIGH-STAKES TESTING, STANDARDS, THE STRUGGLE FOR CURRICULUM RENEWAL IN NEW YORK CITY, AND CONSEQUENCES FOR DEMOCRACY IN EDUCATION

As part of the Children First Reform Agenda (CFRA) passed by the New York City Department of Education (NYCDOE), New York City public schools underwent a major structural reorganization. Four elements of the CFRA include

- Adoption of a single, coherent systemwide approach for instruction in reading, writing, and math that is supported by strong professional development;
- Establishment of a new parent support system to make schools more welcoming to students' families and to give families the access and tools they need to be full partners in the education of their children;
- Development of principals as the key instructional leaders of their schools through unprecedented leadership development programs at the new Leadership Academy; and
- Reorganization of the Department of Education's management structure into a unified, streamlined system dedicated to instruction and design to drive resources from bureaucratic offices into the classroom (www.nycboe .net/Administration/Childrenfirst/CFAgenda.htm).

Joel Klein, considered by many the most powerful city school chancellor in decades, was appointed head of the 1.1 million student school system. As a former antitrust lawyer, Klein, with the New York City mayor's backing, instituted radical changes to the then Board of Education. Forty school districts were replaced with regional divisions. Further, he mandated a new standard curriculum be adopted in all but 208 exempt (top performing schools), and fired scores of principals (*New York voices: Education reform*, 2003).

The aforementioned four elements of the CRFA have been met by mixed results in terms of their implementation. The first element, for instance, has met particularly strong opposition. McFayden (2005) reported some teacher opposition as follows:

> The principal of IS 230 in Queens gave stopwatches to math and English teachers this October to help keep their mini-lessons to the allotted 10 minutes. . . . These episodes encapsulate the rigidity, disrespect and obsession with picayune detail that drove a majority of staff in 95 schools in Region 4 to vote to present a letter of censure to [the] Superintendent. . . .
>
> "The pedagogical staff members in region 4 have been subjected to working in an atmosphere that stifles their professional judgment and impedes their ability to provide the safest environment and the best possible education for their students," the statement of censure said.
>
> The educators in the schools spelled out their concerns in the four page letter. Among the core issues were
>
> - The mandatory use of the "workshop model" for all lessons, particularly in secondary schools. . . .
> - The rigid interpretation of "flow of the day" and bulletin board policy.
> - Problems with Teachers College professional development, including the scheduling of training during teachers' instructional time and during their prep periods and lunches. (p. 3)

Efforts by business-minded noneducators such as Mayor Michael Bloomberg, schools Chancellor Joel I. Klein, and his staff find justification and authority within a larger national movement to standardize both what takes place in classrooms and in the ways colleges, schools, or departments of education prepare teachers (Cochran-Smith, 2003).

Teacher educators' and practicing school administrators' efforts are under assault by those business and political leaders who profess that they know better ways to nurture and develop the requisite knowledge, skills, and dispositions of future and current educators. Thomas Nelson (2003), editor of the *Teacher Education Quarterly*, recently lamented, "[P]eople in power who are clearly not experts in the field of education . . . control . . . what content is deemed appropriate and how that content is to be taught" (p. 3). He continues:

To believe that all students should be learning the same material in the same way at the same time (as seen in teachers using formula-based curriculum scripts written by others), taught by teachers who are prepared under the same exact standards (which are minimal at best), is to believe in the end of a truly public education system. (p. 4)

There have always been those who wish to standardize teaching and view learning in the narrowest sense. Unfortunately many educators, in particular, have not learned from the recent and distant past. Teaching cannot be standardized or reduced into ready-made recipes or prescriptions (Chomsky, 2002).

Teaching is a highly complex and contextual intellectual activity that challenges and engages learners with concrete experiences, intellectual discourse, and reflective thought. Qualified teachers understand that knowledge is temporary, socially constructed, culturally mediated, and developmental. Learning, from such a constructivist perspective, becomes a self-regulated process whereby students resolve their own cognitive conflicts with the keen guidance of teachers (Foote, Vermette, & Battaglia, 2001; Mintrop, 2002; Rodgers, 2002).

Apparently those individuals who call for accountability and favor high-stakes testing do not appreciate the complexities of teaching and learning (Neill, 2003; O'Day, 2002). Measuring student learning simplistically by relying predominantly on scores gleaned from standardized tests relegates teachers to mere technicians who simply deliver content to students. The consequences for supervision are similarly striking. Supervision, in this context, is relegated to an administrative function aimed at inspection rather than at improving instruction.

The position advocated here is not against raising expectations for student learning and improving teaching and supervisory practice in the classroom. Setting standards for performance and even using standardized tests as one measure, among many others, is warranted. Also warranted are efforts to weed out incompetent teachers. Teacher and school autonomy indeed must be earned by successful performance.

More serious though are those who misuse and abuse results from standardized tests and attempt to blame declines in reading and math scores on the shoulders of teachers and those who train them. Their motives are suspect because they appear not to understand the complexity of educational reform.

Jean Anyon (1997), scholar and educator, reminds us that school reform without social and economic reform is like washing air on one side of a screen door—it makes no sense and accomplishes nothing. The proposals offered by the mayor and chancellor are devoid of considering the complexity and encompassing nature of meaningful reform (Anyon, 1997; Mirel, 1993).

Larry Cuban (1993) demonstrates and reminds us that top-down driven change has not had a remarkable history.

In New York City, in particular, while top-down changes have been prolific, their staying power has been ephemeral (Ravitch, 1974). Reform efforts are likely to fail when reforms do not address the underlying bureaucratic structure of schooling and the social and economic structures that support them (Tyack, 1974). A prominent impediment, for example, to a collaborative, democratically functioning educational paradigm is the seemingly immutable, hierarchical, top-heavy bureaucracy that operates to stifle the autonomy and professionalism of members of a school system (Glanz, 1991).

Bureaucracy in New York City has a long, inglorious history, and reform efforts have paid scant attention to developing ways to mitigate its negative influences. Current proposals, couched to some degree in increased parental involvement and elimination of some bureaucratic and inefficient layers of bureaucracy, do not go far enough to dismantle a dysfunctional system of schooling.

Mirel's (1993) astute observation, cited earlier, that "urban schools are the most troubled part of the American educational enterprise" (p. vii) finds relevance here. Even a cursory examination of school systems in cities such as Chicago, San Francisco, and Atlanta (Hogan, 1985; Peterson, 1985; Weir, 1985) attest to the plethora of troubling reports including unparalleled dropout rates, uncontrolled student misbehavior, poor teacher morale, dearth of parental involvement, and declining student scores on standardized tests.

A history of urban education reveals competing ideological interests among teacher unions, school boards, other community members, politicians, and even federal and state courts. Such political contests did not bode well for urban schools and, especially, for students attending them. Interests of children seemed to always come second to vested political interests. Entrenched bureaucratic structures and policies, along with politics that do not consider needs of children first and foremost, contributed, in large measure, to the decay of urban schools in the twentieth century.

It was not always like that however. At the turn of the twentieth century the situation was not bleak. City schools, even in the 1940s and 1950s, enjoyed an excellent reputation for administrative efficiency and considerable levels of student achievement. The situation today, in contrast, is bleak. Acknowledging this view, Edson (1994) observed, "As the perceived quality of instruction and student achievement reach historic lows, public confidence in urban schools has eroded to the degree that some suggest that they are not worth saving" (p. 34).

Others have posited explanations for urban education's turmoil and misfortune (e.g., Mirel, 1993). Explanations range from racist assertions that urban schools deteriorated due to an increased presence of Black and other minorities, to appalling socioeconomic conditions, conservative politicians who eschewed the funding of social and educational programs, inequities in school finance, and continually changing curricular reforms.

Contributing, in part, to this discussion, this chapter examines the recently introduced reforms in New York City to reconfigure the urban school system with a more centralized governance base. Placing the current sweeping reform efforts in New York City in historical context, we point to the confluence of urban politics and entrenched school bureaucracy with efforts to improve education for 1.1 million students attending public schools.

Drawing on the national currents to standardize curriculum and recent calls for greater accountability via high-stakes testing, this chapter sharply criticizes the recent politically motivated reformers for ahistoricism, their imposition of business ideology to solve educational problems, and their myopic view of educational reform.

Educational standardization in New York City began when Chancellor Klein mandated a uniform curriculum for all but 208 of the city's schools in January and February, 2003. UFT president Randy Weingarten, who welcomed the mayor's control over urban schools (in large measure due to her greater distaste for central Board of Education officials and local school district administrators and principals—non-UFT members), complained that the New York City Department of Education (renamed for the Board of Education) had created an "artificial benchmark" to identify the "top" 208 city schools.

Weingarten reacted because the UFT was receiving complaints from parents and teachers whose schools were not on the list of schools exempt from the mandated curricula. The proposal to identify the top 208 city schools had unwittingly created an elite group of schools that not only will serve to further divide a troubled school system but might serve to exacerbate racial tensions in the city. After all, as we will highlight below, few, if any, of the schools included in the "top" list were minority.

The motivation for mandating a common school curriculum for most of New York City schools by Department of Education officials came from an analysis of declining standardized scores in reading and mathematics. Chancellor Klein's proposals are myopic because he based his decisions solely on examination of passing rates on standardized tests over a two-year period.

Decisions regarding the high schools were made from an analysis of passing rates on English and math Regents examinations. For the top schools, according to Klein, "it wouldn't make sense to impose a core curriculum on them" (Reifer, 2003, p. A1). School officials whose schools made the top list were elated.

In one, unnamed school, the principal disseminated a letter to the P.S. X Family as follows: "This honor is clearly a tribute to all teachers, paraprofessionals, support staff, and our assistant principals. . . . Your consciousness and dedication to your profession has brought success and honor to our school. . . . In closing, I would like to tell you how proud I am to be the principal of such a great school." One wonders how teachers and other support staff at schools that did not make the list might have felt.

Schools that did not make the list were mandated to follow various curriculum programs: "Month by Month Phonics" for grades K–3, published by Carson-Dellosa Publishing Co., Inc.; "Everyday Mathematics" for grades K–5, published by Everyday Learning and developed by the University of Chicago Mathematics Program; "Impact Mathematics" for grades 6–8, created by the authors of "Everyday Mathematics"; and "New York Math A: An Integrated Approach" for high school students, published by Prentice-Hall. Parenthetically, few, if any, studies are available to demonstrate the efficacy of these programs.

Critically important is the fact that a vast majority of the 208 top schools were from middle-class and wealthy neighborhoods of Manhattan, Brooklyn, Queens, and Staten Island. District 5 in Harlem and most of the Bronx were not included at all, nor were schools in East New York or the Ocean Hill-Brownsville sections of Brooklyn. The test scores in these schools were generally lower than the scores in middle-class schools on the list. For example, according to the *New York Times*, "at P.S. 33 in central Bronx, whose students are overwhelmingly poor, less than half passed standardized reading tests last year" (Goodnough & Medina, 2003, A1).

The national movement toward standards-based education, including high-stakes testing, has served to legitimize and bolster local reform proposals such as those mandated in New York City. Raising standards and promoting uniformity of curricular offerings to raise academic achievement has been a long-established reform proposal (Seguel, 1966).

Present efforts at establishing national or state standards should be viewed within a historic context. The first significant attempt to improve and "modernize" the American curriculum occurred in the 1890s. The Committee of Ten issued its report in 1892 under the leadership of Charles W. Eliot, the president of Harvard University. The committee sought to establish new curriculum standards for high school students. Standards were established to enable all students to receive a high-quality academic curriculum (Kliebard, 1987).

Notwithstanding the lofty aims of this committee, it wasn't until the establishment of the Commission on the Reorganization of Secondary Education that the school curriculum actually changed. The commission issued its report in 1918 and advocated a diversified curriculum that made allowances for a variety of curriculum "tracks" for the varied abilities of students. Known as the "Cardinal Principles of Education," the findings of this commission endorsed a differentiated curriculum that emphasized, in part, the importance of vocational training for a large segment of students (Krug, 1964).

During the first half of the twentieth century, the College Entrance Examination Board (formed in the 1890s), the Scholastic Aptitude Test (the first SAT was administered in 1926), and the American College Testing Program (established in 1959) were the guardians of standards, as applied to the academic curriculum. As a result of the Russian launch of the first artificial satellite (Sputnik) in 1957, American education was attacked vociferously.

Only months after the Sputnik launching, Congress passed the National Defense Education Act (NDEA), which poured millions of dollars into mathematics, sciences, and engineering. For several years following Sputnik, enrollments in high schools increased dramatically as did achievement scores in many academic areas. Academic standards, until this time, continued to be driven by levels of student achievement and assessed by national standardized tests (Ravitch, 1995).

By the mid-1960s, however, the American school curriculum shifted from an academic orientation to a nonacademic one. Prompted by political and social reforms, educational reformers reconsidered their longstanding emphasis on academic curriculum standards. The easing of high school graduation and college entrance requirements were just two of many effects of educational reforms during this tumultuous era.

Yet, by the late 1970s criticism of nonacademic curricula focused on declining SAT scores and what was perceived of as a general lowering of standards. With the election of Ronald Reagan in 1980, an era of unprecedented educational reform, focusing on a conservative political and educational agenda, was about to begin.

With the publication of the *A Nation at Risk: The Imperative for Educational Reform* report by the National Commission on Excellence in Education (1983), attention was drawn to the assertion that schools had lowered their standards too much and that American students were not competitive with their international counterparts. The authors of this 1983 report were perturbed by the fact that American schoolchildren lagged behind students in other industrialized nations.

The National Commission on Excellence in Education reported that, among students from various industrialized nations, U.S. students scored lowest on 7 of 19 academic tests and failed to score first or second on any test. Similar results were reported by the Educational Testing Service (1992). Moreover, the study found that nearly 40 percent of U.S. 17-year-olds couldn't perform higher-order thinking skills.

Pressure to improve the quality of American education by articulating con-crete standards for performance increased. Consequently, a spate of national and state reports continued through the 1980s, each advocating fundamental educational change. Commitment to democratic ideals and the influence of public education was reinforced once again in 1986 with the publication of a report sponsored by the Carnegie Foundation, *A Nation Prepared: Teachers for the 21st Century* (Carnegie Forum on Education and the Economy, 1986), and the Holmes (1986) report. The national curriculum reform movement was catapulted into prominence and action with the Education Summit held in 1989 by then President George Bush and state governors.

A year later, in his State of the Union Address, President Bush affirmed his commitment to excellence in education by establishing six national education goals to be achieved by the year 2000. Signed into law by Congress during the Clinton administration on March 31, 1994, Goals 2000 proclaimed, in part, that by the year 2000 "U.S. students will be first in the world in science and mathematics achievement" and "Every school will be free of drugs and violence and will offer a disciplined environment conducive to learning."

The adoption of national goals has been a major impetus for the increased attention to standards at the state level. In 1991, the U.S. Congress established the National Council on Educational Standards and Testing (NCEST) that encouraged educators and politicians to translate somewhat vague national goals into content curriculum standards. NCEST recommended that educa-tors establish specific standards in specific subject areas.

The National Council of Teachers of Mathematics (NCTM) led the way by publishing standards that quickly influenced textbook companies and testing agencies. These national curriculum reforms inevitably affected state educa-tional reforms. More than 40 states have revised their curricula to reflect the standards they established.

Continuing in the tradition of standards-based education, President George W. Bush signed into law the No Child Left Behind Act of 2001, a reauthori-zation of the Elementary and Secondary Education Act of 1965. The purpose of the new legislation was to redefine the federal role in K–12 education and to help raise student achievement, especially for disadvantaged and minor-ity students. Four basic principles were evident: stronger accountability for results, increased flexibility and local control, expanded options for parents, and an emphasis on teaching methods that presumably have been proven to work.

What can the history of standards-based education teach us about the cur-rent interest in revising curriculum and raising standards in New York City? Striking is the persistence of reform efforts and the influence of political and ideological agenda on national and state educational policies. Since the emergence of public education, attempts to improve curricular standards have abounded. Over the past hundred years or so, the American school curriculum has been influenced by different philosophies and ideological frameworks (Pinar, Reynolds, Slattery, & Taubman, 1995).

Yet, since the election of President Reagan in 1980, an essentialist and perennialist orientation has held sway in education that was not thwarted by the election and reelection of President Clinton. This ideological commitment, spurred on by conservative political alliances, explains why so much emphasis has been placed on a call for the return to traditional academic content, usually in the form of core curriculum standards.

With the exploding knowledge and information ages and the rapid changes in technology, a growing demand for internationally competitive workers placed inordinate pressures on schools. Schools have been continually pressured to confront society's economic and social crises.

Consequently, an advocacy for standards has been promulgated. Myopic stakeholders have not considered the complexities of school reform. Even Ravitch (1995), an advocate of standards, reminds us that "a system of standards . . . no matter how reliable, will not solve all the problems of American education. It will not substitute for the protection of a loving family, it will not guard children against the violence of the streets, it will not alleviate poverty, and it will not turn off the television at night" (p. 186).

Standards-based reform efforts have been criticized from many quarters for different reasons. Hostetler (2003), a teacher educator, laments our slavish adherence to standards. Overreliance on a "technicist conception of teaching," he says, is a detriment to sound pedagogy (p. 61). Smith and O'Day (1991) decry the emphasis on teaching-for-the-test practices among educators to meet specified standards.

Furthermore, they contend that standards-based reforms do not advocate assessment of complex thinking and problem solving but rather rely on assessments of lower-level skills. Amrein and Berliner (2003), in a wide-scale research study involving data collected in 18 states, criticize high-stakes testing for having a detrimental effect on student motivation and achievement. They say the current reform efforts by policy makers did not create high-stakes testing, but the No Child Left Behind Act of 2001 made it "more pervasive than ever before, mandating annual testing of students in grades 3–8 in reading and math" (p. 32).

The aim of federal legislators was that high-stakes tests would improve student motivation and achievement, yet the authors conclude that "the evidence shows that such tests actually decrease student motivation and increase the proportion of students who leave school early" (p. 32). Making the point even stronger, they state, "As we think about testing policies, we should remember the wisdom in the farmer's comment that weighing a pig every day won't ever make the pig any fatter. Eventually, you have to feed the pig" (p. 37).

The authors also assert, "Weighing or assessing may not work, but everyone looks busy doing it, and it costs much less than providing all students, including poor and minority students with high-quality preschools, small class sizes in the early grades, well-qualified teachers, adequate medical attention, and so forth" (p. 37). Those who recently criticized the Amrein and Berliner study, still, at best, conclude that evidence suggests that high-stakes testing "so far has had neither the dramatic beneficial effects hoped for by its proponents nor the catastrophic ones feared by its detractors" (Steinberg, 2002, p. 34). Democracy is best understood within this larger context.

CONCLUSION: DEWEYAN DEMOCRACY AND THE FUTURE OF NCLB

Perusal of comments by our survey respondents (see chapter 8) clearly indicates that John Dewey would consider NCLB anathema to the plight of maintaining and furthering the ideals of democracy. Respondents also indicate that NCLB, having bipartisan support in Congress, is likely to remain with us for some time.

Dewey's voice was muted in his own time. Nothing indicates that the situation is different now. Given the recent economic catastrophe, democracy has taken a further hit. Many align the vices of "unbridled freedoms" as a main cause for unrestrained capitalism, which led in turn to near economic collapse in America and around the world, especially among democratic nations. The future is bleak, or is it?

It is in times such as these that iconoclastic and idealistic thinking find expression. Opposition of NCLB and its concomitant effects resound from many quarters. Such undercurrents of dissent will, in our view, gain momentum in the years ahead as the effects of NCLB worsen.

Can we base our expectations on hard data? No, we cannot. Rather, our optimism is echoed in our understanding of historical trends accompanied by economic and political vicissitudes. What these circumstances are that have potential to alter the course of NCLB remain unclear. What is clear, however, is an abiding faith in those who believe in democracy.

Discussion Questions

1. Why is New York City's experience helpful for illuminating the challenges of NCLB?

2. What and who have driven the movement to reform New York City's school system?
3. The authors allege that the reforms are predicated on ahistoricism. What does that mean?
4. In what subjects and ways were the curricula standardized in New York City?
5. What does history teach us about the current reform efforts?

Further Reflection

1. In what ways does your own school experience reflect or differ from the changes outlined in this chapter?
2. Reflect on how politics drives school reform. Discuss the pros and cons.

Chapter Ten

Combating Poverty in Light of the Attack on Deweyan Democracy

It is false to claim that higher standards, more testing and accountability, and better school leadership can close the achievement gap. . . . They may be able to narrow it some; by how much remains to be determined.

—Rothstein (2004, p. 132)

When a quality education is denied to children at birth because of their parents' skin color or income, it is not only bad policy, it is immoral.

—Arthur E. Levine (Rothstein, 2004, p. x, preface)

Those who desire improvements in classroom learning must realize and acknowledge that school reform cannot easily succeed if it ignores the circumstances of their out-of-school lives.

—Rothstein (2004, p. 59)

Effective school reform must take into account poverty and social class. While principals cannot control all aspects of the external environment, they can develop enhanced school-community relations to combat some of the deleterious effects of poverty. Seizing on the suggestions of author Richard Rothstein (2004), this chapter presents recommendations for principals establishing partnerships with other social agencies within the community to tackle problems such as learning deficits. Because NCLB does nothing to address systemic poverty, and in fact promotes a market approach to educational reform that may, in the long run, exacerbate social inequalities, the principal's role in establishing community partnerships is crucial for providing the highest quality of education to all students regardless of socioeconomic background.

Focus Questions

1. How does poverty affect schools?
2. What is the connection between poverty and NCLB?
3. What might Dewey advise us today in terms of combating poverty?
4. What strategies or programs are you familiar with to combat poverty?

We find Richard Gibboney's (2008) scathing critique of NCLB compelling and most relevant in light of providing an example of an onerous way in which Deweyan democracy is further eroded. Gibboney claims that "unchecked capitalism is destroying our nation's public schools, and NCLB is the final nail in their coffin" (p. 21). He further asserts that use of accountability stringencies by "right-wing, pro-business forces" has been "willfully undermining the democratic right of all children to a free, high-quality education" (p. 21).

Gibboney (2008) decries punitive efforts by schools under NCLB aimed to disenfranchise "poverty-stricken cities" that fail "to work educational miracles." In doing so, he continues, "they are eroding the promise of our democracy" (p. 21). It is misbegotten, he says, to expect schools to close an achievement gap based on economic inequalities. He states:

> Most children at the bottom of the economic ladder start their formal education years behind middle-class children in language development, social behavior, and general knowledge of the world. . . . No system of schools—public or private—has ever demonstrated that it can close this poverty-induced learning gap for most children. (p. 22)

Then why, he queries, have the "corporate elite and their political allies" placed inordinate "pressure on schools with a harsh accountability system"? (p. 22). Gibboney unabashedly places blame on the nation's educators who "have stood by and let all this happen. He explains: "Instead of relying on the energizing principles of democracy—equity, opportunity, and fairness—to fight this law and the mindset it grows out of, educators have taken political and professional cover in technicalities" (p. 22).

After lambasting unions and educational groups, Gibboney draws his attention to the work of Dewey and the extent to which we have "abandoned" his ideals. Dewey, he explains, feared that "without intelligent vigilance, the few would take over from the many, the rich would dominate the poor, and the common good would be replaced by plutocratic corporate private interest."

More starkly, he says plainly,

> Sadly, Dewey's fears are being realized. I can only conclude that educators have been seduced by the viewpoint that considers only the economic value

of schooling as a training ground for workers and not the centrality of public education of the survival of democracy. In the endless parade of education "reforms," a focus on technical skills has replaced the pursuit of leads, democratic ideals, and civic courage. (p. 24)

We think that many of the respondents to our survey quoted earlier in chapter 8 would concur with Gibboney's assessment that NCLB is not only a technical or political problem, but, at its most fundamental level, a "grave threat to democracy and public education" (p. 24). Quoting economist Duncan Foley, he says "capitalism creates income inequality, tolerates poverty, and is hostile to the physical and democratic environment" (p. 23). We must, he reiterates, preserve our democratic ideals.

THE CASE OF POVERTY: RECOMMENDATIONS

One in eight children never graduates from high school. Two in five never complete a single year of college, and every nine seconds a public high school student drops out of school. We spend more money on prisoners than we do to educate our children. Barriers to learning include increased levels of violence, teen pregnancies, depression, eating disorders, sleeping disorders, not having a family member who cares, and so forth. Good teaching is certainly necessary, but it's not enough.

Research has demonstrated that social class differences affect student achievement (Rothstein, 2004). Rothstein explains that "parents of different social classes often have different styles of childrearing, different ways of disciplining their children, different ways of communicating expectations, and even different ways of reading to their children" (p. 2). Although he admits that these social class differences "do not express themselves consistently or in the case of every family" (p. 2), patterns or family tendencies on the average can be noted. He explains further:

That there would be personality and childrearing differences, on average, between families in different social classes makes sense when you think about it: If upper-middle-class parents have jobs where they are expected to collaborate with fellow employees, create new solutions to problems, or wonder how to improve their contributions, they are more likely to talk to their children in ways that differ from the ways of lower-class parents whose own jobs simply require them to follow instructions without question. Children who are raised by parents who are professional will, on average, have more inquisitive attitudes toward the material presented by their teachers than will children who are raised by working-class parents. As a result, no matter how competent the teacher, the academic achievement of lower-class children will, on average, almost inevitably be less than that of middle-class children. The probability of this reduced achievement increases as the characteristics of lower-social-class families accumulate. (p. 2)

He goes on to explain that these social and economic realities can impact student learning. "Lower-class children, on average, have poorer vision than middle-class children, . . . have poorer oral hygiene, more lead poisoning, more asthma, poorer nutrition, less adequate pediatric care, more exposure to smoke" (p. 3), and the list continues. All these conditions affect learning, as Rothstein documents brilliantly in his groundbreaking book.

Rothstein goes on to highlight other social class characteristics that can affect student achievement. For instance, inadequate housing facilities (e.g., lower-class children are more likely to live in transitory housing accommodations that can lead to poorer attendance rates in school) is an important social factor to consider. Another factor is wealth. Black students from low-income families fare poorer than their White counterparts, for instance. Rothstein explains:

It is easier to understand this pattern when we recognize that children can have similar family incomes but be ranked differently in the social class structure, even in economic terms: black families with low income in any year are likely to have been poor for longer than white families with similar income in that year. White families are likely to own far more assets that support their children's achievement than are black families at the same current income level. (p. 3)

In sum, Rothstein posits, children from lower-class families will likely exhibit lower achievement levels than middle-class children. He argues that much of this academic difference in achievement can be attributed to social class characteristics. Rothstein links cultural characteristics with social factors. Cultural differences, for instance, as reflected in the value of education, are rooted in social and economic conditions experienced by students from lower classes. He explains: "[B]lack students may value education less than white students because a discriminatory labor market has not historically rewarded black workers for their education—but values persist independently and outlast the economic circumstances that gave rise to them" (p. 4).

Underscoring Rothstein's emphasis on social and economic factors that affect achievement is the premise that good teaching, high expectations, rigorous standards, accountability, and inspiration are not enough to close the Black-White achievement gap. Although these in-school factors can go a long way toward closing the gap, by themselves they are inadequate. Teachers cannot go it alone. Despite best efforts some students will not succeed.

They will not succeed, in all likelihood, due to social and economic forces beyond the immediate control of a school. Rothstein cautions his readers:

> Readers should not misinterpret this emphasis as implying that better schools are not important, or that school improvement will not make a contribution to narrowing the achievement gap. Better school practices can probably narrow the gap. School reform, however, is not enough. (p. 9)

If social and economic factors play a considerable role in helping to narrow that gap so that all students can learn to the best of their abilities, a critical question must be raised for the school principal. What role do principals play in school and community to narrow this gap and help ensure that all students achieve their academic potential? But of equal importance is the question: What can principals do to influence factors external to the school via school-community relations that might also contribute to narrowing this achievement gap?

In other words, school-community relations may play a critical role in influencing social agencies, for instance, to play a significant role in assisting school officials (principals, teachers, and counselors) to help each child learn to the best of her or his ability. Clearly, principals cannot influence certain factors such as parental income levels or access to adequate living quarters.

But, through the use of an effective campaign of school-community relations a principal can bring to bear a number of social agencies through partnerships. Principals can also strengthen after-school programs to provide needed assistance. Although educators cannot, by themselves, raise achievement of lower-class children, they can do much via school-community program development and services.

The following best practices are based on Rothstein's research and suggestions.

Best Practice #1: School-Community Clinics

According to Rothstein (2004), "Without fully adequate health care for lower-class children and their parents, there is little hope of fully closing the achievement gap" (p. 138). Principals therefore can assist, although not completely solve this problem, by making connections with local health-care facilities to establish a health clinic at the school to serve children from disadvantaged homes.

Principals can familiarize themselves with health services in general by consulting these websites: www.mayoclinic.com/; www.narhc.org/; www.1-800-schedule.com/; and others. Principals may visit a local health clinic, establish rapport with local officials, and reach out to local politicians for assistance. Also, providing family health support is an added way that the school can contribute to the health of students and families attending the school. Rothstein (2004) explains the kind of services that could be included:

> Clinics associated with schools in lower-class communities should include obstetric and gynecological services for pregnant and postpartum women, pediatric services for children through their high school years, physicians to serve parents of all school-age children, nurses to support these medical services, dentists and hygienists to see both parents and children semi-annually, optometrists and vision therapists to serve those who require treatment for their sight, social workers to refer families to other services, community health educators, and psychologists or therapists to assist families and children who are experiencing excessive stress and other emotional difficulties. (pp. 138–139)

Some would argue that such programs could be costly. According to Rothstein (2004), "[P]utting dental and vision clinics in schools serving low-income children would cost only about $400 per pupil. . . . This is a lot less money than is often proposed for school reforms like teacher professional development or class size reduction. Schools might get a bigger test score jump, for less money, from dental and vision clinics than from more expensive instructional reforms" (p. 139).

Best Practice #2: Early Childhood Education Centers

The importance of early childhood education in terms of establishing the necessary prerequisites for future student and, even, adult learning is axiomatic. Rothstein (2004) advocates extending early childhood services. Principals can help educate parents in their community about the importance of early childhood education. Rothstein suggests

> [s]etting up early childhood education centers and services. Research demonstrates that formal education experiences for low-income children that begin at six-months of age and continues throughout the pre-school years can play a significant role in advanced student achievement in later years of schooling. (specific research cited by Rothstein, 2004)

What can principals do to ensure that children come prepared to learn?

Forward thinking school-community principal leaders will reach out to parents of the community to make them aware of such programs. Affiliations or collaborations with local churches, civic associations, or health centers will give principals access to parents of preschool children in order to share such information. Serving as guest lecturers, principals can review with parents the plethora of early childhood research that demonstrates the impact of toddler and preschool experiences on academic achievement in school.

Principals can explain to them that day-care settings do not offer the necessary enrichment their children will need to succeed. Formal early childhood programs are more content rich and are usually staffed with licensed, credentialed teachers. Rothstein (2004) states, "To narrow the achievement gap later in life, lower-class toddlers probably should begin early childhood programs at six months of age, and attend for a full day" (p. 140). The principal can also serve as an advocate in interactions with local politicians to urge them to support such early childhood programs.

Best Practice #3: After-school Programs

Research demonstrates consistently that structured after-school programs contribute to narrowing the achievement gap (Rothstein, 2004). Fashola's (2002) in-depth treatment of after-school programs provides a rationale for their importance, cites examples of effective programs, and offers concrete suggestions for implementation. Fashola highlights the following benefits of attending such programs in concise fashion:

- Improves academic performance across content areas
- Provides academic enrichment
- Offers social, cultural, and recreational activities

Too often, however, these programs lack academic rigor and become little more than "baby-sitting" services. Moreover, these after-school programs are usually disconnected to curricula offered during the regular school day. Principals can do much here by solidifying this connection thus ensuring continuity between day and after-school programs.

Moreover, the principal can and should insist that such programs and activities meet the highest academic standards in curriculum and instruction. Principals can offer supervision (Sullivan & Glanz, 2009) to these after-school programs so that highest standards of instruction are maintained. Certainly, some might argue that to suggest that already overworked principals should oversee after-school programs is as much impractical as it is idealistic.

Still, school-community leadership that is aimed at comprehensive reforms in and out of school, even before and after school, is more likely to have a lasting impact on closing the achievement gap and thus ensuring high achievement for all students. As transformation school-community leaders, principals must take the assertive stance by either paying attention to these after-school programs that can, when done well, support during-the-day instruction in the school, or work toward creating effective after-school programs. Fashola (2002) identifies the following steps in creating after-school programs:

- Create and conduct a needs assessment.
  As principal, you can proactively assess community-school needs by speaking with parents, teachers, students, and other community partners to ascertain the specific academic needs of students who attend after-school programs. For instance, for students who do not possess computers at home, after-school workshops or classes can be offered to teach students PowerPoint, databasing, and word processing. A needs assessment, conducted in various ways, can provide substance and guidance for such programs. Fashola cautions educators to involve all parties in designing such programs. He explains:

  > For example, a program might decide to create a well-rounded, after-school program and set the hours of the program from 2:30 p.m. to 5 p.m., but forget to consult with the parents of the students. This could be a problem because of the hours of operation. Parents may like the program and actually be in need of the services, but the hours of operation could be a hindrance to the participation of the students. Involving parents in the goals by setting sessions that address stakeholders' wants, needs, and concerns would encourage the program to address transportation issues by either extending the hours of the program or by providing some transportation option for the participants. (pp. 58–59)

- Create committees and execute goals.
  Establishing goals is critical to a program's success. Solicit involvement from interested parties. Fashola explains:

  > For example, if one of the goals was to improve the reading skills of students, the academics committee—headed by a staff member with training in the area of reading programs—would be responsible for the curriculum, materials, and training of other staff members. (p. 59)

- Create the components.
  Many decisions have to be made about the program, including, among others, who will attend, who will serve as staff, what funding is required, how to recruit, train, and retain staff, and so on. Fashola identifies three major components that need attention during program implementation: academic, recreational, and cultural. Only the academic component is alluded to below since such programs have the most direct impact on student achievement levels in order to narrow the achievement gap.

  Fashola states: "The school or community center must decide whether the goal of its academic component is to improve the school-day performance of children through activities tied to the school curriculum, through enrichment activities, or through both" (p. 60). He goes on to say that careful attention to hiring qualified educators to teach in the program should be a top priority. Research that Fashola reviews indicates that successful after-school academic programs have "clear goals, well-developed procedures for attaining those goals, and extensive professional development" (p. 61).

Establishing meaningful and content-rich after-school programs in the school can go far toward making an academic difference. Proactive principals pay attention to as many factors that affect student achievement as possible. The school-community leader realizes the important value of such an effort.

Educational leaders need to reinvest in the idea of a democratic purpose of education. In other words, educational policy must reflect a democratic theory of education, and that such theory should guide policy is axiomatic. The cultivation of democratic ideals is the end-all. If we had such a theory educators would not wallow in mediocrity and remain vulnerable to the vicissitudes of politics and interest groups. Dewey's work, as relevant as ever, is a critical guidepost.

CONCLUSION

As a society we have not been willing to commit to fundamental change to provide the highest quality education to all students regardless of socioeconomic background. Educational reform, although important, is inadequate, by itself, to meet the needs of all students. Current proposals, couched to some degree in increased parental and community involvement and elimination of some bureaucratic and inefficient layers of administration, do not go far enough to dismantle a dysfunctional system of schooling.

So what can principals do? Principals should serve as transformative school-community leaders. Young (2004) affirms such a role for the principal. "Principals must be accountable to their communities and make citizens aware of the inadequacies and unfairness of a system that continually privileges the rich over the poor." He continues, "Principals have the social power and influence to make a difference." He concludes by admonishing principals to "speak up and make people aware of the realities we know so well" (p. 109).

Principals of the twenty-first century are no longer merely maintainers and sustainers of the status quo. As school-community leaders, principals' moral commitment to ensuring the highest educational opportunities for all students is more critical than ever. Principals remain committed to doing everything and anything in their power to support high achievement for all students.

They rally educational and social support, even political, to raise the consciousness of the school community and the community at large to engage in comprehensive reform. As school-community leaders, principals are staunch spokespersons for justice, equity, and opportunity for all. Such thinking is founded on developing a comprehensive and democratic theory of education, as advocated by John Dewey.

Discussion Questions

1. How do economic inequalities relate to school reform?
2. Articulate how social class relates to school preparedness. Of all the factors, which is the most important to you for school success?
3. Describe the importance of the principal for affecting schoolwide changes.
4. What solutions does Rothstein provide for narrowing the achievement gap?
5. How does democracy fit in with these recommendations?

Further Reflection

1. What objections do you foresee to these recommendations?
2. Brainstorm other societal challenges that may also affect the achievement gap. How would you address these challenges?

Part Three

THE DEWEY SCHOOLS

Chapter Eleven

Democracy and Education for All Children

The whole boy goes to school; therefore school should stimulate his whole being.

—Aikin (1942, p. 17)

Dewey's influence was massive. His thinking fed directly into many American schools, particularly in Chicago where one of Dewey's associates eventually became superintendent of schools.

—Darling (1994, p. 32)

The recognition that schools—as communities—offer hope and possiblility, and intellectual competence, especially for those families who live lives of quiet despair, is particularly needed. Children have never been reared in more anonymous and estranged settings—divorced from the adult communities beyond immediate families and like-minded peers, and voracious media that feed their narrowest narcissism. The sheer neighborliness that once went with public schools—even the interchangeable ones—no longer comes naturally. Schools must literally help create communities, rather than expect to live off them.

—Meier (2000, p. ix)

Beginning with Dewey's laboratory school at the University of Chicago in the late nineteenth century, dozens of private schools around the United States have embraced Dewey's progressive education, some for over 100 years. In the 1970s, innovative and daring educators advocated for a similar democratic-style education for marginalized and at-risk, inner-city youths. With the creation of Central Park East Elementary School in New York City in 1974, a movement was launched to value and develop the interests of mainly poor, Hispanic, and Black students in an effort to combat high dropout levels, low achievement, and abysmal graduation rates. The success of Central Park East spawned the creation of similar schools and eventually led to an international movement to bring Dewey's ideals to the masses.

Focus Questions

1. What makes Dewey's philosophy democratic?
2. What are some established practices in schools that promote democratic learning today?
3. What type of interests do students bring to school?
4. Why do you believe some private schools adopted Dewey's philosophy and practices long before any public schools?

——— ✿ ———

One of the lasting impressions made on the young John Dewey was the drudgery and boredom associated with his traditional primary and secondary education. Dewey began his education in Burlington, Vermont, at the age of seven shortly after the U.S. Civil War had ended and life in most places was attempting to return to some state of normalcy.

As one of Dewey's biographers described, because of the Civil War, conditions "had deteriorated to a degree little short of scandalous. Crowded classrooms, low standards, lax discipline, irregular attendance, poorly prepared teachers, run-down school buildings were the general rule" (Dykhuizen, 1959, pp. 518–519). In his second year of attending school, the district had managed to improve conditions considerably.

When he entered high school in 1872, at the age of 12, Dewey selected the college course of study over the English plan, because he had some interest in furthering his education beyond high school. The college preparatory course incorporated an emphasis on the classics such as Latin and Greek, together with mathematics, English literature, and a few electives (Dykhuizen, 1959).

Despite evidence that Dewey was a student of high achievement, much of what he experienced during his grade school and high school years was based on a traditional system of memorization and recitation, something that Dewey repugnantly recalled numerous times in his justification for a new type of democratic education (Dewey, 1913, 1938, 2001, 1916/2007a, 1910/2007b).

Dewey's education also represented more than drudgery to him; he viewed traditional ideas and practices of pedagogy and curriculum as a means to preserve the power and institutions of a bygone era. In *Democracy and Education* (1916/2007a), he waxed, "The philosophy of learning has been duly dominated by a false psychology. It is frequently stated that a person learns by merely having the qualities of things impressed upon his mind through the gateway of the senses" (p. 27).

And when addressing the traditional curriculum he further lamented, "Nowhere, however, is there greater danger that subject matter will be accepted as appropriate educational material simply because it has become customary to teach and learn it" (p. 158). And as he systematically presented his reform case offering arguments to why traditional education was antithetical to a modern democracy, he masterfully concluded, "Since custom and traditionary beliefs held men in bondage, the struggle of reason for its legitimate supremacy could be won only by showing the inherently unstable and inadequate nature of experience" (p. 194).

And it was from a quality experience characterized by instability and inadequacy—and facilitated with the expertise of an effective teacher—that students made meaning in a social context as explained in some detail in chapter 5. Dewey's philosophy of democratic education has been embraced by nearly every educational institution in the world to some degree, but some have embraced it more than others.

While progressive education—or the "New Education," as Dewey referred to it—has existed in some private schools for over 100 years, it was not until the 1970s that poor and marginalized students had the opportunity to immerse themselves in this democratic type of learning in public schools. Central Park East in New York City was the first alternative school dedicated to bringing Dewey's ideals to poor, inner-city youth. Today, the school has managed to stay true to its mission and flourish in the era of high-stakes testing.

DEWEY'S LABORATORY SCHOOL

It would be a mistake to underestimate how much John Dewey influenced the educational system in the United States, and perhaps even the world. From his university appointments, he commanded great respect and gravitas. He was a prolific author throughout his long lifetime and frequent speaker both within the United States and abroad.

When he established the first laboratory school at the University of Chicago, his pragmatic ideals rippled across the city of Chicago, and then radiated to distant places. The idea of starting a school for experimental purposes connected with an institution for higher education was a novel idea that the president of the University of Chicago, William R. Harper, enthusiastically embraced. In fact, as Tanner (1997) remarked,

> Everything new seemed to be happening at the new University of Chicago in the 1890s. Never before had there been such a department in an American university.

College professors in pedagogy, teachers in normal schools, city school supervisors, and superintendents either had to begin their work with inadequate preparation or study in Germany. (p. 16)

In January of 1896 the school opened with 16 students between the ages of six and nine. When Dewey left the school in 1904, enrollment had increased to 140 students with a total of 33 teachers and staff members. More significantly, the school had launched a movement within the United States to change education forever.

Although learner-centered education was not new to the history of Western civilization, and indeed even to the United States, the unification and scope of ideas emanating from Dewey's school are extensive. Tanner (1997) culled a list of 25 lessons learned from the school where at least some—if not most—are evident in every school in America:

1. It is organized as a social community; children are learning in the active setting of a miniature community.
2. There is a developmental curriculum that begins in kindergarten with children's natural interests and abilities.
3. The curriculum has two dimensions, the child's side (activities) and the teacher's side (facts and generalizations in the major fields of knowledge).
4. The teachers are specialists in their subject fields.
5. The social significance of subject matter is brought out in instruction.
6. Children have hands-on experiences in the manual arts.
7. Children are engaged in solving real problems, past and present. The subjects in the curriculum are integrated in the way that they work and are synthesized in the real world.
8. There is a powerful organizing vertical theme.
9. Curriculum thought is vertical; teachers have a longitudinal view of the curriculum.
10. Teachers work together in planning theme-related activities.
11. Teachers confer frequently, informally and formally.
12. The school is imbued with a test-and-see (experimental) attitude.
13. The curriculum is continually being developed and plans are modified as new difficulties and potentials are found.
14. There is a close relationship with a university.
15. Classes are small enough to give individual attention to each child.
16. The child's attention is self-impelled.
17. Regarding discipline, appropriate behavior is determined by the nature of the work to be done.

18. In the case of individual discipline problems, the child is redirected into a different activity with the same objective.
19. Younger groups begin the day by reviewing what was accomplished the day before and planning the day's work cooperatively; older children start right in on their independent projects.
20. Children are free to move around in the room and seek help from others.
21. The teacher is viewed by the children as a fellow worker in the activities in progress instead of as an all-powerful ruler.
22. Children are developing habits of cooperation and service to the community.
23. Teachers support the child's aspirations.
24. The school takes advantage of cultural and educational institutions in the community to enrich the curriculum and children's lives; Dewey's idea that there is no lower or higher education, just education, is in operation.
25. The children are happy. (pp. 177–178)

Remembering that these lessons were considered quite radical in early twentieth-century America, combined with the fact that local entities governed the schools, in the immediate aftermath of the school's origins the effects were felt most acutely around Chicago and other urban centers. Moreover, grass-roots initiatives emerged around the United States creating places such as the School of Organic Education in Fairhope, Alabama, and the Presidio High School in San Francisco, California.

In the early twentieth century, Dewey's ideas were encapsulated in the Progressive Education reform movement, which over the ensuing decades, sometimes triumphed in the public consciousness, and at other moments, suffered from the perception of promoting lax standards, weak rigor, and general academic decay.

From the beginning, the schools that adopted progressive principles were private organizations that served mostly affluent students. However, beginning in the 1960s and into the 1970s, a new reform movement coalesced around the notion of child-centered instruction in public schools for poor and marginalized students predicated on progressive ideals and calls for social justice and equity.

PROGRESSIVE EDUCATION

Shortly before the commencement of World War I, Dewey's daughter, Evelyn, visited experimental schools around the United States in preparation for *Schools of To-morrow* (1915), a book she coauthored with her father. Dewey wrote about visiting only one school, so it was most likely Evelyn who traveled down to Fairhope, Alabama, to investigate the School of Organic Education founded in 1907 by a former Minnesota school teacher, Marietta Johnson.

Together with other schools sprouting up around the United States such as the Cottage School in Riverside, Illinois, the Organic School of Education was one of the first progressive schools following Rousseau's child-centered philosophy and practicing Dewey's pragmatic instrumentalism. Rousseau was the first widely read philosopher who advocated for the natural development of the child, to which Dewey and his daughter explained, "It meant that education is not something to be forced upon children and youth from without, but is the growth of capacities with which human beings are endowed at birth" (p. 2).

Nestled within the utopian community of Fairhope, Alabama, situated along the eastern shore of Mobile Bay, Marietta Johnson, with the encouragement of friends and family, opened the doors to the School of Organic Education. Populated mainly by progressive Midwesterners, Fairhope formed in 1894 as a socialist colony predicated on a "single tax," meaning that the colony owned the land and the settlers paid rents on 99-year leases to finance parks and public services.

Within this receptive and tolerant environment, Mrs. Johnson named her school, "organic," because it allowed for the natural development of the child. She not only shunned the graded curriculum, but she also banned the use of a numbered grading system. Instead, the school employed the term "life classes," which corresponded roughly with childhood periods of development. Specifically, she created the primary life class to correspond with the ages of 8 and 9 years; the secondary for those of 11 and 12 years of age; and the subsequent designations as high school (Dewey & Dewey, 1915; Newman, 1997).

The concept of life classes also implied another motive, which was the idea that students did not fail the graded curriculum at the Organic School because it did not exist. Children were not forced to study, do homework, nor did they take traditional examinations. Rather, through their natural interests and inclinations they embarked on various investigations. Mrs. Johnson believed that following a natural path led to a love of learning, and increased motivation to perform in school, overall. As Dewey and Dewey (1915) observed,

> At Fairhope the children do the work, and the teacher is there to help them to know, not to have them give back what they have memorized. Tests are often conducted with the books open, since they are not to show the teacher what the child can remember, but rather to discover his progress in ability to use books. Lessons are not assigned, but the books are open in the hands of the pupils and

with the teacher they discuss the text, getting out of it all the joy and informa-tion possible. This stimulates a real love of books, so that these children, who have never been assigned a lesson to study, voluntarily study the text after the class work. They are not tempted to cheat, for they are not put in the position of having to show off. (pp. 28–29)

According to the authors, this system resulted in motivated students with minimal discipline problems. Likewise, as Dewey was to articulate in minute detail in *Democracy and Education*, which was originally published in 1916 only one year after the publication of *Schools of To-morrow*, the teachers at the Organic School used social occupations as a vehicle for creating meaning-ful and quality learning experiences juxtaposed in the natural world.

Within the natural environment children played, exercised, and most im-portantly, learned in the spirit of democratic community and mutual coop-eration. Undoubtedly, Marietta Johnson learned some things from Dewey's laboratory school and copious writings, and at the same time, Dewey discov-ered a vibrant validation of his philosophical musings. Further, Dewey and Johnson were to form a lifelong alliance by becoming founding members of the Progressive Education Association.

DEWEY AND THE PROGRESSIVE EDUCATION MOVEMENT

The book Dewey and his daughter coauthored, *Schools of To-morrow* (1915), proved to be immensely successful and popular. Within a decade of its publi-cation, it was reprinted 14 times and helped to establish Dewey as a national leader of the somewhat ubiquitous progressive education movement, which meant many things to many different types of people from the settlement house movement to the reform of city governments.

In education, progressive reform manifested as a revolt against the formal, traditional curriculum and instruction. With the entry of the United States into World War I at about the same time as the publication of the Deweys' book, disparate reform elements united to form the Progressive Education Association in 1919, and John Dewey emerged as its most influential speaker (Cremin, 1959).

In the 1920s a new brand of progressive reformist emerged, and whereas Dewey had critically linked education reform to democracy, this new type of reformist connected education improvement to self-expression and creativity, part of an ideological current roaring throughout the decade. Implicit in this new approach was the centrality of the child's interests and the perception that adult guidance interfered with those interests.

Dewey vociferously objected, or as Cremin (1959) wrote, "Baby, Dewey insisted, does not know best!" (p. 166). In fact, while Dewey considered his new education child-centered, he also defended the necessity of a formal curriculum and the crucial role for teachers in providing and guiding children through learning experiences. Ironically, when Dewey's ideas came under attack throughout his lifetime and beyond, particularly in the 1960s and 1970s, the attacks were attributed to his critics' lack of understanding of what Dewey meant by interests (Pring, 2007).

According to Dewey, interests were not temporary whims; they were something the child controlled. Further, they were part of a child's natural being, something to be nurtured, not suffocated. Additionally, interests were explored in a social environment in the pursuit of activities.

And while younger children have a limited number of interests, Dewey believed it was the teacher's responsibility—and indeed, moral obligation—to expand those interests drawing on professional expertise and the teacher's lifetime of wider experiences. Dewey's version of child-centered education was much different from that of the progressive reformists of the 1920s, who considered teacher interventions an impediment to natural growth (Pring, 2007).

During the 1930s, while the Great Depression enveloped the world, a more radical progressive reform element came into vogue. Again, Dewey emerged as a leading proponent of a moderately collaborative form of democratic education, which prepared young people for community life, and with even more emphasis, advocated for social progress at a time of immense deprivation and suffering.

Further, according to Dewey, in a complex industrial society such as the United States, schools would never be the decisive factor for any kind of meaningful political, social, or economic upheaval. Rather, teachers could harness the power of the forces changing society by identifying new scientific discoveries, technologies, and other types of forces to aid social progress.

Clearly, Dewey had in mind his theory of learning based on social occupations and teachers creating qualitative and continuous experiences for learning. He was attacked by both extremes: traditionalists accused him of betraying the truths of the past, and radical progressive reformers attacked him for advocating adult interference with children's natural interests (Cremin, 1959).

In 1938, Dewey published *Experience and Education*, a recapitulation of the main points of *Democracy and Education* (1916/2007a), which he had written over two decades earlier. As Cremin (1959) described, "By 1938, Dewey the sensitive observer could already note, probably with a measure of sadness, that the movement was devoting too much of its energy to internecine ideological conflict and too little, perhaps, to the advancement of its own cause" (p. 169). Dewey, the affected observer, praised the new education labeled "progressive" and also warned of lurking dangers over the rest of his lifetime.

In one of his final publications shortly before his death in 1952, he lauded changes in pedagogy that took into account the interests of children as well as the more affectionate relationship between students and teachers. At the same time, he warned of the potential dangers of formalizing the ideals and goals of the progressive education movement, which was built on the whole notion of embracing changes and rejecting formalistic rigidity, something that could degenerate into a means for subjugating others and threatening the very foundations of democracy (Cremin, 1959).

Throughout the decades following his death, he became a symbol of reform, and at the same time, a symbol of everything that went wrong with education. His name inexplicably became attached to the child-centered movement in the 1960s that came under conservative attack here and abroad, most notably in England (Darling, 1994; Pring, 2007).

Since the establishment of Dewey's laboratory school in 1896, pockets of progressive schools flourished around the United States as private institutions more likely to serve students with comfortable or wealthy, politically liberal parents. However, with the rise of the socially conscious 1960s and the accompanying ideological forces attacking poverty and racism, liberal reformers advocated for progressive education for inner-city students, who were often poor and mainly of color.

DEMOCRATIC EDUCATION FOR DISADVANTAGED AND MARGINALIZED STUDENTS

Rising above the malaise of early-1970s New York City, some brave educators and parents dared to challenge existing norms that poor children were doomed to live lives of poverty and engage in substandard learning. The War on Poverty, began under the Johnson administration in the 1960s, was based on the assumption that poverty must be solved before other social ills could be attacked, including the myriad problems of inner-city schools such as violence, high dropout rates, and low achievement levels.

Beginning with the establishment of Central Park East in 1974, a movement was launched to educate the whole student in places where many thought it would not be possible. Today, Central Park East is thriving under NCLB, and the movement has blossomed to include networks of schools at all levels around the United States.

Central Park East Elementary School in New York City

Central Park East (CPE) Elementary School is located in a densely populated inner-city neighborhood about one block from Central Park in the East Harlem section of Manhattan. In the early 1970s, New York City school officials sanctioned CPE as the city's first alternative school in District 4—and most likely, the first in the nation—as a reaction to low attendance, below grade level achievement, and stratospheric dropout rates. As the first director of New York City's Office of Alternative Schools, Seymour Fliegel (1994) described conditions at the time:

> Only 16 percent of School District Four's children were reading at or above grade level; morning attendance at Benjamin Franklin High School on East 116th Street was 44 percent of enrollment, and by graduation time 93 percent of the high school's ninth graders had dropped out. (para. 1)

Under these dire conditions, the District 4 school superintendent, Anthony Alvarado, asked an exceptional educator named Deborah Meier to direct a new type of school.

Born into an affluent Jewish family in Westchester County, New York, a wealthy enclave just north of New York City, Meier seemed like an unlikely candidate to spearhead the first Dewey-type school in New York City for inner-city youths. Educated in elite private schools around New York City, Meier subsequently attended Antioch College, and then completed her graduate work at the University of Chicago in history, which in the 1950s would have surely been steeped yet in Deweyan thought and influence.

Her foray into teaching occurred while she was living in Chicago with her husband and three children when she began substituting in various public schools. Following a family move to Philadelphia, she continued to substitute in the public school system. Later, after moving back to the New York City area, she worked full-time as a kindergarten teacher, and then later, accepted a position at the City University of New York at City College. Her work with teachers who were dealing with challenging students caught the eye of district officials such as Superintendent Alvarado, who tapped her to become the director of the first alternative school in District 4 (Bensman, 2000; Fliegel, 1994).

Her work at City College led to efforts to create "open classrooms" at some schools, and as Fliegel (1994) remarked, "She had developed an educational method which she believed reflected the cognitive development of children, combining John Dewey's learning theory with more recent psychological investigations of Jean Piaget" (para. 11).

With a clear vision, Meier proposed a Dewey school where the teachers would use social occupations, hands-on activities, and play to guide and develop student interests. The school would become a small community, unlike the typical New York City school at the time, which was bulging with huge enrollment.

Meier and other administrators began with the idea of keeping the school purposely small. They started with the premise that the only way to reform the system was to develop a warm, nurturing community based on mutual respect, not just respect between the teachers and students, but also respect between teachers and administrators and respect among family members, teachers, and administrators. Evidence of this respect manifested in the policy of addressing teachers and students on a first-name basis, which continues to this day.

Meier also insisted that she have complete control over hiring, and she demanded that the staff members be allowed to develop their own curricula. The curricula began with student interests, and equally importantly, valued the type of knowledge and skills that the predominantly minority inner-city students brought to the school. Beginning with just two kindergartens and one first grade class, the inaugural body of 1974 consisted of 32 students comprising 12 in each of the kindergarten classes and only 8 in the first grade class. Soon after the school year commenced, word had spread, and the school accepted more children while a waiting list was created for the next year (Bensman, 1994, 2000; Fliegel, 1994).

Despite the appearance of initial success on nearly all measures—parent interest, small class sizes, and District 4 support—the first few years were also contentious as certain people began to question the wisdom of the new ways as well as raise doubts about Meier's authority. As Fliegel (1994) reported from his investigation:

> As the year went on, strains within the staff began to mount. The democratic staff organization that had seemed to work so well the year before was now breaking down. From the beginning Meier had brought staff together to function as a sort of teacher collective. . . . But in practice, the staff's search for consensus consumed more and more time. While the teachers acted as if all were equal, they held Meier responsible for solving major problems. And while Meier professed a belief in functioning democratically, she believed she had the right to act unilaterally when it came to make-or-break issues affecting the school's best interests. (para. 20)

In addition to the fledgling problems with the school staff, Meier was also encountering parent opposition from those who distrusted "a white Jewish lady" (Fliegel, para. 19) with strong convictions. She also fought over resources with members from the other school housed in the same building, and the teacher's union voiced objections to her independent power.

On a much smaller scale than Dewey, Meier was experiencing much of the same conservative backlash for her insistence on following the New Education. Moreover, in spite of these early challenges, Fliegel recommended that the superintendent support Meier unconditionally because he concluded that students were engaged and learning in a highly supportive environment (Fliegel, 1994).

In the early 1980s, Meier went on to found two other similar preK–6 schools in the district following the success of CPE. As Meier (2007) described this seminal moment:

> Little did I suspect that the New Wave of Reform would soon transmorph into an intensification of all that was wrong with the old ways of educating. Our little network of elementary schools in East Harlem's District 4 had managed to operate with a degree of freedom to try new things otherwise unknown in NYC. Thanks to an unusual superintendent and a distant central bureaucracy, we created three small preK–6 schools that reinvented progressive education for public school children. Long a staple of NYC's finest and most expensive elite private schools, we offered progressive education (against everyone's advice) to the poorest of Latino and African American children. (para. 1)

Meier was not just speaking anecdotally because subsequent investigations confirmed that students were motivated to learn and succeeding at CPE.

In 1994, Bensman published the results of a follow-up study to determine whether the school offered an effective education by examining school records and surveying the graduates of CPE who attended during the years from 1978 through 1983. He was able to obtain the records and interview about 87 percent of the students from those years, which translated into 117 out of the total 135 former pupils.

What he reported was nothing short of astounding with 98 of 117 students graduated from high school, another 13 eventually earned a GED, and a mere 5 never graduated; 1 was still in school at the time of his 1990 data collection. Keeping in mind that only about 7 percent of all students made it to graduation at one of the neighborhood high schools, the evidence was compelling. In the in-depth interviews, moreover, the researcher reported that the students also cited emotional and social growth, in addition to academic achievement, as some of the outcomes from their attending CPE.

The themes that emerged from the interviews specifically centered on three factors supporting a positive learning environment: First, teachers identified and expanded student interests to motivate them to learn. Second, teachers cultivated warm personal relationships with the students providing a sense of belonging. And third, teachers applied their own innovative methods to teaching while increasing parent participation at the school. Many of these findings were recently echoed in a conversation that I had with the current principal of the school, Julie Zuckerman.

CPE in the Era of NCLB

In 2009, CPE celebrated its thirty-fifth anniversary, and at the same time, under the direction of Principal Julie Zuckerman, earned an A grade designation under the auspices of the State of New York, NCLB, and adequate yearly progress (AYP). About 61 percent of the 201 students who attended the school in the 2008–2009 school year qualified for free or reduced lunch. Further, as revealed in the census data, the student population consisted of 55 percent females and 45 percent males with 44 percent of the students reporting as Black, 21 percent Hispanic, 22 percent White, 5 percent Asian/Pacific, and 8 percent not revealing any status.

As in the past, the school today is a choice school, which means that children apply through a lottery system for admittance. The selection process gives preference to students who live in the neighborhood. The school typically enrolls about 200 students in prekindergarten through the fifth grade.

The mission statement of the school emphasizes educating the whole student, promoting not only academic success but emotional and social growth as well. The social element also carries over to the pedagogical philosophy of the school with a focus on inclusion, cross-age classrooms, active learning, and an integrated curriculum where the students engage daily in physical activities and the fine arts. The entire curriculum is propelled by student interests.

Learning at CPE

Before school begins at 8:30 a.m. each morning, the students are served breakfast in the cafeteria, and then the teachers arrive to escort them upstairs for a day brimming with activities. For the midmorning snack, groups of students will prepare nutritious foods based on research and perhaps family recipes. On Monday mornings, the students go to the auditorium for the All School Sing.

Every day the students engage in independent projects for about an hour to an hour and a half. In pure Deweyan fashion, most of the curricula—including the students' projects—are conceptualized around the social studies and student interests, providing the direct links between students' existing experiences and the wider curriculum. The projects and general activities integrate other subject areas such as ELA, science, mathematics, and the fine arts.

The arts are an integral part of the students' learning experiences; every student participates in the theater program and movement exercises. Expression in all forms—written, bodily, and verbal—is highly valued at CPE.

Moreover, students engage in common schoolwide investigations, which in the past have included disciplined inquiry of the neighborhood, ancient Egypt, and the New York natural environment.

Similar to the Dewey laboratory school a century earlier, many of the activities and disciplined inquiries at CPE are intimately connected with the natural world. The prekindergarten children visit the Bronx Zoo and Pelham Bay Park to conduct investigations of plants, insects, and animals at regular intervals while the older students conduct more sophisticated studies integrating charts, graphs, written reports, and oral presentations. Many of the investigations also begin in Central Park where, throughout the winter, the students go ice skating once a week.

Once a year the upper grade students in the third through fifth grades embark on a camping trip outside of the city where they are able to investigate natural phenomena as a collaborative community. The students gain firsthand experiences with the water cycle, food chains, and geography. They begin planning for the trip by creating maps of the visited areas and reading. Throughout the adventure, they record observations and engage in storytelling, creative writing, and poetry.

Students are required to complete a major research project and written reflection before the school graduates them at the end of the fifth grade. The research project can be anything that the student chooses and usually involves exploring some topic or earlier project in greater depth. Upon completion of the research endeavor, the student delivers a written and oral presentation of the findings.

Additionally, the student also must produce a lengthy written reflection on what she or he valued in learning over the years. Students often draw on a variety of sources including portfolios, journals, and notebooks. The effectiveness of the inquiries and activities is reflected in the yearly survey data, which factors into the school's grade and the calculation of adequate yearly progress under NCLB. The data have consistently indicated that parents and teachers believe that the school offers a highly supportive learning environment.

Testing and Assessing Students at CPE

In addition to the federally mandated high-stakes tests in English language arts and mathematics, New York State requires that students take a science test in the fourth grade as well as a social studies exam in the beginning of the fifth grade. The social studies assessment is considered a fourth grade test because it is administered in the beginning of the fifth grade school year.

CPE students' progress is also measured using other traditional and authentic assessments. Beginning in kindergarten, the district requires that teachers assess literacy development. As the students progress through the graded curriculum, each teacher collects samples of student work and places them in a portfolio. The portfolios are meant to provide evidence of individual growth during the course of the academic year as well as provide evidence of grade-level learning.

At the end of each quarterly marking period, the teachers also evaluate students through checklists and narrative reports. The teachers do not "grade" students. According to the school principal, teachers are discouraged from using drill activities, rote learning, and "teaching to the test," although before the exams they are encouraged to teach and practice test-taking skills (J. Zuckerman, personal communication, October 2, 2009).

CPE's School Grade and Adequate Yearly Progress

In the 2008–2009 academic year, the state graded Central Park East Elementary School as an A school. The school staff had embarked on an ambitious program to raise attendance rates and target low-performing students in mathematics and English language arts (ELA). In the last iteration of state tests, attendance was calculated at 93.3 percent, 72.6 percent of the students were scoring at grade level in ELA, and about 85 percent were scoring in the acceptable range in mathematics.

More surprisingly, about 94 percent of the bottom one-third of student performers had made or exceeded one grade level of progress. Just two years earlier, the school was graded as a D school, with an attendance rate of 92.1 percent and acceptable ELA and mathematics achievement at 40 percent and 45 percent respectively. Moreover, the bottom one-third actually performed worse the year before. In two years time, the staff aggressively targeted the struggling learners. One intervention involved the convening of a special committee, which met about every other week to devise strategies and interventions for struggling and at-risk students.

Despite the challenges with NCLB and high-stakes testing, the school was able to stay true to its mission and provide an education for the whole student. However, one question remained: What would happen to the CPE students after they graduated from the elementary school? The current principal, Julie Zuckerman, voiced this concern recently much as Deborah Meier had done so over 30 years earlier (J. Zuckerman, personal communication, October 2, 2009).

Meier, at the time, addressed the need by founding some upper grade schools based on the same Deweyan, progressive principles as CPE. She joined forces with Theodore Sizer, former dean of the Harvard Graduate School of Education. Even though CPE graduates transitioned smoothly to the new progressive schools, ultimately the schools failed because the bulk of the students channeled from traditional schools.

One of the major lessons gleaned from the failure was that students who were conditioned with a traditional style of learning were not able to adapt effectively to the interest-driven and open-inquiry format. However, the lessons learned became part of a reform movement resulting in the Coalition of Essential Schools (CES).

Coalition of Essential Schools

In 1984, the same year that Sizer published *Horace's Compromise*, a groundbreaking five-year study chronicling the shortcomings of American high schools, CES was launched in response to the study's findings. Sizer lambasted the traditional high school class schedule of 50-minute blocks as promoting superficial and disconnected learning. He also criticized the wide array of electives that most schools offered, which, he contended, diluted meaningful learning of the core curriculum.

Likewise, he asserted that the didactic instructional methods common to most schools inhibited student interest and, hence, stymied learning. While chastising how most schools elevated sports to a central role in the schools, he also employed the metaphor of good teaching as teachers acting like coaches to facilitate student learning. Beginning with 11 schools in six states, the coalition was voluntarily formed based on a common set of principles, rather than from compulsory mandates (Sizer, 1984). In essence, the schools agreed to adopt many of Dewey's approaches to learning.

Over the years, CES has grown to be an inclusive confederation of hundreds of public and private schools representing urban, suburban, and rural areas from around the United States. All the schools adhere to 10 common principles as follow:

1. Learning to use one's mind well
2. Less is more, depth over coverage
3. Goals apply to all students
4. Personalization
5. Student-as-worker, teacher-as-coach
6. Demonstration of mastery
7. A tone of decency and trust
8. Commitment to the entire school
9. Resources dedicated to teaching and learning
10. Democracy and equity (Coalition of Essential Schools, 2006, paras. 2–11)

Perhaps what seemed so revolutionary over 25 years ago has become the mainstay of best practices for all schools. The principles are intentionally broad in scope, which allows coalition schools to develop their own unique communities reflective of neighborhood and regional values. Over the years, various studies have validated the effectiveness of the schools in creating motivated and capable learners (for examples, see www.essentialschools.org/horace_issues).

Similar to the outcomes of CPE, a recent metastudy examined the effectiveness of CES schools by combining three smaller studies centered on three urban areas in Minnesota, New York, and Boston. Using an extensive variety of measures such as assessment data, motivation measures, dropout rates, retention, and many others, the researchers concluded a pattern of positive outcomes.

Also like CPE, students in CES schools do better on the tests, stay in school, and attend college at higher rates than their peers in traditional school settings. Specifically, the investigators cited data showing that students in the Boston Pilot Schools performed 9 to 26 percent better on standardized tests than similar students at traditional schools; New York City students at CES schools increased their college attendance rates by 17.7 percent while decreasing the dropout rate by 9.7 percent; and the Minnesota students not only performed statistically significantly better than their peers on standardized tests such as the ACT and SAT, they also recorded 10 percent more emotional and behavioral activity with the schools as indicated by increased autonomy and positive goal orientation. Recently, similar movements have also proliferated.

The Big Picture

In 1995, a former New Hampshire high school principal, Dennis Littky, cofounded Big Picture Learning with Elliot Washor, who had run some award-winning professional development programs at the same high school. According to the organization's mission statement,

> Big Picture Learning's mission is to lead vital changes in education, both in the United States and internationally, by generating and sustaining innovative, personalized schools that work in tandem with the real world of the greater community. We believe that in order to sustain successful schools where authentic and relevant learning takes place, we must continually innovate techniques and test learning tools to make our schools better and more rigorous. Lastly, we believe that in order to create and influence the schools of the future, we must use the lessons learned through our practice and research to give us added leverage to impact changes in public policy. (Big Picture Learning, 2009, para. 1)

In this regard, Big Picture Learning is not a management organization. Rather, it is a reform movement that is based on the same ideals of small learning communities, the development of students' interests in authentic ways and real-world contexts, and meaningful reflection like CPE students practiced and what Dewey advocated. The Rhode Island legislature approved the formation of Big Picture Learning's first six schools in 1995, which continue today to primarily serve Hispanic and Black inner-city youth in Providence.

The schools are collectively called "The Met." In a relatively short span of time, the schools were deemed highly successful because nearly all the students graduated high school and were accepted into higher education institutions. Within 15 years, the movement has spread to about 60 schools around the United States and the world.

CONCLUSION

While private Dewey schools such as the School of Organic Education, Presidio High School, and many others have flourished for nearly a century, progressive education did not arrive for marginalized and at-risk inner-city youth until the bold experiments in East Harlem in the 1970s. Beginning with Deborah Meier and her staff, democratic teaching and learning have resulted in students staying in school and many going to college in places where many never thought possible.

We also know that when the correct balance is found—whether or not we agree with the intent of high-stakes tests—students in these schools can score at levels indicating education excellence. As reported throughout this book, current research in authentic intellectual work and interactive instruction helps explicate these results.

One part of the story that often goes untold when talking about the success of CPE and some of the other progressive reform movements is the professionalism and expertise of the teachers. Teachers are charged with helping students identify their interests, and then the teachers must expand those interests while somehow encapsulating the core curriculum and tested standards.

This student-centered approach is best captured by the large Chicago studies from the late 1990s, which concluded that better-prepared teachers use interactive instruction more often than a didactic approach (Smith, Lee, & Newmann, 2001), and that students engage in authentic intellectual work when they activate prior knowledge, practice open inquiry, apply the knowledge to new circumstances, and then communicate the results, which "motivate and sustain students in the hard work that learning requires" (Newmann, Bryk, & Nagaoka, 2001, p. 30). This research captures and validates precisely the democratic type of teaching and learning in the Dewey schools.

In one final thought about the Dewey schools, clearly many of the reforms established by Meier and other progressive movement founders have been claimed in the current educational climate by others. In New York City, the mayor and superintendent have fought bitterly to give public education a private character under the guise of democratic freedom. As Meier (2007) has pointed out,

> Today, 20 years later, our slogans have been co-opted by the big guys—Michael Bloomberg, Joel Klein, the Gates Foundation, and so on—but our own stories and lessons too often have been forgotten. The slogans persist, in greater numbers than before we began our work, but even at their best, they too are stunted by the new paradigm, in which children are tools for beating the foreign competition. (para. 2)

We must never forget the lessons learned.

Discussion Questions

1. How did Dewey's personal educational experiences inform his philosophy?
2. What made Dewey's laboratory school unique at the time?
3. Peruse the list of 25 lessons learned from Dewey's school. Make a list of those innovations practiced or embraced in a school you have worked at or attended. Did your school embrace all 25 of the innovations? How do you explain your results?
4. What did Dewey learn from Rousseau?
5. In what ways is the School of Organic Education progressive?
6. How did progressive education change over the years? How did Dewey's interpretation differ from other reformists?
7. Why did it take so long for progressive education to come to the masses?
8. Compare and contrast the lessons learned from Dewey's laboratory school with the activities and practices at Central Park East Elementary School. What are the most important practices for each?
9. Why did the original progressive high schools begun in the early 1980s in New York City fail?
10. Should all schools adopt the same model of progressive education? Why?

Further Reflection

1. What explains the success of Central Park East Elementary School in the era of high-stakes testing?

2. Just like there were many lessons learned at Dewey's laboratory school, what are the lessons that we can learn from places such as Central Park East, the Coalition of Essential Schools, and the Big Picture?
3. Do you think that NCLB aids or impedes the development of progressive education? Why?

References

Aikin, W. M. (1942). *The story of the eight-year study, with conclusions and recom-mendations.* New York: Harper.

Al-Bataineh, A., Anderson, S., Toledo, C., & Wellinski, S. (2008). A study of tech-nology integration in the classroom. *International Journal of Instructional Media, 35*(4), 381–387.

Alexander, H. A. (2001). *Reclaiming goodness: Education and the spiritual quest.* Notre Dame, IN: University of Notre Dame Press.

Alexander, P. A. (2006). What would Dewey say? Channeling Dewey on the issue of specificity of epistemic beliefs: A response to Muis, Bendixen, and Haerle (2006). *Educational Psychology Review, 18*(1), 55–65.

Alfonso, R. J., & Firth, G. R. (1990). Supervision: Needed research. *Journal of Cur-riculum and Supervision, 5*, 189–193.

Amrein, A. L., & Berliner, D. C. (2002a). High-stakes testing, uncertainty, and stu-dent learning. *Education Policy Analysis Archives, 10*(18). Retrieved from epaa .asu.edu/epaa/v10n18/.

Amrein, A. L., & Berliner, D. C. (2002b). The impact of high-stakes tests on student academic performance: An analysis of NAEP results in states with high-stakes tests and ACT, SAT, and AP test results in states with high school graduation exams. Retrieved from epsl.asu.edu/epru/documents/EPSL-0211–126-EPRU.pdf.

Amrein, A. L., & Berliner, D. C. (2003). The effects of high-stakes testing on student motivation and learning. *Educational Leadership, 60*(5), 32–38.

Anderman, L. H., & Kaplan, A. (2008). The role of interpersonal relationships in student motivation: Introduction to the special issue. *The Journal of Experimental Education, 76*(2), 115–119.

Anyon, J. (1981). Social class and the hidden curriculum of work. In H. A. Giroux, A. N. Penn, & W. F. Pinar (Eds.), *Curriculum and instruction: Alternatives in educa-tion.* Berkeley. CA: McCutchan Publishers.

Anyon, J. (1997). *Ghetto schooling: A political economy of urban educational re-form.* New York: Teachers College Press.

Apple, M. W. (1986). *Teachers and text: A political economy of class and gender.* London: Routledge.

Apple, M. W. (2007). Ideological success, educational failure? On the politics of No Child Left Behind. *Journal of Teacher Education, 58*(2), 108–116.

Arlington, A. (1972). *An historical analysis of the development of supervision in the public schools in the United States from 1870 to 1970.* Unpublished doctoral dissertation, George Washington University.

Arroyos-Jurado, E., & Savage, T. A. (2008). Intervention strategies for serving students with traumatic brain injury. *Intervention in School and Clinic, 43*(4), 252–254.

Arts Education Partnership. (2005). No subject left behind: A guide to arts education opportunities in the 2001 NCLB act. Retrieved from www.aep-arts.org/files/NoSubjectLeftBehindAug2005.pdf.

Ashford, E. (2003). The dangerous schools "No Child Left Behind." *The Education Digest, 68*(5), 12–15.

Au, W. (2007). High-stakes testing and curricular control: A qualitative metasynthesis. *Educational Researcher, 36*(5), 258–267.

August, D., & Shanahan, T. (2006). Executive summary. Developing literacy in second-language learners: Report of the National Literacy Panel on language-minority children and youth. Retrieved from www.cal.org/projects/archive/nlp reports/Executive_Summary.pdf.

Balfanz, R., Legters, N., & Jordan, W. (2004). Catching up: Effect of the talent development ninth-grade instructional interventions in reading and mathematics in high-poverty high schools. *NASSP Bulletin, 88*(641), 3–30.

Banks, J. A. (1997). *Educating citizens in a multicultural society.* New York: Teachers College Press.

Banks, J. A. (2004). *Multicultural education: Theory and practice* (3rd ed.). Boston: Allyn & Bacon.

Banks, J. A., & Banks, C. A. (2007). *Multicultural education: Issues and perspectives* (6th ed.). Indianapolis, IN: Wiley Publishing.

Barr, A. S. (1925). Scientific analysis of teaching procedures. *The Journal of Educational Method, 4*, 361–366.

Barr, A. S. (1931). *An introduction to the scientific study of classroom supervision.* New York: D. Appleton and Company.

Barr, A. S., Burton, W. H., & Brueckner, L. J. (1947). *Supervision: Democratic leadership in the improvement of learning* (2nd ed.). New York: Appleton-Century-Crofts.

Barrow, L. H. (2006). A brief history of inquiry: From Dewey to standards. *Journal of Science Teacher Education, 17*(3), 265–278.

Beck, L. G. (1994). *Reclaiming educational administration as a caring profession.* New York: Teachers College Press.

Bensman, D. (1994). Direct assessment of a progressive public elementary school: Graduates of Central Park East. Retrieved from ERIC database (ED374182).

Bensman, D. (2000). *Central Park East and its graduates.* New York: Teachers College Press.

Bent, S. (1922, November 26). University head derides delusion of democracy, *New York Times*, p. 111.

Big Picture Learning. (2009). About us. Retrieved from www.bigpicture.org/about -us/.

Blackmore, J. (1993). In the shadow of man: The historical construction of educational administration as a "masculinist" enterprise. In J. Blackmore & J. Kenway (Eds.), *Gender matters in educational administration and policy* (pp. 27–48). London: The Falmer Press.

Block, A. A. (2008). Why should I be a teacher? *Journal of Teacher Education, 59*(5), 416–427.

Bobbitt, F. (1913). Some general principles of management applied to the problems of city school systems. In twelfth yearbook of the National Society for the Study of Education, part I: *The supervision of city schools* (pp. 7–96). Chicago: University of Chicago Press.

Bogotch, I. E. (2000). *Educational leadership and social justice: Theory into practice.* Revised version of paper presented at the annual conference of the University Council for Educational Administration, Albuquerque, NM. ERIC document no. ED452585.

Bolin, F., & Panaritis, P. (1992). Searching for a common purpose: A perspective on the history of supervision. In C. D. Glickman (Ed.), *Supervision in transition* (pp. 30–43). Alexandria, VA: Association for Supervision and Curriculum Development.

Bowers, C. A. (2001). *Educating for eco-justice and community.* Athens: University of Georgia Press.

Bowers, C. A., & Flinders, D. J. (1991). *Culturally responsive teaching and supervision: A handbook for staff development.* New York: Teachers College Press.

Boyer, J. B., & Baptiste Jr., H. P. (1996). *Transforming the curriculum for multicultural understandings: A practitioner's handbook.* San Francisco, CA: Caddo Gap Press.

Bransford, J. D., Brown, A. L., & Cocking, R. R. (Eds.). (1999). *How people learn: Brain, mind, experience, and school.* Washington, DC: National Academy Press.

Bridgeland, J. M., DiJulio, J. J., & Morison, K. B. (2006). The silent epidemic: Perspectives of high school dropouts. Retrieved from www.gatesfoundation.org/nr/ downloads/ed/TheSilentEpidemic3–06FINAL.pdf.

Brim, O. G. (1930). Changing and conflicting conceptions of supervision. *Education, 53*.

Brown, J. S., & Duguid, P. (1991). Organizational learning and communities of practice: Toward a unified view of working, learning, and innovation. *Organization Science, 2*, 40–57.

Brown, K. (2004). Leadership for social justice and equity: Weaving a transformative framework and pedagogy. *Educational Administration Quarterly, 40*(1), 79–110.

Brown, L. C. (2009). Share the music across disciplines. *The National Association of Music Education.* Retrieved from www.menc.org/v/general_music/share-the -music-across-disciplines.

Burton, W. H. (1930). Probable next steps in the progress of supervision. *Educational Method, 9*, 401–405.

Burton, W. H., & Brueckner, L. J. (1955). *Supervision: A social process.* New York: Appleton.

Button, H. W. (1961). *A history of supervision in the public schools, 1870–1950.* Unpublished doctoral dissertation, Washington University.

Caplan, N., Choy, M. H., & Whitmore, J. K. (1991). *Children of the boat people: A study of educational success.* Ann Arbor: The University of Michigan Press.

Capps, R. (2007). U.S. immigrant workers and families: Demographics, labor market participation, and children's education. *Virginia Journal of Social Policy & the Law, 14*(2), 170–205.

Carnegie Forum on Education and the Economy. (1986). *A nation prepared: Teachers for the 21st century.* New York: Carnegie Corporation.

Cassirer, E. (1953). *An essay on man: An introduction to a philosophy of human culture.* New York: Doubleday & Co.

Center on Education Policy. (2007). Choices, changes, and challenges: Curriculum and instruction in the NCLB era. Retrieved from www.cep-dc.org/_data/n_0001/resources/live/07107%20Curriculum-WEB%20FINAL%207%2031%2007.pdf.

Center on Education Policy. (2008). Instructional time in elementary schools: A closer look at changes for specific subjects. Retrieved from www.cep-dc.org/document/docWindow.cfm?fuseaction=document.viewDocument&documentid=234&documentFormatId=3713.

Center on Education Policy. (2009). How state and federal accountability policies have influenced curriculum and instruction in three states: Common findings from Rhode Island, Illinois, and Washington. Retrieved from www.cep-dc.org/document/docWindow.cfm?fuseaction=document.viewDocument&documentid=296&documentFormatId=4396.

Chomsky, N. (2002). Chomsky offers advice to teachers on the use of science. Retrieved from www.justresponse.net/chomsky_offers_advice.html.

Clarke, M., Shore, A., Rhoades, K., Abrams, L., Miao, J., & Li, J. (2003). Perceived effects of state-mandated testing programs on teaching and learning: Findings from interviews with educators in low-, medium-, and high-stakes states. Retrieved from ERIC database (ED474867).

Coalition of Essential Schools. (2006). The CES common principles. Retrieved from www.essentialschools.org/pub/ces_docs/about/phil/10cps/10cps.html.

Cochran-Smith, M. (2003). The unforgiving complexity of teaching: Avoiding simplicity in the age of accountability. *Journal of Teacher Education, 54*, 3–5.

Cogan, M. L. (1973). *Clinical supervision.* Boston: Houghton Mifflin.

Connell, R. W. (1993). *Schools and social justice.* Philadelphia, PA: Temple University Press.

Costa, A., & Garmston, R. (1994). *Cognitive coaching: Approaching renaissance schools.* Norwood, MA: Christopher-Gordon Publishing.

Courtis, S. A. (1928). Ideals in supervision. *The Journal of Educational Method, 7*, 339.

Covington Clarkson, L. M. (2008). Demographic data and immigrant student achievement. *Theory into Practice, 47*(1), 20–26.

Cremin, L. A. (1959). John Dewey and the progressive-education movement, 1915–1952. *The School Review, 67*(2), 160–173.

Cuban, L. (1993). *How teachers taught: Constancy and change in American classrooms, 1890–1990* (2nd ed.). New York: Teachers College Press.

Cuban, L. (2001). *Oversold and underused: Computers in the classroom.* Cambridge, MA: Harvard University Press.

Cuban, L., Kirkpatrick, H., & Peck, C. (2001). High access and low use of technologies in high school classrooms: Explaining an apparent paradox. *American Educational Research Journal, 38*(4), 813–834.

Danforth, S. (2008). John Dewey's contributions to an educational philosophy of intellectual disability. *Educational Theory, 58*(1), 45–62.

Darling, J. (1994). *Child-centered education and its critics.* London: Paul Chapman Publishing Ltd.

Darling-Hammond, L., & Goodwin, A. L. (1993). Progress toward professionalism in teaching. In G. Cawelti (Ed.), *Challenges and achievements of American education* (pp. 19–52). Alexandria, VA: ASCD.

David, J. L. (2007). What research says about classroom walk-throughs. *Educational Leadership, 65*(4), 81–82.

Davis Jr., O. L. (1998). Beyond beginnings: From "hands-on" to "minds-on." *Journal of Curriculum and Supervision, 13,* 119–122.

DeCapua, A., Smathers, W., & Tang, L. F. (2007). Schooling interrupted. *Educational Leadership, 64*(6), 40–46.

Denzin, N. K., & Lincoln, Y. S. (1998). *Strategies of qualitative inquiry.* Thousand Oaks, CA: Sage.

Department of Homeland Security. (2009). 2008 yearbook of immigration statistics. Retrieved from www.dhs.gov/xlibrary/assets/statistics/yearbook/2008/ois_yb_2008.pdf.

DeVary, S. (2008). Educational gaming: Interactive edutainment. *Distance Learning, 5*(3), 35–44.

Dewey, J. (1900). Science in elementary education. *Elementary School Record, 1*(6), 153–166.

Dewey, J. (1913). *Interest and effort in education.* New York: Houghton Mifflin Company.

Dewey, J. (1918). Nationalizing education. In M. G. Fulton (Ed.), *National ideals and problems: Essays for college English* (pp. 282–290). New York: The Macmillan Company.

Dewey, J. (1922). An undemocratic proposal. In E. P. Cubberley & E. C. Elliott (Eds.), *State and county school administration source book* (vol. II, pp. 365–369). New York: The Macmillan Company.

Dewey, J. (1929). *The sources of a science of education.* New York: Liveright.

Dewey, J. (1938). *Experience and education.* New York: Touchstone.

Dewey, J. (1945). Democratic versus coercive international organization: The realism of Jane Addams. In J. Addams (Ed.), *Peace and bread in time of war* (pp. ix–xx). New York: King's Crown Press.

Dewey, J. (1954). *The public and its problems.* Athens, OH: Swallow Press. (Original work published in 1927.)

Dewey, J. (1964). My pedagogic creed. In R. D. Archambault (Ed.), *John Dewey on education: Selected works*. Chicago: University of Chicago Press. (Original work published in 1897.)

Dewey, J. (1967). The ethics of democracy. In J. A. Boydston (Ed.), *John Dewey: The early works, 1882–1898*. Carbondale: Southern Illinois University Press.

Dewey, J. (1976a). Ethics. In J. A. Boydston (Ed.), *John Dewey: The middle works, 1899–1924* (pp. 364–379). Carbondale: Southern Illinois University Press.

Dewey, J. (1976b). Individuality, equality, and superiority. In J. A. Boydston (Ed.), *John Dewey: The middle works, 1899–1924* (vol. 13, pp. 295–300). Carbondale: Southern Illinois University Press.

Dewey, J. (1976c). Mediocrity and individuality. In J. A. Boydston (Ed.), *John Dewey: The middle works, 1899–1924* (vol. 13, pp. 289–294). Carbondale: Southern Illinois University Press.

Dewey, J. (1976d). The school as social centre. In J. A. Boydston (Ed.), *The middle works, 1899–1952* (vol. 2, pp. 80–93). Carbondale: Southern Illinois University Press.

Dewey, J. (1981). Creative democracy: The task before us. In J. A. Boydston (Ed.), *John Dewey: The later works, 1925–1953*. Carbondale: Southern Illinois University Press.

Dewey, J. (2001). *The school and society & the child and the curriculum*. Mineola, NY: Dover Publications, Inc. (Original works published 1899 and 1902.)

Dewey, J. (2005). *Art as experience*. New York: Penguin Group, Inc. (Original work published 1934.)

Dewey, J. (2007a). *Democracy and education*. Middlesex, UK: The Echo Library. (Original work published 1916.)

Dewey, J. (2007b). *How we think*. Champaign, IL: Book Jungle. (Original work published 1910.)

Dewey, J. (2008). *Logic: The theory of inquiry*. New York: Holt.

Dewey, J., & Dewey, E. (1915). *Schools of to-morrow*. New York: E. P. Dutton.

Dewey, J., & Tufts, J. H. (1909). Ethics. In J. Ratner (Ed.), *Intelligence in the modern world: John Dewey's philosophy*. New York: The Modern Library.

Diket, R. M. (2003). The arts contribution to adolescent learning. *Kappa Delta Pi Record, 39*(4), 173–177.

Dougherty, J. P. (2007). Using the past to rescue the future. *Modern Age, 49*(1), 3–11.

Downey, C. J., Steffy, B. E., English, F. W., Frase, L. E., & Poston Jr., W. K. (2004). *The three-minute classroom walk-through*. Thousand Oaks, CA: Corwin Press.

Dunn, R. (1995). A meta-analytic validation of the Dunn and Dunn Model of Learning-Styles Preferences. *Journal of Educational Research, 88*(6), 353–362.

Dykhuizen, G. (1959). John Dewey: The Vermont years. *Journal of the History of Ideas, 20*(4), 515–544.

Dynarski, M., Agodini, R., Heaviside, S., Novak, T., Carey, N., Campuzano, L., et al. (2007). Effectiveness of reading and mathematics software products: Findings from the first student cohort. Retrieved from ies.ed.gov/ncee/pdf/20074006.pdf.

Edson, C. H. (1994). Detroit's demise. *Educational Researcher, 23*, 34–35.

Educational Testing Service. (1992). *The second international assessment of educational progress.* Princeton, NJ: Educational Testing Service.

Education Trust. (2003). Disaggregated data and NCLB: What's required to be publicly reported and by when? Retrieved from www.ewa.org/files/docs/disagdata.pdf.

Eick, C. J. (2002). Science curriculum in practice: Student teachers' use of hands-on activities in high-stakes testing schools. *NASSP Bulletin, 86*(630), 72–85.

Eisele, J. C. (1975). John Dewey and the immigrants. *History of Education Quarterly, 15*(1), 67–85.

EM exclusive: Riverdeep tops Simba's 2005 software publisher index. (2006). *Educational Marketer, 37*(14), 3–5.

English, F. W. (2007). From the president: Toward re-founding the field of educational administration. *UCEA Review*, fall issue.

Erikson, E. (1995). *Childhood and society* (rev. ed.). New York: Vintage.

Ertmer, P. A. (2005). Teacher pedagogical beliefs: The final frontier in our quest for technology integration? *Educational Technology Research and Development, 53*(4), 25–39.

Etuk, N. (2008). Educational gaming—from edutainment to bona fide 21st century teaching tool. *MultiMedia & Internet@Schools, 15*(6), 10–13.

Fallace, T. (2009). John Dewey's influence on the origins of the social studies: An analysis of the historiography and new interpretation. *Review of Educational Research, 79*(2), 601–624.

Fashola, O. S. (2002). *Building effective afterschool programs.* Thousand Oaks, CA: Corwin Press.

Ferguson, K. E. (1984). *The feminist case against bureaucracy.* Philadelphia, PA: Temple University Press.

Fesmire, S. (2003). *John Dewey and moral imagination: Pragmatism in ethics.* Bloomington, IN: Indiana University Press.

Feuer, L. S. (1959). John Dewey and the back to the people movement in American thought. *Journal of the History of Ideas, 20*(4), 545–568.

Finn Jr., C. E., & Ravitch, D. (2008). Seeds of competitiveness. *Hoover Digest*(1).

Firth, G. R., & Eiken, K. P. (1982). Impact of the schools' bureaucratic structure on supervision. In T. J. Sergiovanni (Ed.), *Supervision of teaching* (pp. 153–169). Washington, DC: ASCD.

Fliegel, S. (1994). Debbie Meier and the dawn of Central Park East: When teachers take charge of schooling. *City Journal, 4*(1). Retrieved from www.city-journal.org/article01.php?aid=1414.

Foote, C. S., Vermette, P. J., & Battaglia, C. F. (2001). *Constructivist strategies: Meeting standards and engaging adolescent minds.* Larchmont, NY: Eye on Education.

Franklin, C. (2007). Factors that influence elementary teachers' use of computers. *Journal of Technology and Teacher Education, 15*(2), 267–293.

Furman, G. C., & Shields, C. M. (2005). How can educational leaders promote and support social justice and democratic community in schools? In W. A. Firestone & C. Riehl (Eds.), *A new agenda for research in educational leadership* (pp. 119–137). New York: Teachers College Press.

Geier, R., Blumenfeld, P. C., Marx, R. W., Krajcik, J. S., Fishman, B., Soloway, E., et al. (2008). Standardized test outcomes for students engaged in inquiry-based science curricula in the context of urban reform. *Journal of Research in Science Teaching, 45*(8), 922–939.

Genesee, F., & Harper, C. (2008). Standards for the recognition of initial programs in p-12 ESL teacher education. Retrieved from www.tesol.org/s_tesol/bin .asp?CID=219&DID-10697&DOC=FILE.PDF.

George, P. S. (2005). A rationale for differentiating instruction in the regular classroom. *Theory Into Practice, 44*(3), 185–193.

Gibboney, R. A. (2006). Intelligence by design: Thorndike versus Dewey. *Phi Delta Kappan, 88*(2), 170–172.

Gibboney, R. (2008). Why an undemocratic capitalism has brought public education to its knees: A MANIFESTO. *Phi Delta Kappan, 90*(1), 21. Retrieved from https:// yulib002.mc.yu.edu:8443/login?url=proquest.umi.com/pqdweb?did=1595730491 &Fmt=7&clientId=13170&RQT=309&VName=PQD.

Gilligan, C. (1993). *In a different voice: Psychological theory and women's development.* Cambridge, MA: Harvard University Press.

Ginott, H. (1993). *Teacher and child: A book for parents and teachers.* New York: Macmillan.

Giroux, H. A. (Ed.). (1991). *Postmodernism, feminism, and cultural politics.* Albany, NY: SUNY Press.

Glanz, J. (1977). *Bureaucracy and professionalism: An historical interpretation of public school supervision in the United States, 1875–1937.* Unpublished doctoral dissertation, Teachers College, Columbia University.

Glanz, J. (1991). *Bureaucracy and professionalism: The evolution of public school supervision in the United States, 1875–1937.* Unpublished doctoral dissertation, Teachers College, Columbia University.

Glanz, J. (1992). Curriculum development and supervision: Antecedents for collaboration and future possibilities. *Journal of Curriculum and Supervision, 7,* 226–244.

Glanz, J. (1995). Exploring supervision history: An invitation and agenda. *Journal of Curriculum and Supervision, 10,* 95–113.

Glanz, J. (1998). Histories, antecedents, and legacies of school supervision. In G. R. Firth & E. F. Pajak (Eds.), *Handbook of research on school supervision* (pp. 39–79). New York: Macmillan.

Glanz, J. (2000). Clandestine schooling during the Holocaust. *Journal of Curriculum and Supervision, 16*(1), 48–69.

Glickman, C. D. (1981). *Developmental supervision.* Boston: Allyn & Bacon.

Goldhammer, R. (1969). *Clinical supervision: Special methods for the supervision of teachers.* New York: Holt, Rinehart and Winston.

Good, T. L., & Brophy, J. E. (2007). *Looking in classrooms* (10th ed.). Boston: Allyn & Bacon.

Goodnough, A., & Medina, J. (2003, February 15). Joy and danger greet list of top city schools. *New York Times,* pp. A1, B4.

Gulek, C. (2003). Preparing for high-stakes testing. *Theory into Practice, 42*(1), 42–50.

Hannafin, R. D., & Foshay, W. R. (2008). Computer-based instruction's (CBI) redis-covered role in K–12: An evaluation case study of one high school's use of CBI to improve pass rates on high-stakes tests. *Educational Technology Research and Development, 56*(2), 147–160.

Hansen-Thomas, H. (2008). Sheltered instruction: Best practices for ELLs in the mainstream. *Kappa Delta Pi Record, 44*(4), 165–169.

Hardman, M. L., & Dawson, S. (2008). The impact of federal public policy on cur-riculum and instruction for students with disabilities in the general classroom. *Preventing School Failure, 52*(2), 5–11.

Henry, M. (1996). *Parent-school collaboration: Feminist organizational structures and school leadership.* New York: State University of New York Press.

Hermans, R., Tondeur, J., van Braak, J., & Valcke, M. (2008). The impact of primary school teachers' educational beliefs on the classroom use of computers. *Computers & Education, 51*(4).

Hetland, L., & Winner, E. (2002). Cognitive transfer from arts education to non-arts outcomes: Research evidence and policy implications. Retrieved from www2.bc.edu/~winner/pdf/cognitive_transfer.pdf.

Hickman, L. A. (2001). *Philosophical tools for technological culture: Putting prag-matism to work.* Bloomington, IN: Indiana University Press.

Hill, S. (1918). Defects of supervision and constructive suggestions thereon. *National Educational Association Proceedings, 56,* 347–350.

Hoefer, M., Rytina, N., & Baker, B. C. (2009). Estimates of the unauthorized immi-grant population residing in the United States: January 2008. Retrieved from www.dhs.gov/xlibrary/assets/statistics/publications/ois_ill_pe_2008.pdf.

Hoetker, W. J., & Ahlbrand, W. P. (1969). The persistence of the recitation. *American Educational Research Journal, 6,* 152–176.

Hogan, D. (1985). *Class and reform: School and society in Chicago, 1880–1930.* Philadelphia: University of Pennsylvania Press.

Hohlfeld, T. N., Ritzhaupt, A. D., Barron, A. E., & Kemker, K. (2008). Examining the digital divide in K–12 public schools: Four-year trends for supporting ICT literacy in Florida. *Computers & Education, 51,* 1648–1663.

Holmes Group. (1986). *Tomorrow's teachers: A report of the Holmes Group.* East Lansing, MI: Holmes Group, Inc.

Hosic, J. F. (1920). The democratization of supervision. *School and Society, 11,* 331–336.

Hostetler, K. D. (2003). Responding to the technicist challenge to practical wis-dom in teaching: The case of INTASC standards. *Educational Foundations, 16,* 45–64.

Howard, G. R. (2007). As diversity grows so must we. *Educational Leadership, 64*(6), 16–22.

Huebner, D. (1996). Teaching as moral activity. *Journal of Curriculum and Supervi-sion, 13*(3), 267–275.

Hung, D. (2002). Metaphorical ideas as mediating artifacts for the social construction of knowledge: Implications from the writings of Dewey and Vygotsky. *Interna-tional Journal of Instructional Media, 29*(2), 197–214.

Institute on Community Integration. (2009). About developmental disabilities. Retrieved August 31, 2009, from www.ici.umn.edu/related resources/definition.html.

International Society for Technology in Education. (2007). The ISTE national educational technology standards (NETS-S) and performance indicators for students. Retrieved from www.iste.org/Content/NavigationMenu/NETS/ForStudents/2007Standards/NETS_for_Students_2007_Standards.pdf.

International Society for Technology in Education. (2008). The ISTE national educational standards (NETS-T) and performance indicators for teachers. Retrieved from www.iste.org/Content/NavigationMenu/NETS/ForTeachers/2008Standards/NETS_T_Standards_Final.pdf.

Igo, C., Moore, D. M., Ramsey, J., & Ricketts, J. C. (2008). The problem-solving approach. *Techniques, 83*(1), 52–55.

Itkonen, T. (2007). PL 94-142: Policy, evolution, and landscape shift. *Issues in Teacher Education, 16*(2), 7–17.

Ito, M. (2006). Engineering play: Children's software and the cultural politics of edutainment. *Discourse: Studies in the Cultural Politics of Education, 27*(2), 139–160.

Jacobson, L. (2006). Current events: After-school special. *Teacher Magazine, 17*(5), 9–10.

Jerald, C. D. (2006a). *"Teach to the test"? Just say no.* Retrieved from www.centerforcsri.org/files/CenterIssueBriefJuly06.pdf.

Jerald, C. D. (2006b). Using data: The math's not the hard part. Retrieved from www.centerforcsri.org/files/Center_IB_Sept06B.pdf.

Jimenez, T. C., Graf, V. L., & Rose, E. (2007). Gaining access to general education: The promise of universal design for learning. *Issues in Teacher Education, 16*(2), 41–54.

Johnsen, S. K. (2009). Best practices for identifying gifted students. *Principal, 88*(5), 8–14.

Johnson, D. W., Johnson, R. T., & Johnson-Holubec, E. (1994). *Cooperative learning in the classroom.* Alexandria, VA: Association for Supervision and Curriculum Development.

Jordan Irvine, J. (2001). The critical elements of cultural responsive pedagogy: A synthesis of research. In J. Jordan Irvine & B. Armento (Eds.), *Culturally responsive teaching: Lesson plans for elementary and middle grades* (pp. 2–17). New York: McGraw-Hill.

Jordan Irvine, J. J., & Armento, B. J. (2003). *Culturally responsive teaching.* Boston: McGraw-Hill.

Judd, C. H. (1920). The high school manager. *National Association of Secondary School Principals*, 30–31.

Kaplan, L. S., & Owings, W. A. (2002). The politics of teacher quality: Implications for principals. *National Association of Secondary School Principals. NASSP Bulletin, 86*(633), 22–41.

Karier, C. J. (1975). John Dewey and the new liberalism: Some reflections and responses. *History of Education Quarterly, 15*(4), 417–443.

Katz, M. S., Noddings, N., & Strike, K. A. (Eds.). (1999). *Justice and caring: The search for common ground in education.* New York: Teachers College Press.

Kessler, R. (2000). *The soul of education: Helping students find connection, compassion, and character at school.* Alexandria, VA: Association for Supervision and Curriculum Development.

Killian, J. E., & Post, D. M. (1998). Scientific dimensions of supervision. In G. R. Firth & E. F. Pajak (Eds.), *Handbook of research on school supervision* (pp. 1032–1054). New York: Macmillan.

Kivinen, O., & Ristela, P. (2003). From constructivism to a pragmatist conception of learning. *Oxford Review of Education, 29*(3), 363–375.

Kliebard, H. M. (1987). *The struggle for the American curriculum: 1893–1958.* New York: Routledge & Kegan Paul.

Koth, C. W., Bradshaw, C. P., & Leaf, P. J. (2008). A multilevel study of predictors of student perceptions of school climate: The effect of classroom-level factors. *Journal of Educational Psychology, 100*(1), 96–104.

Kozol, J. (1991). *Savage inequalities.* New York: Crown Publishers.

Krug, E. A. (1964). *The shaping of the American high school, 1890–1920.* New York: Harper & Row.

Kummel, F. (1966). Time as succession and the problem of duration. In J. T. Fraser (Ed.), *The voices of time* (pp. 31–55). New York: George Braziller.

Ladson-Billings, G. (1994). *The dreamkeepers.* San Francisco: Jossey-Bass.

Lambert, N. M., & McCombs, B. L. (Eds.). (2000). *How students learn: Reforming schools through learner-centered education.* Washington, DC: American Psychological Association.

Langer, J. A. (2002). *Effective literacy instruction: Building successful reading and writing programs.* Urbana, IL: National Council of Teachers of English.

Layton, C. A., & Lock, R. H. (2007). Use authentic assessment techniques to fulfill the promise of No Child Left Behind. *Intervention in School and Clinic, 42*(3), 169–173.

Lazear, E. P. (2006). Speeding, terrorism, and teaching to the test. *The Quarterly Journal of Economics, 121*(3), 1029–1061.

Levine, A. E. (2004). Preface. In R. Rothstein, *Class and schools: Using social, economic, and educational reform to close the black-white achievement gap* (pp. x–xi). New York: Teachers College Press.

Lewis, E. E. (1923). Scientific school supervision. *American School Board Journal, 16.*

Liethwood, K., & Jantzi, D. (1990). *Transformational leadership.* Chapter presented at the meeting of the American Educational Research Association, Boston.

Lindsey, R. B., Roberts, L. M., & Campbell Jones, F. (2005). *The culturally proficient school: An implementation guide for school leaders.* Thousand Oaks, CA: Corwin Press.

Lowther, D. L., Inan, F. A., Strahl, D. J., & Ross, S. M. (2008). Does technology integration "work" when key barriers are removed? *Educational Media International, 45*(3), 195–213.

Lucio, W. H., & McNeil, J. D. (1969). *Supervision: A synthesis of theory and action* (2nd ed.). New York: McGraw-Hill.

Lynch, S., Kuipers, J., Pyke, C., & Szesze, M. (2005). Examining the effects of a highly rated science curriculum unit on diverse students: Results from a planning grant. *Journal of Research in Science Teaching, 42*(8), 912–946.

Madaus, G. F. (1988). The influence of testing on the curriculum. In L. Tanner (Ed.), *Eighty-seventh yearbook of the National Society for the Study of Education, part II.* Chicago: University of Chicago Press.

Marshall, C., Patterson, J. A., Rogers, D. L., & Steele, J. R. (1996). Caring as career: An alternative perspective for educational administration. *Educational Administration Quarterly, 32*, 271–294.

Marshall, K. (2003). Recovering from HSPS (Hyperactive Superficial Principal Syndrome): A progress report. *Phi Delta Kappan, 84*(9), 701–709.

Marzano, R. J. (2007). *The art and science of teaching: A comprehensive framework for effective instruction.* Alexandria, VA: ASCD.

Mathews, J. (2006). Let's teach to the test. *Washington Post*, p. A21.

Mayer, R. E. (1998). Cognitive, metacognitive, and motivational aspects of problem solving. *Instructional Science, 26*(1), 49–63.

Mayhew, K. C., & Edwards, A. C. (1965). *The Dewey School: The laboratory school of the University of Chicago, 1896–1903.* New York: Atherton Press.

McDermott, J. J. (1992). Isolation as starvation: John Dewey and a philosophy of the handicapped. In J. E. Tiles (Ed.), *John Dewey: Critical assessments.* New York: Routledge.

McFayden, D. (2005). Don't stop us from teaching our kids. *New York Teacher/City Edition, 46*(7), 3–4.

McTighe, J., Seif, E., & Wiggins, G. (2004). You can teach for meaning. *Educational Leadership, 62*(1), 26–31.

Medina, J. (2009, January 25). In school for the first time, teenage immigrants struggle. *New York Times*, p. A1.

Menken, K. (2006). Teaching to the test: How No Child Left Behind impacts language policy, curriculum, and instruction for English language learners. *Bilingual Research Journal, 30*(2), 521–546.

Meier, D. (2000). Foreword. In D. Bensman (Ed.), *Central Park East and its graduates* (pp. vii–ix). New York: Teachers College Press.

Meier, D. (2007). How much is learned when we're not looking: The promise of CES elementary schools. *Horace, 23*(3). Retrieved from www.essentialschools.org/cs/resources/view/ces_res/431.

Merriam, S. B. (1998). *Qualitative research and case study applications.* San Francisco: Jossey-Bass.

Mintrop, H. (2002). Educating student teachers to teach in a constructivist way: Can it all be done? *Teachers College Record.* Retrieved from www.tcrecord.org/Contentasp?ContentID+10726.

Mirel, J. (1993). *The rise and fall of an urban school system: Detroit, 1907–81.* Ann Arbor: The University of Michigan Press.

Monger, R., & Rytina, N. (2009). U.S. legal permanent residents: 2008. Retrieved from www.dhs.gov/xlibrary/assets/statistics/publications/lpr_fr_2008.pdf.

Morse, S. C., & Ludovina, F. S. (1999). Responding to undocumented children in the schools. Retrieved from http:/www.ericdigests.org/2000–2/schools.htm.

Mouza, C. (2008). Learning with laptops: Implementation and outcomes in an urban, under-privileged school. *Journal of Research on Technology in Education, 40*(4), 447–472.

Nalder, N. L. (2007). *Cooperative learning in an inclusive classroom: The impact on students with special needs.* Dissertation Abstracts. Retrieved from www .amazon.com/Cooperative-learning-inclusive-classroom-Dissertation/dp/B000 GKHR8M/ref=sr_1_2/103-1694125-4367017?ie=UTF8&s=books&qid=1188996 703&sr=8-2.

National Commission on Excellence in Education. (1983). *A nation at risk: The imperative for educational reform.* Washington, DC: U.S. Department of Education.

National Council for the Social Studies. (2009). Powerful and purposeful teaching and learning in elementary school social studies. Retrieved from www.social studies.org/positions/powerfulandpurposeful.

Neill, M. (2003). The dangers of testing. *Educational Leadership, 60*, 43–46.

Nelson, J. L. (2003). Academic freedom, institutional integrity, and teacher education. *Teacher Education Quarterly, 30*, 65–72.

Nelson, M. R., & Debacker, T. K. (2008). Achievement motivation in adolescents: The role of peer climate and best friends. *The Journal of Experimental Education, 76*(2), 170–189.

Nelson, T. (2003). Editor's introduction: In response to increasing state and national control over the teacher education profession. *Teacher Education Quarterly, 30*, 3–8.

Newlon, J. H. (1934). *Educational administration as school policy.* New York: C. Scribner's Sons.

Newman, J. W. (1997). Experimental school, experimental community: The Marietta Johnson School of Organic Education. Retrieved from www.theharbinger.org/ xvi/971007/newman.html.

Newmann, F. M., Bryk, A. S., & Nagaoka, J. K. (2001). Authentic intellectual work and standardized tests: Conflict or coexistence? Retrieved from ccsr.uchicago.edu/ publications/p0a02.pdf.

New York City Department of Education. (2003, January 15). Letter from Mayor Bloomberg and Chancellor Klein. Retrieved from www.nycenet.edu/whatsnew/ ParentLetters/default.asp.

New York State Department of Education. (2002). Traumatic brain injury: A guidebook for educators. Retrieved from www.vesid.nysed.gov/specialed/tbi/guidebook .pdf.

New York voices: Education reform. (2003). Retrieved December 1, 2009, from www .thirteen.org/nyvoices/features/educationreform.html.

Nichols, S. L. (2008). An exploration of students' belongingness beliefs in one middle school. *The Journal of Experimental Education, 76*(2), 145–169.

Nichols, S. L., & Berliner, D. C. (2007). *Collateral damage: How high-stakes testing corrupts America's schools.* Cambridge, MA: Harvard Education Press.

Noddings, N. (1984). *Caring: A feminist approach to ethics and moral education.* Berkeley: University of California Press.

Noddings, N. (1986). Fidelity in teaching, teacher education, and research for teaching. *Harvard Educational Review, 56*, 496–510.

Noddings, N. (1992). *The challenge to care in schools: An alternative approach to education.* New York: Teachers College Press.

Noddings, N. (2003). *Caring: A feminine approach to ethics and moral education* (2nd ed.). Berkeley: University of California Press.

North Central Regional Educational Laboratory. (2004a). Critical issue: Using scientifically based research to guide educational decisions. Retrieved from www.ncrel .org/sdrs/areas/issues/envrnmnt/go/go900.htm.

North Central Regional Educational Laboratory. (2004b). Summary of Goals 2000: Educate America Act. Retrieved from www.ncrel.org/sdrs/areas/issues/envrnmnt/ stw/sw0goals.htm.

Null, J. W. (2007). William C. Bagley and the founding of essentialism: An untold story in American educational history. *Teachers College Record, 109*(4), 1013–1055.

Oakes, J. (1985). *Keeping track: How schools structure inequality.* New Haven, CT: Yale University Press.

Obama, B. (2008). *Full text of President Obama's education speech.* Retrieved November 19, 2009, from origin.denverpost.com/headlines/ci_9405199.

O'Day, J. A. (2002). Complexity, accountability, and school improvement. *Harvard Educational Review, 72*(3), 293–329.

Odom, S. L., Brantlinger, E., Gersten, R., Horner, R. H., Thompson, B., & Harris, K. R. (2005). Research in special education: Scientific methods and evidence-based practices. *Exceptional Children, 71*(2), 137–148.

Ogbu, J. U. (1978). *Minority education and the caste: The American system in cross cultural perspective.* San Diego, CA: Academic Press.

Ogbu, J. U. (2003). *Black American students in an affluent suburb: A study of academic disengagement.* Mahwah, NJ: Erlbaum.

Okan, Z. (2003). Edutainment: Is learning at risk? *British Journal of Educational Technology, 34*(3), 255–264.

Oliveira, E., & Sarmento, L. (2002). Emotional valence-based mechanisms and agent personality. Retrieved from 209.85.215.104/search?q=cache:WnJFCWp RlEIJ:www.fe.up.pt/~eol/PUBLICATIONS/2002/personality7.ps+define+ achievement+valence&hl=en&ct=clnk&cd=5&gl=us&client=firefox-a.

O'Steen, B. (2008). Are Dewey's ideas alive and well in New Zealand undergraduate education? Kiwi case studies of inquiry-based learning. *Journal of Experiential Education, 30*(3), 299–303.

Ovando, M. N. (1995). Enhancing teaching and learning through collaborative supervision. *People and Education, 3*(2).

Ovando, M. N. (2000). Collaborative supervision: Implications for supervision research & enquiry. In Author & L. Behar-Horenstein (Eds.), *Paradigm debates in curriculum and supervision: Modern and postmodern perspectives* (pp. 108–125). Westport, CT: Bergin & Garvey.

Ovando, M. N., & Harris, B. M. (1992). Collaborative supervision and the developmental evaluation of teaching. *Journal of School Administrators Association of New York State, 23*(1).

Pajak, E. (1993a). *Approaches to clinical supervision: Alternatives for improving instruction.* Norwood, MA: Christopher-Gordon.

Pajak, E. (1993b). Change and continuity in supervision and leadership. In G. Cawelti (Ed.), *Challenges and achievements of American education* (pp. 158–186). Alexandria, VA: ASCD.

Pajak, E. (2000). *Approaches to clinical supervision: Alternatives for improving instruction.* Norwood, MA: Christopher-Gordon.

Parkay, F. W., & Stanford, B. H. (2006). *Becoming a teacher* (7th ed.). Boston: Allyn & Bacon.

Passel, J. S., & Cohn, D. V. (2009). A portrait of unauthorized immigrants in the United States. Retrieved from pewhispanic.org/files/reports/107.pdf.

Patrick, H., Mantzicopoulos, P., Samarapungavan, A., & French, B. F. (2008). Patterns of young children's motivation for science and teacher-child relationships. *The Journal of Experimental Education, 76*(2), 121–144.

Patterson, D. S., Jolivette, K., & Crosby, S. (2006). Social skills training for students who demonstrate poor self-control. *Beyond Behavior, 15*(3), 23–27.

Peterson, P. (1985). *The politics of school reform 1870–1940.* Chicago: University of Chicago Press.

Pew Research Center. (2009). Generations online in 2009. Retrieved from www.pewinternet.org/Reports/2009/Generations-Online-in-2009.aspx.

Phelps, R. P. (2006). Characteristics of an effective student testing system. *Educational Horizons, 85*(1), 19–29.

Piaget, J. (1936). *Origins of intelligence in the child.* London: Routledge & Kegan Paul.

Pinar, W. F., Reynolds, W. M., Slattery, P., & Taubman, P. M. (1995). *Understanding curriculum: An introduction to the study of historical and contemporary curriculum discourses.* New York: Peter Lang Publishers.

Polanyi, M. (1964). *Science, faith, and society.* Chicago: University of Chicago Press.

Popham, W. J. (2001). Teaching to the test? *Educational Leadership, 58*(6), 16–20.

Popham, W. J. (2004). "Teaching to the test" an expression to eliminate. *Educational Leadership, 62*(3), 82–83.

Posner, D. (2004). What's wrong with teaching to the test? *Phi Delta Kappan, 85*(10), 749–751.

Prawat, R. S. (1998). Current self-regulation views of learning and motivation viewed through a Deweyan lens: The problems with dualism. *American Educational Research Journal, 35*(2), 199–224.

Pring, R. (2007). *John Dewey: A philosopher of education for our time?* London: Continuum International Publishing Group.

Rance-Roney, J. (2009). Best practices for adolescent ELLs. *Educational Leadership, 66*(7), 32–37.

Rapp, D. (2002). Social justice and the importance of rebellious, oppositional imaginations. *Journal of School Leadership, 12*(3), 226–245.

Ravitch, D. (1974). *The great school wars: New York City, 1805–1973.* New York: Basic Books.

Ravitch, D. (1995). *National standards in American education: A citizen's guide.* Washington, DC: The Brookings Institution.

Rawls, J. (1971). *A theory of justice.* Cambridge, MA: Harvard University Press.

Reese, M., Gordon, S. P., & Price, L. R. (2004). Teachers' perceptions of high-stakes testing. *Journal of School Leadership, 14*(5), 464–496.

Regan, H. B. (1990). Not for women only: School administration as a feminist activity. *Teachers College Record, 91*, 565–577.

Reichle, J. (1997). Communication intervention with persons who have severe disabilities. *The Journal of Special Education, 31*(1), 110–134.

Reifer, J. L. (2003, February 15). 17 Island public schools making the grade? *Staten Island Advance*, p. A1.

Richardson, J. G., & Parker, T. L. (1993). The institutional genesis of special education: The American case. *American Journal of Education, 101*(4), 359–392.

Rist, R. (1970). Student social class and teacher expectations: The self-fulfilling prophecy in ghetto education. *Harvard Educational Review, 40*(3), 411–451.

Roberts, S. M., & Pruitt, E. Z. (2003). *Schools as professional learning communities: Collaborative activities and strategies for professional development.* Thousand Oaks, CA: Corwin Press.

Rodgers, C. (2002). Seeing student learning: Teacher change and the role of reflection. *Harvard Educational Review, 72*(2), 230–253.

Rogers, S. J. (2000). Interventions that facilitate socialization in children with autism. *Journal of Autism and Developmental Disorders, 30*(5), 399–409.

Rosenthal, R., & Jacobson, L. (1968). *Pygmalion in the classroom: Teacher expectation and pupils' intellectual development.* New York: Holt, Rinehart and Winston.

Ross, D. B., & Driscoll, R. (2006). *Test anxiety: Age appropriate interventions.* Paper presented at the American Counseling Association Southern Region Leadership Conference, Huntsville, AL. Retrieved from ERIC database (ED493897).

Rothstein, R. (2004). *Class and schools: Using social, economic, and educational reform to close the black-white achievement gap.* New York: Teachers College Press.

Rousmaniere, K. (1992). *City teachers: Teaching in New York City schools in the 1920s.* Unpublished doctoral dissertation, Columbia University.

Rudolph, J. L. (2005). Inquiry, instrumentalism, and the public understanding of science. *Science Education, 89*(5), 803–821.

Russell, M., & Abrams, L. (2004). Instructional uses of computers for writing: The effect of state testing programs. *Teachers College Record, 106*(6), 1332–1357.

Russell, M., O'Dwyer, L. M., Bebell, D., & Tao, W. (2007). How teachers' uses of technology vary by tenure and longevity. *Journal of Educational Computing Research, 37*(4), 393–417.

Ryan, K. E., Ryan, A. M., Arbuthnot, K., & Samuels, M. (2007). Students' motivation for standardized math exams. *Educational Researcher, 36*(1), 5–13.

Sadker, M., & Sadker, D. (1994). *Failing at fairness: How our schools cheat girls.* New York: Simon & Schuster Publishers.

Santos, M. (2007). Students with interrupted formal education (SIFE) strand. Retrieved from www.hunter.cuny.edu/msibetac/docs/workshops/SIFE/SABESIFEDOE_3_2_07.pdf.

Sarason, S. B. (1996). *Revisiting "The culture of the school and the problem of change."* New York: Teachers College Press.

Scheurman, G., & Newmann, F. M. (1998). Authentic intellectual work in social studies: Putting performance before pedagogy. Retrieved from www.learner.org/workshops/socialstudies/pdf/session4/4.AuthIntellectualWork.pdf.

Schroeder, C. M., Scott, T. P., Tolson, H., Huang, T.-Y., & Lee, Y.-H. (2007). A meta-analysis of national research: Effects of teaching strategies on student achievement in science in the United States. *Journal of Research in Science Teaching, 44*(10), 1436–1460.

Scot, T. P., Callahan, C. M., & Urquhart, J. (2009). Paint-by-number teachers and cookie-cutter students: The unintended effects of high-stakes testing on the education of gifted students. *Roeper Review, 31*(1), 40–52. Retrieved from doi:10.1080/02783190802527364.

Scott, P., & Mouza, C. (2007). The impact of professional development on teacher learning, practice and leadership skills: A study on the integration of technology in the teaching of writing. *Journal of Educational Computing Research, 37*(3), 229–266.

Seguel, M. L. (1966). *The curriculum field: Its formative years.* New York: Teachers College Press.

Sergiovanni, T. J. (1992). Moral authority and the regeneration of supervision. In C. D. Glickman (Ed.), *Supervision in transition: 1992 yearbook of the Association for Supervision and Curriculum Development* (pp. 203–214). Alexandria, VA: ASCD.

Seyfried, S. (1998). Academic achievement of African-American preadolescents: The influence of teacher perceptions. *American Journal of Community Psychology, 26,* 381–402.

Shapiro, S. (2008). It's time for a progressive vision of education! *Tikkun, 23*(1), 17.

Shapiro, J. P., & Stefkovich, J. A. (2005). *Ethical leadership and decision making in education: Applying theoretical perspectives to complex dilemmas* (2nd ed.). Mahwah, NJ: Erlbaum Associates.

Shepard, L. A. (1990). "Inflated test score gains": Is it old norms or teaching to the test? Retrieved from www.cse.ucla.edu/products/Reports/TR307.pdf.

Simpson, R. L. (2005). Evidence-based practices and students with autism spectrum disorders. *Focus on Autism and Other Developmental Disabilities, 20*(3), 140–149.

Sizer, T. R. (1984). *Horace's compromise: The dilemma of the American high school.* New York: Houghton Mifflin Company.

Skrtic, T. M. (2005). A political economy of learning disabilities. *Learning Disability Quarterly, 28*(2), 149–155.

Slattery, P. (1995). *Curriculum development in the postmodern era.* New York: Garland.

Sloane, F. C., & Kelly, A. E. (2003). Issues in high-stakes testing programs. *Theory into Practice, 42*(1), 12–17.

Smith, J. B., Lee, V. E., & Newmann, F. M. (2001). Instruction and achievement in Chicago elementary schools. Retrieved from ccsr.uchicago.edu/publications/p0f01.pdf.

Smith, M., & O'Day, J. (1991). Systemic school reform. In S. Fuhrman & B. Malen (Eds.), *The politics of curriculum and testing* (pp. 233–265). Philadelphia, PA: Falmer Press.

Smith, R. A. (2005). Aesthetic education: Questions and issues. *Arts Education Policy Review, 106*(3), 19–34.

Smith, W. A. (1934). Dictatorship and democracy in education from a teacher's viewpoint. *School and Society, 39*, 614.

Smyth, J. (1991). Instructional supervision and the redefinition of who does it in schools. *Journal of Curriculum and Supervision, 7*, 90–99.

Sobel, A., & Kuglar, E. G. (2007). Building partnerships with immigrant parents. *Educational Leadership, 64*(6), 62–66.

Spring, J. (1994). *The American school, 1642–1993* (3rd ed.). New York: McGraw-Hill Publishers.

Stallones, J. (2006). Struggle for the soul of John Dewey: Religion and progressive education. *American Educational History Journal, 33*(1), 19–28.

Steinberg, L. (2002). Does high-stakes testing hurt students: Read early evidence with caution. *Education Week, 22*, 48.

Steiner, D. M. (2004). Aesthetics between philosophy and pedagogy. *Journal of Education, 184*(1), 39–56.

Sternberg, R. (2008). Applying psychological theories to educational practice. *American Educational Research Journal, 45*(1), 150–165.

Stichter, J. P., Randolph, J., Gage, N., & Schmidt, C. (2007). A review of recommended social competency programs for students with autism spectrum disorders. *Exceptionality, 15*(4), 219–232.

Strike, K. A. (1991). The moral role of schooling in a liberal democratic society. In G. Grant (Ed.), *Review of research in education*. Washington, DC: American Educational Research Association.

Strike, K. A. (2007). *Ethical leadership in schools: Creating community in an environment of accountability*. Thousand Oaks, CA: Corwin Press.

Strike, K. A., & Soltis, J. F. (1992). *The ethics of teaching* (2nd ed.). New York: Teachers College Press.

Strober, M. M., & Tyack, D. B. (1980). Why do women teach and men manage? *Signs*, n.a.

Stullich, S., Eisner, E., & McCrary, J. (2007). National assessment of Title I: Final report. Retrieved from ies.ed.gov/ncee/pdf/20084012_rev.pdf.

Sullivan, S. (2006). Monitoring under the guise of reflective practice. *Supervision and Instructional Leadership AERA SIG Newsletter*, pp. 2–3.

Sullivan, S., & Glanz, J. (2009). *Supervision that improves teaching: Strategies and techniques* (3rd ed.). Thousand Oaks, CA: Corwin Press.

Sullivan, S., Shulman, V., & Glanz, J. (2005, October 29). *Instructional supervision in a standards-based environment: Retrospective, perspective, and prospective.* Presented at the annual meeting of the Council of Professors of Instructional Supervision.

Superfine, B. M. (2005). The politics of accountability: The rise and fall of Goals 2000. *American Journal of Education, 112*(1), 10–43.

Supervision in Transition. (1992). Alexandria, VA: ASCD.

Sutinen, A. (2008). Constructivism and education: Education as an interpretative transformational process. *Studies in Philosophy and Education, 27*(1), 1–14.

Tal, T., Krajcik, J. S., & Blumenfeld, P. C. (2006). Urban schools' teachers enacting project-based science. *Journal of Research in Science Teaching, 43*(7), 722–745.

Tanner, L. N. (1997). *Dewey's laboratory school: Lessons for today.* New York: Teachers College Press.

Tauber, R. T. (1997). *Self-fulfilling prophecy: A practical guide to its use in education.* Westport, CT: Praeger.

Taylor, F. W. (1911). *The principles of scientific management.* New York: Harper and Brothers.

Taylor, J. A. (2004). Teaching children who have immigrated: The new legislation, research, and trends in immigration which affect teachers of diverse student populations. *Multicultural Education, 11*(3), 43–44.

Theoharis, G. (2007). Navigating rough waters: A synthesis of the countervailing pressures against leading for social justice. *Journal of School Leadership, 17*(1), 4–27.

Tomlinson, C. (2001). Differentiated instruction in the regular classroom: What does it mean? How does it look? *Understanding Our Gifted, 14*(1), 3–6.

Tomlinson, C. (2003). *Fulfilling the promise of the differentiated classroom.* Alexandria, VA: ASCD.

Tomlinson, C. (2005). This issue. *Theory Into Practice, 44*(3), 183–184.

Tomlinson, S. (1997). Edward Lee Thorndike and John Dewey on the science of education. *Oxford Review of Education, 23*(3), 365–383.

Trifonas, P. P., & Ghiraldelli Jr., P. (2004). Experience, reason, and education. *JCT, 20*(4), 141.

Twomey Fosnot, C. (2005). *Constructivism: Theory, perspectives and practice.* New York: Teachers College Press.

Tyack, D. B. (1974). *The one best system: A history of American education.* Cambridge, MA: Harvard University Press.

Udvari-Solner, A., & Kluth, P. (2007). *Joyful learning: Active and collaborative learning in inclusive classrooms.* Thousand Oaks, CA: Corwin Press.

U.S. Department of Education. (2002a). Choice provisions in No Child Left Behind. Retrieved from www.ed.gov/admins/comm/choice/choice02/edlite-slide001.html.

U.S. Department of Education. (2002b). No Child Left Behind: A desktop reference. Retrieved from www.ed.gov/admins/lead/account/nclbreference/reference.pdf.

U.S. Department of Education. (2003). Identifying and treating attention deficit hyperactivity disorder: A resource for school and home. Retrieved from www.ed.gov/offices/OSERS/OSEP/.

U.S. Department of Education. (2008). *No Child Left Behind* provision gives schools new flexibility and ensures accountability for students with disabilities. Retrieved from www.ed.gov/nclb/freedom/local/specedfactsheet.html.

Villegas, A. M., & Lucas, T. (2007). The culturally responsive teacher. *Educational Leadership, 64*(6), 28–33.

Vogler, K. E., & Virtue, D. (2007). "Just the facts, ma'am": Teaching social studies in the era of standards and high-stakes testing. *The Social Studies, 98*(2), 54–58.

Volante, L. (2004). Teaching to the test: What every educator and policy-maker should know. *Canadian Journal of Educational Administration and Policy, 35.* Retrieved from https://www.umanitoba.ca/publications/cjeap/articles/volante.html.

Volker, M. A., & Lopata, C. (2008). Autism: A review of biological bases, assessment, and intervention. *School Psychology Quarterly, 23*(2), 258–270.

Vygotsky, L. (1986). *Thought and language.* Cambridge, MA: MIT Press. (Original work published 1934.)

Waber, D. P., Gerber, E. B., Turcios, V. Y., Wagner, E. R., & Forbes, P. W. (2006). Executive functions and performance on high-stakes testing in children from urban schools. *Developmental Neuropsychology, 29*(3), 459–477.

Wadsworth, D., & Remaley, M. H. (2007). What families want. *Educational Leadership, 64*(6), 23–27.

Waks, L. J. (2001). Computer mediated experience and education. *Educational Theory, 51*(4), 415–432.

Weir, M. (1985). *Schooling for all.* New York: Basic Books.

Weiss, S. G., DeFalco, A. A., & Weiss, E. M. (2005). Progressive = permissive? Not according to John Dewey . . . subjects matter! Retrieved from www.usca.edu/essays/vol142005/defalco.pdf.

Westbrook, R. B. (1991). *John Dewey and American democracy.* Ithaca, NY: Cornell University Press.

Willerman, M., McNeely, S. L., & Koffman, E. C. (1991). *Teachers helping teachers: Peer observation and assistance.* New York: Praeger.

Windschitl, M. (2002). Framing constructivism, in practice as the negotiation of dilemmas: An analysis of the conceptual, pedagogical, cultural, and political challenges facing teachers. *Review of Educational Research, 72,* 131–175.

Winner, E. (1993). Exceptional artistic development: The role of visual thinking. *Journal of Aesthetic Education, 27*(4), 31–44.

Winzer, M. A. (1993). *The history of special education: From isolation to integration.* Washington, DC: Gallaudet University Press.

Yonezawa, S., & Jones, M. (2006). Students' perspectives on tracking and detracking. *Theory into Practice, 45*(1), 15–23.

Young, P. G. (2004). *You have to go to school—You're the principal: 101 tips to make it better for your students, your staff, and yourself.* Thousand Oaks, CA: Corwin Press.

Zukav, G. (2000). *Soul stories.* New York: Simon & Schuster.

About the Authors

Daniel W. Stuckart is assistant professor of secondary education at Wagner College in New York City and is currently serving as chair for the Small College and University Faculty Forum of the National Council for the Social Studies. His research interests focus on the nexus of school reform, technology, and social studies practice and pedagogy.

Jeffrey Glanz is professor and holder of the Silverstein Chair in Professional Ethics and Values in the Azrieli Graduate School of Jewish Education and Administration at Yeshiva University. His recent research interests include ethics and educational leadership.

	DATE DUE		